D1072013

This book details the results of the authors' research using laboratory animals to investigate individual choice theory in economics, particularly consumer-demand and labor-supply behavior and choice under uncertainty. The use of laboratory animals provides the opportunity to conduct controlled experiments involving precise and demanding tests of economic theory with rewards and punishments of real consequence. Economic models are compared with psychological and biological choice models along with the results of experiments testing between these competing explanations. Results of animal experiments are used to address questions of social policy importance. A number of new experimental results are reported along with summaries of the authors' previously published studies and related research.

ECONOMIC CHOICE THEORY

Economic choice theory

An experimental analysis of animal behavior

JOHN H. KAGEL
University of Pittsburgh

RAYMOND C. BATTALIO
Texas A&M University

LEONARD GREEN
Washington University

CAMBRIDGE
UNIVERSITY PRESS

Published by the Press Syndicate of the University of Cambridge
The Pitt Building, Trumpington Street, Cambridge CB2 1RP
40 West 20th Street, New York, NY 10011-4211, USA
10 Stamford Road, Oakleigh, Melbourne, 3166, Australia

© Cambridge University Press 1995

First published 1995

Printed in the United States of America

Library of Congress Cataloging-in-Publication Data
Kagel, John H. (John Henry), 1942–
Economic choice theory: an experimental model of animal behavior / John H.
Kagel, Raymond C. Battalio, Leonard Green.

p.   cm.

ISBN 0-521-45488-3

1. Consumption (Economics).   2. Consumer behavior.   3. Human
behavior–Animal models.   I. Battalio, Raymond Charles.   II. Green,
Leonard.   III. Title.
HB801.K28   1994
339.4'7—dc20   94-4
                                                                          CIP

A catalog record for this book is available from the British Library.

ISBN 0-521-45488-3 hardback

CONTENTS

PREFACE

This book provides a unified treatment of our research and related research on models of individual choice drawn from economics, psychology, and behavioral biology. The unique aspect of this research from the perspective of economics is its use of laboratory experimental methods and nonhuman subjects to study economic choice theory. The unique aspect of the research from the perspective of psychology is its application of economic concepts to the analysis of individual behavior.

The book is intended for economists, psychologists, and behavioral biologists. It includes a brief, self-contained exposition of the relevant theoretical concepts and relationships for each substantive research area covered. These sections rely on graphical methods with limited algebraic derivations. The book is written at the level of an intermediate to upper-level undergraduate price theory text in economics or a learning text in psychology.

Significant parts of the book are based on a series of published papers. We have expanded upon these by including relevant data from a number of previously unpublished studies of our own, and by analyzing data from our earlier experiments in ways that we had thought about for some time but had never gotten around to, and by establishing clear connections between our work and related research in psychology and biology. Finally, the book has provided a focus for closing some of the more obvious gaps in our analyses.

Acknowledgments

From its inception, the research has been supported by a series of grants from the National Science Foundation, with additional funding from the National Institutes of Health and the National Institute of Mental Health. We are most grateful for this support. An Earhart Foundation Fellowship to Kagel provided partial support for writing the book. In addition, the University of Pittsburgh has provided generous secretarial support.

Our research has truly been collaborative. A number of colleagues participated, and the able assistance of graduate and undergraduate students who helped run the animal laboratories at Texas A&M University and Washington University was essential. Much of the early research was conducted in close collaboration with Howard Rachlin, to whom we owe a special debt of gratitude and appreciation. The work on choice under uncertainty was done in collaboration with Don MacDonald. Mike Ormiston helped establish the relationship between consumer choice theory and the marginal value theorem reported in the appendix to Chapter 2. Bob Bassman gave us the vision and the wherewithall to ask and answer many of the questions underlying the research. Students who provided significant support for the research both inside and outside the laboratory include Jimmie Walker, Paul Thistle, Carl Kogut, Komain Jirankul, and the Psychonomy Cabal at Washington University. Last, but not least, we thank Mary Gromicko for editorial and secretarial support while we were writing the manuscript and Sharon Bangert for editing the final manuscript.

All of our experiments were conducted under the supervision and approval of the laboratory animal care committees, operating under the guidelines of the National Institutes of Health, where the research was performed.

JHK

RCB

LG

1

Introduction

Choices of economic agents – consumer-demand and labor-supply behavior, choice under uncertainty – are central to the study of economics and to the performance of economic institutions. In economics, empirical studies of individual choice are usually based on field data collected by government agencies. But such data are of limited value because of the difficulty in obtaining appropriate observations in relation to the theoretical constructs that the theory employs. To overcome this limitation, we embarked on a research program of gathering our own data using experimental laboratory methods. One distinctive feature of this experimental methodology has been the use of nonhuman subjects, primarily rats and pigeons.

Our initial motivation for using rats and pigeons in these experiments was that they provide an economically efficient method of investigating questions about individual choice behavior. The methodology for conducting these experiments was originally developed by experimental psychologists, and we have applied it to questions of interest to economists. We took this step after concluding, on the basis of ample evidence from existing psychological and biological research, that other animals besides humans respond to the basic hedonistic (cost – benefit) calculations underlying economic theory. The fundamental question guiding our initial inquiries was whether the individual choice behavior of these subjects was consistent with more precise implications of economic theory, and if not, what kind of theoretical adaptations would be required to account for the data. As the studies progressed, several major themes emerged.

One theme underlying the research, and a major reason it has gained acceptance in some economic circles is that it constitutes a branch of economic imperialism, whereby economic theory is extended to organize data lying outside the traditional purview of economics (that being goods and services traded in the marketplace). Economic analyses have been extended to such diverse areas

1

of life as love and marriage (Manser and Brown, 1980; Becker, 1981), medieval agriculture (McCloskey, 1989), slavery (Engerman and Fogel, 1974), and crime and punishment (Becker, 1968; Ehrlich, 1973). However, such extensions are often criticized on the grounds that behavior in these areas is dominated by non-rational considerations. In extending economic choice theory to nonhuman animal behavior, we are presumably operating at the extreme end of these kinds of studies. However, the fact that, when put to the test, rats and pigeons conform to elementary principles of economic theory provides rather striking support for the theory and, indirectly, refutes the argument that the theory cannot be extended to nonmarket behavior because such behavior is guided by nonrational considerations.

However, these objections lead immediately to a second major theme of the research: the importance of testing between economic explanations for the data and alternative hypotheses. Alternative hypotheses include nonrational explanations drawn from the economics literature (for example, random behavior models; see Becker, 1962), optimal foraging models from behavioral biology, and, most contentiously, rival explanations from animal psychologists. After all, this particular exercise in economic imperialism tramples most directly on the psychologists' turf, since it adapts their experimental technologies to the study of economic behavior. A leading quantitative choice model put forth by psychologists is the matching law (Herrnstein, 1970; Herrnstein and Prelec, 1991). Our research has shown that economic choice theory is not only capable of organizing the stylized facts underlying the matching law (see Section 3.2b) but it can also account for anomalies in existing data (Section 5.2b). More important, and even more damaging to the matching law, economic choice theory specifies circumstances under which the predictions of the matching law will be reversed (what we call antimatching) (Sections 3.2c and 5.2a). Many of these results have been reported in psychology journals. This book brings them together under one roof and makes them accessible to economists, psychologists, and other interested readers.

One exciting aspect of theory rooted in experimentation is that it is always possible to develop new experiments and produce new data to discredit rival explanations. As might be expected, adherents of the matching law have done just that. The text follows some of these developments (Sections 5.2c and 7.5), with a view to demonstrating how experimentation and theory interact to provide a better understanding of behavior.

On a more basic level, the studies reported constitute (arguably) the first real tests of consumer-demand theory. Most tests of consumer-demand theory use time-series and cross-sectional data of the sort usually available to economists. However, this approach leads to some serious problems. First, predictions of the model break down when applied to aggregates or across individuals except under the most stringent of aggregation requirements. And, as we demonstrate, these requirements do not hold even under the most favorable of conditions (see Sections 3.4 and 5.3d). Second, tests of the theories' predictions are conditional on the validity of the functional form of the estimating equations. And these equations are typically at the center of considerable controversy in their own right. All too often, this creates an awkward situation for econometric studies that use field data to test static models of labor supply. In a number of instances, responses to (income-compensated) wage changes are opposite in sign to those predicted by the model, yet this prediction constitutes *the* important implication of the model. The model is then "rescued" by arguing that the string of auxiliary hypotheses required to apply the theory to field data (assumptions about functional forms, the measurement of variables, etc.) does not hold. However, the problem with this defense is that these auxiliary hypotheses are continuously being called on to "save" the theory, so that we are left with a model that has yet to be seriously tested (for arguments to this effect, see Pencavel, 1986). Not all economists would agree with this characterization of the current status of labor-supply theory; perhaps only a small minority do. But as we see it, there are inherent problems in testing individual choice theory using field data. These problems were the springboard for the laboratory experiments reported in this volume.[1]

Once we established the relevance of animal experiments to economics, there was a foundation for testing between interesting and plausible competing hypotheses for which there is little consensus among economists. To give a brief idea of some of the highlights of this work, we demonstrated the existence of Giffen goods, at least on the level of individual subject demand (Section 2.4b); identified Allais-type violations of expected utility theory similar to those reported with human subjects and also rejected the "fanning out" hypothesis (Machina, 1982) designed to explain these violations, a hypothesis that underlies a number of nonexpected utility formulations (Section 6.4); and investigated the "cycle-of-poverty" hypothesis – which posits that consumers with smaller incomes have a higher preference for present over future income (Section 7.3; our data tend to support the *converse* of the cycle-of-poverty hypothesis).

1.1 **On using animal experiments to understand human behavior**

Questions naturally arise as to whether experiments with animal subjects can shed light on human behavior, much less complicated social issues. We believe that there is behavioral as well as physiological continuity across species. This notion of behavioral continuity is well established in psychology and behavioral biology, both of which have well-developed subdisciplines that make extensive use of animal experimentation.

Animals provide a way of testing *elementary* microeconomic principles. For some questions, we would argue, animal models are the only practical means to investigate an issue. They allow us to conduct precise, controlled, and demanding *experiments* using rewards and punishments of real consequence to test individual choice theory. This is impossible, or impractical, to do with human subjects in a number of areas of individual choice theory. The question then becomes, if it is the case that basic economic principles do *not* apply to the relatively simple choice situations involved in our experiments, how can these principles be relied upon in substantially more complex situations?

The basic difficulty in using animal experiments to elucidate issues of general interest to economists lies in deciding whether the results obtained with other species are applicable to humans (Lea, 1981). In studying the consumer-demand and labor-supply behavior of rats, we are not studying the behavior of simplified humans. The behavior of a given species is constrained by its psychological and biological characteristics and by its ecological niche. As a result, there can be no general answer to the species extrapolation problem. What can be assumed, however, is that a theory that works well across species has a greater likelihood of being valid than one that works well with only one, or a limited set of, species. In applying animal models to the study of economic behavior, we are following much the same approach used in biomedicine, where animal models are accepted with few reservations.

In this book we go beyond looking at simple principles of economic behavior. We use our animal model to address complicated social issues – such as the "cycle-of-poverty" and the "welfare trap" hypothesis. Here the results are surely bound to be more contentious. How do we justify examining such questions with animals? What can be learned from such investigations that might inform our understanding of human behavior? The answer is that theories about welfare traps and cycles of poverty deal with the effects that wide differences in income and extremely low levels of income have on individual behavior; an experimental treatment cannot adequately approximate these conditions with human volunteer subjects (to say nothing about the huge expense such experiments would entail). With rats and pigeons, however, one can impose large differences in income for extended periods of time to address directly the effects on behavior.

Our goal in addressing complicated social issues is relatively modest, however, as we can illustrate with the cycle-of-poverty hypothesis. Economists have conjectured that time bias varies inversely with income and wealth. That is to say, because the preference for immediate payoffs is stronger at lower income levels, there is *proportionately* less saving and investment in physical human capital at those levels, and poverty is thereby perpetuated. In investigating this question experimentally, we cannot hope to recreate the full set of cultural and socioeconomic conditions that characterize poverty in national economic systems. Rather, we focus exclusively on the wealth effects of poverty by establishing wealth differences between subjects in the laboratory, and then we determine the effects of this treatment variable on time discounting. If we can support the cycle-of-poverty hypothesis under these conditions, we have direct evidence favoring a wealth-induced effect on time preferences, which to us, at least, is at the heart of the conjecture. If we find no such effect on discount rates, then the data compel us to look to other conditions associated with poverty, such as discrimination and poor schooling, as explanations for the presence of poverty cycles within national economies. It is essential to distinguish between these potential sources of poverty since only a correct diagnosis will allow us to design effective policies to alleviate poverty.

Needless to say, our studies (or any single study for that matter, whether experimental or not) are hardly the last word on the questions they investigate. Some would argue that this is particularly true with respect to studies using nonhuman consumers since questions inevitably arise regarding the generalizability of the results to human consumers (particularly when the nonhuman data contradict someone's pet hypothesis). Because we are sensitive to and interested in questions of generalizability, we have conducted parallel studies of choice under uncertainty with human consumers and looked at parallel data from national economies regarding the social issues investigated. Nevertheless, we would argue that our results put the burden of proof on those who support a particular position for which our data are incompatible. It is they who must show how our results are not applicable, or are irrelevant, to the human condition. But there is a danger here – providing answers to these questions often requires further experimentation, sometimes even using pigeons and rats.

1.2 Summary of chapter contents

Chapter 2 is concerned with consumer-choice behavior, that is to say, the choice between alternative commodities (different edibles). Subjects operate under a budget constraint, which limits their consumption opportunities. The subjects are then required to make trade-offs in what and how much to consume. The chapter begins with a review of basic economic concepts and relations underlying the experiments and provides details of the procedures used to investigate the theory. Basic tests of the theory are reported. They deal with (a) the effects of income-compensated price changes, (b) the "law of demand" for normal goods, and (c) the existence of a Giffen good (a positive relationship between price and the amount of the commodity consumed.) Section 2.5 turns to optimal foraging behavior, an area of concern to both biologists and psychologists. A technical appendix to Chapter 2 relates the economist's commodity choice model to the marginal value theorem, a mainstay of the optimal foraging literature. The appendix shows that the full implications of the marginal value theorem hold only in the absence of a time constraint on foraging, or when foragers are satiated, conditions that are rarely satisfied in laboratory, seminaturalistic, and naturalistic environments. The bias inherent in the marginal value theorem when foraging time is limited is specified along with its observable implications.

Chapter 3 takes up the important issue of testing between alternative explanations of the behavior reported. We test between random choice models, the matching law from the operant psychology literature, and between bliss-points and minimum-needs specifications of underlying motivational processes. Section 3.4 examines the "representative consumer" hypothesis, which refers to the degree to which tastes are sufficiently similar across individuals so that aggregate per capita data, of the sort usually available to economists, are reflective of individual choice. Section 3.5 uses consumer-choice theory to distinguish between the incentive effects of different reinforcers, specifically brain stimulation and food. This area of investigation is usually considered the province of physiological psychology and neuroscience.

Chapter 4 moves on to labor-supply behavior. In the experiments discussed here, subjects face a time constraint and are free, within the confines of that constraint, to vary the amount of consumption obtained by varying the amount of work performed. The first part of the chapter extends consumer-choice theory to labor-supply behavior and provides details of the procedures used to investigate the theory. Basic tests of the theory are reported, the most important of which is the effect of income-compensated wage changes on labor supply (response rates). The procedures employed in these experiments have much in common with negative income tax plans and other income transfer schemes associated with modern economic systems. This relationship is explored in both static and dynamic responses to the delivery of large amounts of unearned income.

In Chapter 5 we apply the competing motivational models developed in Chapter 3 to the labor supply of animals. We also construct earnings distribution functions for pigeons and rats and compare the characteristics of these distributions with earnings distributions reported from national economies. In our experiments, we found systematic differences in earnings across individual subjects; the median Gini coefficient was .14. These differences in earnings are evident in economies where virtually all sources of earnings differences, other than those arising from basic differences in tastes for consumption versus leisure, have been controlled for, and where even taste differences have presumably been minimized through genetic inbreeding and similar behavioral histories.

Chapter 6 considers animals' choices over uncertain outcomes. It opens with an explanation of the theoretical concepts underlying the experiments reported and provides details of the experimental procedures. It then discusses tests for risk aversion and transitivity of choices over prospects with differing degrees of risk. Risk preferences under varying levels of resource availability are examined next. This subject is of considerable interest to economists and behavioral biologists alike. Section 6.4 applies the procedures to test whether animal subjects, like human subjects, show Allais-type violations of expected utility theory. These experiments also test for fanning out of indifference curves in previously unexplored areas of the unit probability triangle. Choices over losses/aversive outcomes (where less is better) are reported in Section 6.5. The chapter closes with a review of studies on search and information acquisition by nonhuman subjects.

Chapter 7 is concerned with intertemporal choice. It explains elementary economic concepts of intertemporal choice and the procedures used to measure time discount rates. Section 7.3 reports a new experiment designed to study the effect of differences in income and wealth on the shape of the time-delay gradient. We test, and find wanting, the common conjecture among economists that preference for present over future rewards becomes more intense with lower consumption/wealth levels (the "cycle-of-poverty" hypothesis). Section 7.4 extends the analysis to multiperiod models of consumer choice. Of particular concern here are the conditions under which the single-period, static choice representations developed in Chapters 2–5 remain unaffected when time discounting on the animal's part is taken into account. Section 7.5 looks at the effects of time discounting on procedures discussed in earlier chapters. The chapter also points out some practical implications of the analysis for understanding differences in saving patterns in different token economies and for understanding differences in patterns of self-administered drug use.

Chapter 8 briefly summarizes our major findings.

Notes

1 Another problem that also leads us to claim that our laboratory studies provide the first real tests of consumer-demand theory is that, for an alarming number of economists, mathematical proof of a proposition is sufficient to verify its validity. To quote from correspondence with an unnamed, but sympathetic colleague, "It seems to me your research has been directed at verifying existing economic theory. For example in the paper you sent me you found downward sloping demand curves. In other work you have produced Giffen goods under the conditions dictated by the Slutsky equation. Research of that sort is well suited to establishing the relevancy of animal experiments to economics. For your purposes, that objective is a worthy objective in itself. However, I am a 'true believer' in microeconomic theory, and as a result I am perfectly willing to accept mathematical proofs without experimental verification."

2

Commodity-choice behavior I:
Some initial tests of the theory

In our initial applications of economic theory to animal choice we presented subjects with choices between different edible commodities. This chapter reviews and synthesizes the results from these studies. Sections 2.1 and 2.2 describe the theoretical concepts underlying the experiments and the procedures employed in them. Section 2.3 presents a series of experiments testing for income-compensated (Slutsky) substitution effects, an essential element of consumer-demand theory. Results from both essential and nonessential commodity-choice experiments consistently show reduced consumption in response to income-compensated price increases, as the theory requires.

Section 2.4 reports income-constant demand curves – which represent subjects' responses to changing prices while income is held constant – for both normal and inferior goods. In the case of normal goods, consumption increases when price decreases, as the law of demand requires. For inferior goods, we identify portions of the choice space over which consumption *decreases* as price decreases, at least for some individuals. That is, we confirm the existence of a Giffen good. This has a number of important theoretical implications, which are discussed in Chapter 3.

In Section 2.5 we extend the analysis of commodity-choice behavior to optimal foraging behavior, a subject of concern to both biologists and psychologists. We show how elements of the marginal value theorem, which was developed by biologists to analyze foraging in patchy environments, follows directly from consumer-demand theory. However, a more formal analysis of the mathematical relationship between demand theory and the marginal value theorem reveals some differences (see the appendix to this chapter). The main difference is that the marginal value theorem calculates the optimal foraging strategy in the absence of any type of budget constraint, whereas in nature, animals almost surely face such constraints – for example, in the amount of time that they can allocate to foraging. The different implications of these two approaches are discussed, and some data brought to bear on the question.

The important issue of testing between alternative explanations for the results reported is reserved for Chapter 3.

2.1 Commodity-choice theory: Some basic concepts

A type of behavior economists have traditionally been concerned with is choice between different bundles of consumption goods. In this section we develop the rudimentary concepts of the theory formulated to explain this kind of behavior. This is the theory tested in our initial experiments. A more rigorous specification of the assumptions underlying the theory and its predictions can be found in a number of standard textbooks (Deaton and Muellbauer, 1980; Varian, 1992).

2.1a Consumer preferences: Indifference curves and substitutability

Figure 2.1a shows two commodities, good 1 and good 2, available to consumers. In this scheme, consumers choose between *commodity bundles* that contain various amounts of the two goods. Preferences among commodity bundles are represented by *indifference curves*: these curves indicate the set of commodity bundles that leaves the consumer equally well off, or to which the consumer is indifferent (for example, the two commodity bundles X and Y on indifference curve I_3 are of equal value). The commodity space in Figure 2.1a is assumed to contain an infinite number of indifference curves, which are nonintersecting. This implies that the consumer has well-defined preferences over the entire set of commodity bundles and that preferences are transitive (if commodity bundle X is preferred to W, and Z is preferred to X, then Z must also be preferred to W). Commodity bundles on a higher indifference curve, such as bundle Z, are preferred to those on lower indifference curves, such as X and Y. This follows from the assumption that more goods are preferred to less and that preferences are transitive. The theory can readily be extended to account for instances in which *less* is better, in the case of economic bads (see Chapter 4) or satiation effects (a point beyond which more is no longer better). For the present, however, we will deal with the case in which more is always better.

The slope of an indifference curve at any point indicates the amount of one good required by an individual to exactly compensate for the loss of a small amount of the other good. The slope is called the *marginal rate of substitution* and measures the degree of substitutability at a point. The indifference curves are assumed to be convex to the origin. This assumption corresponds to that of a *diminishing marginal rate of substitution*; that is, the more of good 1 the con-

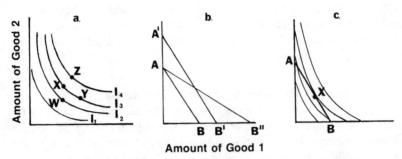

Figure 2.1 Basic concepts. (a) Indifference curves with decreasing marginal rate of substitution between commodities. (b) Changes in the budget line due to increases in income (movement from AB to A'B') and to decreases in p_1 (movement from AB to AB''). (c) Budget line superimposed on a set of indifference curves. Point X represents highest indifference curve attainable (optimal choice), given the budget constraint AB.

sumer has, the smaller the amounts of good 2 he is willing to sacrifice to obtain additional amounts of good 1.

In cases where commodities are perfect substitutes – as they would be, for example, if one was choosing between the same food from two different locations (assuming the consumer has no locational preferences) – then indifference curves are straight lines, so that the marginal rate of substitution does not vary with the consumption pattern. At the other extreme, in cases where goods are completely nonsubstitutable – as would be the case with left and right shoes – the indifference curves would be right-angled, so that having more of one good without more of the other would leave the consumer no better off. Most pairs of real commodities are somewhere between the extremes of complete substitutability and complete nonsubstitutability and are consequently described by indifference curves that are convex to the origin, as in Figure 2.1a. Even such items as food and clothing, which seem nonsubstitutable, may in fact be substitutable to a certain extent. Eating more food when you are cold may keep you slightly warmer. To the extent that food keeps you warm, it is at least somewhat substitutable for clothing. If not having a new hat makes you depressed, perhaps you can forget your troubles with an ice cream soda. Both food and clothing may satisfy some common emotional needs and are therefore substitutable to some extent. Correspondingly, even items that seem completely substitutable, such as pecking the left key and the right key of a two-key pigeon chamber, may be nonsubstitutable to a certain extent, or after a certain point. Different muscles may be used in each activity and it may be important to equalize exercise. Thus, responding to one key may be, to a slight extent, nonsubstitutable for responding on the other key.

2.1b   The budget constraint and optimal choice

The *budget constraint* specifies the set of commodities actually obtainable. It is determined by the prices of the goods, p_1, p_2, and the amount of income, m, that the consumer has available to spend on these goods. The *budget line*, $p_1x_1 + p_2x_2 = m$, forms a boundary between the set of commodity bundles the consumer can afford to buy and those that cannot be purchased given current prices and income. With prices fixed and independent of the quantity of goods purchased, the traditional specification in the economics literature, the budget line is linear, as in Figure 2.1b.

The budget line may be moved about by manipulating income and the relative prices of the two goods. Changing income while holding prices constant moves the budget line up or down parallel to itself (the effect on the budget line of an income increase is illustrated in the movement from AB to A'B' in Figure 2.1b). Changing the price of one of the commodities while holding income constant alters the slope of the budget line (the effect on the budget line of a decrease in the price of good 1 is illustrated in the movement from budget line AB to AB″ in Figure 2.1b). Figure 2.1c shows a budget line superimposed on a set of indifference curves. According to demand theory, the individual will spend his income so as to attain a commodity bundle on the highest possible indifference curve. This commodity bundle, represented by point X in Figure 2.1c, represents the most preferred commodity bundle obtainable, and will ordinarily be at the point where the budget line is tangent to an indifference curve.

If the budget line changes in height, as a result of an income change, or in slope, as a result of a price change, the most preferred commodity bundle attainable will also change. Consumer-demand theory is primarily concerned with shifts in consumption patterns as a function of changes in the budget line. In fact, consumer responses to changes in the budget line are the only data with which to test the theory, since without complete knowledge of the consumer's preferences it is virtually impossible to verify that any particular consumption point constitutes an optimum. The two most frequently studied changes in the budget line are income-compensated and income-constant price changes.

2.1c   Income-compensated price changes

An *income-compensated* price change is illustrated in Figure 2.2a. We start with an initial budget line AB, with equilibrium choice point X. Then a new budget line is established, A'B', with relative prices changed such that $p_1/p_2 > p_1'/p_2'$ (p_1 has been lowered in relation to p_2) *and* income adjusted so that the budget line passes through the original commodity bundle consumed. Note that with respect to point X, only the slope of the budget line has changed, so that the original commodity bundle can continue to be consumed. However, given the convexity of the indifference curves, the response to this change in the budget line *must* result in increased consumption of the commodity whose relative price has decreased, with compensating decreases in consumption of the good whose relative price increased. In Figure 2.2a, the new commodity bundle purchased must be somewhere along the dashed portion of the new budget line (a point such as Y). Compared with what was previously available, the change in relative prices permits increased consumption of good 1 in relation to 2, so that if the commodities are substitutable, the price change will result in more of good 1 being consumed. For sufficiently small price changes, the magnitude of the response to the change in relative prices indicates the curvature of the underlying indifference curve at that point, with a greater change in consumption corresponding to a greater marginal rate of substitution (flatter slope of the indifference curves).

The income-compensated price changes we studied are Slutsky-compensated price changes, as opposed to Hicks-compensated price changes. While both involve changes in relative prices and adjustments in the consumer's income, in the Hicks case the adjustments are made so that the consumer remains on the *original* indifference curve. Since indifference curves are not directly observable, the Slutsky-compensated price changes are more readily implemented.

At this point we provide a brief illustration of the experimental procedures used to study these price changes and the results obtained (more extensive specifications of experimental procedures and results are reported later in the chapter). Consider a rat choosing between root beer and Tom Collins mix (without any alcohol), with ad lib (unrestricted) access to food and water. The rat has two levers it can press on, one of which delivers a small (0.05 ml) cup of root beer, the other of which delivers a 0.05 ml cup of Tom Collins mix (each fluid is delivered immediately following a lever press directly below the lever pressed). The rat has a limited number of lever presses at its disposal (300) that it can distribute in any way it chooses between the two fluids. This establishes a budget constraint like AB in Figure 2.2b, with lever presses serving the role of income (m) in the budget constraint.[1] The rat is exposed to this (baseline) experimental condition for a minimum of 14 days, with conditions changed after 10 consecutive days of stable performance (the "stability criterion").

For the rat shown in Figure 2.2b, average baseline consumption (point X) during the period of stable performance was close to 3 to 1 in favor of root beer (11.1 ml root beer, 3.9 ml of Tom Collins mix) since the rat regularly (and quickly) used all of its lever presses each day. For the next condition, we halved the price of the Tom Collins mix, the less preferred commodity, by doubling its cup size and doubled the price of root beer by halving its cup size. Income compensation was determined by median baseline choices: 78 choices of Tom Collins mix and 222 choices of root beer. Given the price changes, it is a simple matter to compute the income needed for the rat to continue to consume the median baseline consumption bundle – 483 lever presses in this case – resulting in the income-compensated budget line A'B' in Figure 2.2b. Following the

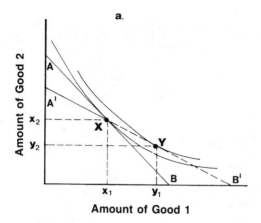

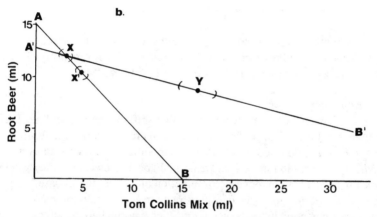

Figure 2.2 Income-compensated price changes. (a) The new budget line (A'B') passes through the original commodity bundle chosen (X). The price of good 1 has decreased relative to good 2, and this change has altered the slope of the budget line. The result is increased consumption of good 1 and decreased consumption of good 2. (b) An application to a rat choosing between root beer and Tom Collins mix. Mean consumption values are reported with brackets indicating ± 1 standard error of the mean.

income-compensated price change, mean consumption favored Tom Collins mix over root beer by a ratio of 2 to 1 (7.9 ml of root beer, 16.5 ml of Tom Collins mix). The rat reduced its consumption of root beer and increased its consumption of Tom Collins mix, as the theory requires. Further, returning prices and income to baseline levels, consumption returned as well (point X' in Figure 2.2b), providing further evidence that the income-compensated price change was re-

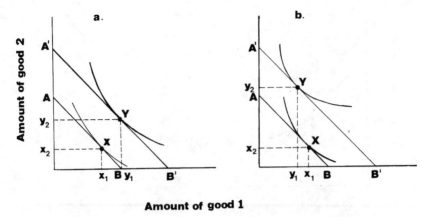

Figure 2.3 Income Effects. (a) The case of normal goods. The consumption of both goods increases when income increases. (b) The case of an inferior good. The consumption of good 1 decreases when income increases.

sponsible for the changes in consumption, rather than some uncontrolled change in experimental conditions or the rats' preferences. This reversibility of behavior permits each rat to serve as its own control (Sidman, 1960).

2.1d Income effects

Changes in income result in parallel shifts in the budget line. This is illustrated in Figure 2.3. In the normal case, increases in income result in increased consumption of a good. Such commodities are referred to as *normal goods*. Both goods in Figure 2.3a are normal goods. However, increases in income may also result in reduced consumption of a good. In this case, the good is called an *inferior good*, the case illustrated in Figure 2.3b for good 1. (Note that at least one good in the choice set must be a normal good – all goods cannot be inferior). It takes some engineering to devise an inferior good in animal choice experiments. We have done it using a quinine solution – a fluid that tastes bad but not so bad that rats avoid it completely (see Section 2.4b). Hastjarjo, Silberberg, and Hursh (1990) devised one using quinine-adulterated food pellets for rats.

2.1e Income-constant price changes

An *income-constant* price change is one in which the price of one good changes while income and the prices of all other goods remain constant. This is shown in Figure 2.4a, where the change from budget line AB to AB″ involves a reduction in p_1. Note that the reduction in p_1 not only alters the relative prices of the two goods (the slope of the budget line), but it also provides the consumer with more real income, in that he or she can afford to buy the same goods as

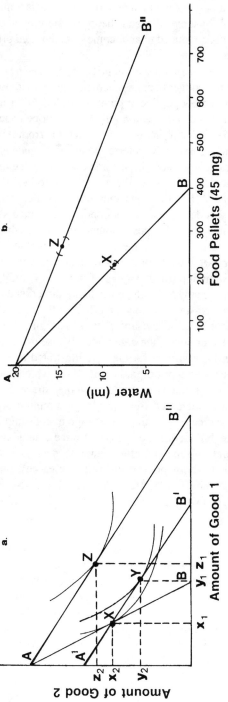

Figure 2.4 Income-constant price changes. (a) The effects of the price change can be broken into two parts, an income-compensated price change (budget line AB to A′B′), referred to as the substitution effect, and an increase in income (budget line A′B′ to AB″), referred to as the income effect. (b) An application to a rat choosing between food and water. Mean consumption values are reported with brackets indicating ± 1 standard error of the mean.

before the price change and still have income left over. This fact underlies the fundamental theorem of consumer-demand theory, namely, that an income-constant price change can be reduced to an income-compensated price change plus a change in income.

Figure 2.4a shows how an income-constant price change can be obtained by two separate changes in the budget line: an income-compensated price change (a change in the slope of the budget line at point X) with equilibrium moving from X to Y (referred to as the *substitution effect* of the price change), and a pure income change (a parallel shift in this new budget line from $A'B'$ to AB'') with equilibrium moving from Y to Z (referred to as the *income effect* of the price change). Note, in decomposing the income-constant price change into an income and a substitution effect, we, the analysts, introduce the income-compensated budget line $A'B'$ (the consumer normally does not see this budget line). However, this decomposition is important for understanding responses to income-constant price changes encountered in field environments.

With income-compensated price changes, the directional predictions of consumer-demand theory are unambiguous; there must be an inverse relation between prices and consumption (the movement from x_1 to y_1 in Figure 2.4a). For income-constant price changes, on the other hand, directional predictions of the theory are ambiguous, since the income effect of the price change (the response to the movement from budget line $A'B'$ to AB'' in 2.4a) may be to increase or decrease consumption of the commodity whose price changed (an increase in consumption from y_1 to z_1 for the case illustrated in Figure 2.4a), and economic theory makes no a priori predictions about which goods will be normal and which inferior. In the case of normal goods, the substitution and income effect both lead to increased (decreased) consumption for the good whose price decreased (increased), so that the change in consumption will be larger than for a comparable income-compensated price change. For inferior goods, on the other hand, the income effect leads to decreased (increased) consumption of the good whose price decreased (increased), which is the opposite response to the substitution effect. As such, the response to an income-constant price change will be smaller than for a corresponding income-compensated price change.

Figure 2.4b illustrates the effect of an income-constant price change for a rat choosing between food and water, with all consumption occurring within the experimental session. Under baseline conditions (budget line AB), 20 presses on the left lever resulted in the delivery of a 0.1 ml cup of water and 20 presses on the right lever delivered 2 (45 mg) Noyes food pellets. Income was fixed at 4,000 lever presses, with the rat free to distribute its income between the two goods. With budget line AB'', the price of food was reduced by increasing the number of food pellets delivered for each 20 lever presses from 2 to 5 pellets. Food consumption increased from 229 pellets a day, on average, to 269 pellets (from point X to point Z). Note that with the price change the rat could continue to purchase its baseline consumption package (229 pellets and 8.6 ml of water) with approximately 1375 lever presses left over to allocate to additional food and water consumption. Thus, unlike an income-compensated price change, in order to reach a higher indifference curve (be better off), there is no need to trade off increased consumption of the good whose relative price decreased (food) against reduced consumption of the other good (water). Rather, since the rat has more "real" income at its disposal, even if it chooses food and water in fixed proportions, it will increase food consumption following the price decrease (see Section 3.1). As such, income-constant price changes for normal goods are a less demanding test of the theory than income-compensated price changes.

2.2 **Experimental procedures**
Our experiments all involve choices between two commodities. In one series of experiments, the essential-commodity experiments, the choice was between food and fluid, and there was no access to any other consumption goods outside the experiment. Hursh (1980) refers to this as a closed economy experiment. In the other series, the nonessential-commodity experiments, the choice was over flavored fluids, such as root beer and Tom Collins mix, with ad lib access to food and water (Hursh's [1980] open-economy experiment.) An elementary knowledge of physiology suggests that indifference curves in the essential-commodity experiments will exhibit a low marginal rate of substitution throughout, whereas the nonessential-commodity experiments will exhibit a high marginal rate of substitution throughout.

Experiments were conducted using both rats and pigeons. In the rat experiments, the budget constraint was effected by using lever presses as a medium of exchange. The pigeon experiments used time as "money." These alternative procedures are explained below.

The use of lever presses as a medium of exchange was illustrated with Figures 2.2b and 2.4b above. Under these procedures, changing the amount of the commodity delivered per payoff, or altering the number of lever presses required per payoff, has the same effect on the budget constraint as a change in prices. Hence, the number of lever presses required per unit of commodity consumed corresponds to the concept of price and is referred to as such. Typically, prices were changed by altering the amount of the commodity per press. In all cases, lever pressing requirements were small in comparison with what rats can perform in experimental chambers (Collier, Hirsch, and Hamlin, 1972) and were not an effective constraint on total consumption. In almost all cases the rats would have readily made more lever presses if they were available (hence our use of consumer-choice terminology in preference to the labor-supply terminology developed in Chapters 4 and 5). White lights, one pair over each lever, remained lit as long as there was income left to be spent. Once the daily income allotment was spent, the lights were automatically extinguished until the next day, when the income allotment was replenished. Most rats quickly learned that pressing the lever was ineffective when the lights over the levers were out.

The experimental situation can be compared to that of a consumer purchasing goods from a two-commodity vending machine. Since, for the particular consumers at hand (rats), operating and handling money or tokens is a difficult behavior to learn, we do not require it to operate the machine. But, as we have described, the rats do have their budget constraint. And, extending the vending machine analogy, delivering smaller quantities per press was commonly used as a way of raising prices. Lever presses are but one of many possible mediums of exchange suitable for setting up the budget constraint. The adage "time is money" suggests another and, in an essential-commodity experiment with pigeons, we used time as the medium of exchange. In this case, the pigeons had access to food and water for a fixed period of time each day. Access to these goods was controlled by separate variable-time schedules. Under a variable-time schedule, commodities become available for a fixed period of time every α seconds, on average. Only one of the variable-time schedules was in operation at any given time, and the pigeon could switch between schedules by a single peck on a choice key. Pecks on this key were not required to continue food or water deliveries, but only to change between the commodities being delivered.

The price of each commodity was varied by altering the average time between deliveries (α) while holding access time per payoff constant. Thus, increasing (decreasing) the average time between food deliveries increases (decreases) its price in terms of the scarce resource time. Income changes were implemented by varying the total time available each day for the delivery of commodities.

Under both of these experimental procedures, the animal "knows" the economic contingencies it faces through experiencing them. There are no price announcements or paychecks to indicate the amount of money available for spending. Economists have argued that these circumstances present the animals with a more difficult choice situation than ordinary consumer-demand theory assumes. While this may be correct, it is not obvious to us that the conditions are more complex than those that human, or animal, consumers face in field environments. In the natural environment, it is costly to obtain information about prices at different locations, and ostensibly identical goods can differ greatly in quality. In contrast, the biological issue is: To what extent do these experiments mimic the animal's natural ecology? Biologists would argue that the more similar the experimental situation to the natural one, the more plausible the assumption that the animal will behave adaptively; adaptive behavior commonly coincides with the "rationality" requirements of consumer-demand theory.

Whatever the difficulty, our subjects responded quite rapidly to changes in price and income parameters. Usually within three observation periods (days), the data revealed major adjustments in their response behavior. In all cases, prices and income were maintained for a minimum number of days (generally 14), and conditions were not changed until subjects satisfied a stability criteria. Unless noted otherwise, all data refer to averages computed over the last several days of an experimental condition for which the stability criteria were satisfied.

Finally, we analyze choices among commodities ignoring lever pressing requirements except as they affect total expenditures. Since lever pressing may be viewed as a job, with leisure (not pressing) a positive argument in the utility function (see Chapters 4 and 5), this amounts to assuming that the utility function is *weakly separable* with respect to consumption and work. That is, while lever pressing requirements will undoubtedly affect how many total payoffs the animal will obtain, the total amount of lever presses required to obtain these payoffs does not affect the *composition* of consumption at any given income level.[2] This seems like a fairly safe assumption given the commodities in question and the minimal lever pressing requirements imposed. But the assumption is supported by both direct tests (Kagel et al., 1975; Thistle, 1983) and indirect tests based on comparing outcomes across experiments with time or lever pressing as the medium of exchange (see the next section).

2.3 Income-compensated price changes: Tests of the fundamental law of demand

The inverse relationship between prices and consumption under an income-compensated price change constitute the fundamental law of demand – the convexity of the indifference curves requires this inverse relationship. In this section we discuss the outcomes reported in various published accounts of these tests, as well as in unpublished follow-up studies. We do this in two ways. First, we report the number of compensated price changes implemented and count the number of times mean consumption decreased for the commodity whose relative price increased. Second, we report own-price elasticity estimates for each series of price changes implemented for a given subject from a given baseline condition. These elasticity estimates provide measures of substitutability for the commodities. (Price elasticities can take on values between 0 and $-\infty$: the smaller the absolute value, the less substitutable the goods are.)

Price elasticities are measured by fitting log linear functions to the data by the method of least squares

$$\log x_{it} = \log a_0 + a_1 \log (p_{it}/p_{jt}) \qquad (2.1)$$

where x_{it} equals the mean quantity of commodity i purchased in experimental period t, p_{it} equals the price of commodity i in time period t, and $\log a_0$ and a_1 are the intercept and slope coefficients. A convenient property of these functions is that the slope coefficient, a_1, provides a single direct measure of elasticity.[3]

Table 2.1. *Income-compensated price change effects*

Commodities employed	Percentage consistent choices[a]	Price elasticities: median (range)	Medium of exchange, procedures	Subjects (no.)
Food-fluid	87.5 (35/40)	−0.08 (−0.18 to 0.05)	Lever pressing; essential commodity	Rats (13)
Food-fluid	81.3 (13/16)	−0.07 (−0.13 to −0.03)	Time; essential commodity	Pigeons (8)
Fluid-fluid	100.0 (4/4)	−0.59 (−2.22 to −0.31)	Lever pressing; nonessential commodity	Rats (3)

[a]Number of consistent choices divided by number of tests shown in parentheses.

2.3a Essential-commodity experiments

Table 2.1 summarizes the results of the income-compensated price change tests. In the essential-commodity studies with rats, 87%, or 35 out of 40, of the compensated price changes resulted in increased consumption of the commodity whose price decreased, as the theory predicts. Assuming that responses to these price changes were strictly random – that is, that there was a 50 percent chance that a compensated price change would result in increased, or decreased, consumption of the commodity whose price changed – the probability of finding these many consistent responses is less than .01 (Conover, 1971, pp. 96–9).

The median price elasticity estimate here is −.08, which is relatively small. Nevertheless, substantial change in the food-to-liquid ratio is reported at times, by virtue of the compensatory nature of the price changes. For example, in one case, the food-to-liquid ratio (grams of food to milliliters of fluid) varied from a low of 0.61 to a high of 1.07, while in another case it changed from a low of 0.26 to a high of 0.82. These changes in the food-to-liquid ratio also resulted in significant weight changes, since rats chose not to defend a given weight level, and their metabolism could not compensate for the fluctuations in food intake. Note that with compensated price changes the budget line always passes through the original commodity bundle consumed, so the rats did not have to change consumption patterns. That they did is indicative of the importance of environmental conditions on feeding behavior and the fact that feeding mechanisms based strictly on momentary deficits and repletions (homeostatic control mechanisms) are inadequate to explain the animals' foraging strategies (for an extended discussion of the relative importance of environmental conditions on feeding behavior compared with traditional homeostatic control mechanisms, see Collier, 1986; and Collier and Johnson, 1990).

The results for the pigeons parallel those for the rats. Eighty-one percent, or 13 out of 16, of the compensated price changes implemented resulted in consistent substitution effects. Here, too, the likelihood of this happening by chance is less than 1 in 100. The price elasticity estimates are similar to the rats, with a median value of $-.07$.

All of these experiments using income-compensated price changes support the fundamental law of demand in that, overwhelmingly, consumption is reduced for commodities whose price increases. However, not all choices were consistent with the fundamental law of demand. One parsimonious explanation for the inconsistencies is that they may be due to stochastic elements in the animals' choices. That is, the commodity choice set varies somewhat from day to day even under constant experimental conditions. Therefore, we might expect some unexplained shifts in consumption that would result in inconsistent choices, particularly in view of the limited substitutability between commodities such as food and water. From this perspective, the key result is the statistical support for the fundamental law of demand.

In looking for some kind of consistent pattern to these inconsistent choices, we are limited by their infrequency. However, the pattern we have been able to identify (in five out of the eight cases) is that the inconsistency occurred over the initial set of compensated price changes studied and involved a shift in consumption such that baseline consumption was not recovered when baseline economic conditions were replicated. Income-compensated price changes that were then implemented on the basis of these adjusted baseline consumption values were consistent. The fact that so many of these inconsistencies occurred between early, rather than later, treatment conditions suggests that learning, or physiological maturation, may have been responsible for the unexplained shift in consumption that resulted in the inconsistency.[4]

2.3b Nonessential-commodity experiments

Table 2.1 also presents results from the nonessential-commodity experiments. In all four of the compensated price changes tried, we find reduced consumption of the commodity whose relative price increased. Price elasticity estimates and changes in consumption patterns are substantially larger than in the essential-commodity experiments. For the three rats studied, the smallest switch in consumption was from root beer to Tom Collins mix in the ratio of 0.48 to 9.23. This greater substitutability between nonessential, as compared with essential, commodities is to be expected in view of the physiological limits on substitution that underlie essential commodity choices.

With nonessential commodities, we have not observed any choices inconsistent with demand theory. Price-induced substitution effects have, apparently, been large enough to mask any minor changes in preference structure or inherent stochastic variability in choice.

2.3c Substitutability and variability over time

Purchase patterns over time under experimental conditions sometimes showed considerably greater variability than during the steady-state conditions used in computing price elasticities. Occasionally this variability meant that an experimental condition had to be maintained for as long as 60 days before our stability criteria were satisfied. This temporal pattern of behavior has two relevant characteristics. First, purchase patterns during the entire experimental condition were not always randomly distributed nor was the degree of variability during the last days of a condition necessarily indicative of the behavior preceding it. Second, the variability in purchase patterns (under a given condition) was positively correlated with the (absolute) size of the Slutsky substitution effect resulting from changes in relative prices.

Table 2.2 illustrates this point. Here, we restrict the analysis to periods with roughly comparable changes in relative prices. Within-period variability is measured in terms of the standard error of the percentage of daily income spent on one of the goods for all but the first five days of an experimental condition (excluding the first five days eliminates confounding from immediate adjustments to changes in experimental conditions).[5] The within-period variability measures show no overlap between essential- and nonessential-commodity experiments, the latter being markedly more variable.[6] This is in keeping with the minimal overlap between price elasticity estimates between the two commodity groups shown in the last column of Table 2.2.

The analysis can be taken one step further for the nonessential-commodity rats. Each of the rats faced identical baseline conditions with respect to incomes and relative prices (300 lever presses, 0.05-cc cups on both dipper mechanisms). This was followed, in each case, by an income-compensated price change of identical magnitude in which the relative price of the commodity that the subjects had been consuming more of during baseline was increased. Further, for N2, following the return to baseline conditions, root beer was introduced into both sides of the dipper mechanism and an income-compensated price change of identical magnitude implemented, in this case increasing the relative price of the favored side.

Table 2.3 shows the baseline variability under these conditions and the increase in consumption of the commodity whose price was reduced. The consumption data provide a direct comparison of substitutability here since commodities are measured in the same units and all subjects experienced identical changes in relative prices. The data show a pronounced positive correlation between variability and substitutability ($r = .87$, $t = 2.50$, d.f. $= 2$, $p <$ .10, 1-tailed t test). Further, with the introduction of root beer on both sides for

Table 2.2 *Substitutability and within-period variability*

Subject	Baseline income[a]	Within-period variability[b]		Price elasticity[c]	
		Baseline prices	Price-change period		
		Essential commodities			
E4	2,500 (133;120)	0.042	0.070; 0.018	−0.153 (liquid)	−0.126 (food)
E5	6,000 (100;143)	0.060	0.043; 0.018	−0.462 (liquid)	−0.177 (food)
E5	4,300 (143)	0.068	0.061		−0.75 (food)
		Nonessential commodities			
N1	300 (120;120)	0.091	0.104; 0.109	−1.25 (Collins mix)	−0.32 (root beer)
N2	300 (120)	0.094	0.204	−3.05 (Collins mix)	
N3	300 (120)	0.325	0.138		−3.61 (root beer)

[a]Percentage change in relative prices in parentheses. Measured as $(p_{i1} - p_{i2})/[(p_{i1} + p_{i2})/2]$, where p_{it} is the relative price of the good whose price changed in period t.
[b]Standard error of the percentage of daily income spent on one of the commodities excluding the first five days of a treatment condition. In case of multiple baselines, standard errors are averaged over periods.
[c]Good whose price changed. Price change period measured against immediately preceding period using equation (2.1) in text and daily data from the stability period for income-compensated price changes.
Source: Kagel, Battalio, Rachlin, and Green (1980).

subject N2, which, by definition, flattens out the indifference curves and increases substitutability, variability increased substantially, as did consumption of the cheaper root beer.

Thiel's (1975) theory of rational random behavior suggests an explanation for this positive correlation between variability and substitutability. Under this theory, the factors responsible for variability consist of the whole set of environmental conditions not completely controlled for in the experiment: for example, changes in temperature and humidity, changes in the physical composition of the commodities over time (shelf-like effects on food pellets), the force required to press the lever, and so on. These changes involve small changes in the cost of consumption, which, since they effectively involve small shifts in the budget

Table 2.3. *Variability and substitutability within nonessential-commodity experiments*

Subject	Variability during baseline[a]	Substitution effect of price change[b]
N1	0.091	13.61
N2	0.094	28.07
(with root beer and Collins mix)		
N2	0.306	53.47
(with root beer both sides)		
N3	0.325	40.67

[a]See note *b* in Table 2.2.
[b]Increase in milliliters of consumption of commodity whose relative price decreased.
Source: Kagel, Battalio, Rachlin, and Green (1980).

line and are essentially random in nature, should result in greater variability in consumption the more substitutable the commodities are. As a result, substitutability as measured in response to experimenter-induced shifts in the budget line should correlate with the within-period variability, and it does.[7]

2.4 Ordinary (uncompensated) price changes

In these experiments, income is no longer adjusted to cause the new budget constraint to pass through the original consumption bundle. Rather, the budget constraint was changed by changing the price of a single commodity while holding constant both the price of the other commodity and nominal income (lever presses). In comparing these results with those of the previous section, it is useful to view this change as having two component parts: (1) a rotation through the original consumption bundle, as in the previous section, and (2) a parallel shift in the budget constraint. That is, we can view the uncompensated price change as a Slutsky-compensated change plus a change in income (recall Figure 2.4a). Viewed from this perspective, if the goods are normal (as in the experiments reported in Section 2.3), own-price elasticity estimates must be greater for uncompensated, compared with compensated, price changes. This prediction provides an additional test of consumer-demand theory.

2.4a Normal goods

For essential-commodity experiments with rats choosing between food and fluid, ordinary demand curves invariably have a negative slope, and price elasticity estimates are considerably larger than for these same rats under income-compensated price changes: the median is -0.20, with a maximum of -0.90 and a minimum of -0.12, whereas with the income-compensated price changes the median was -0.08. Further, food and fluid are *gross complements*, so that reductions in the price of food increase *both* food and fluid consumption. As is shown in Chapter 3, this response pattern is incompatible with the leading quantitative choice model in the psychology literature, the matching law.

For nonessential-commodity experiments in which rats chose between flavored fluids, similar increases in price elasticities, in relation to income-compensated measures, were obtained: They yield a median price elasticity estimate of -1.05, with a maximum of -6.39 and a minimum of -1.02, compared with a median of -0.59 for the income-compensated procedure. For these studies, the two fluids tend to be *gross substitutes*, so that reductions in the price of one fluid tend to *reduce* consumption of the other fluid.

Gross substitutability between nonessential commodities and gross complementarity between essential commodities can be explained in terms of income and substitution effects. All the commodities we are dealing with here are normal goods, so that the income effect of a price decrease for one good results in increased consumption for *both* goods. Further, the substitution effect of a price decrease results in increased consumption of the good whose relative price decreased and *reduced* consumption of the good whose relative price increased (the "other" good; recall Figures 2.2a and 2.4a). Consequently, for normal goods, the substitution effect works in the opposite direction to the income effect for the "other" good. And substitution effects are relatively small for essential as compared to nonessential commodities. The net result is that for essential commodities the income effect of the price change tends to swamp the substitution effect for the "other" good, in which case the goods are gross complements, whereas for nonessential commodities the substitution effect tends to swamp the income effect, in which case the goods are gross substitutes.[8]

The income-constant price changes reported here represent a small fraction of the demand curves for animal consumers that have been reported. Rather extensive studies of income-constant demand curves for normal goods have been published in the psychology and biology literature in terms of animals working for a single commodity (see, e.g., Allison, 1979; Lea, 1978; Hogan and Roper, 1978). These are discussed in Chapter 4, which deals with labor-supply behavior.

2.4b   Inferior/Giffen goods

In the case of inferior goods, when the income effect is larger (in absolute value) than the substitution effect, the net result is a positive relation between prices and consumption: That is to say, as price decreases, consumption decreases as well. In this case, the commodity is referred to as a *Giffen good*. There is some debate in the literature concerning the existence of Giffen goods and the reliability of reputed sightings of the phenomenon in data from national economies (see Dwyer and Lindsay, 1984; Stigler, 1947, 1948;). Further, as an empirical proposition, few would quarrel with Hicks's assertion: "the simple law of demand – the downward slope of the demand curve – turns out to be almost infallible in its working. Exceptions to it are rare and unimportant" (Hicks, 1946, p. 35). Nevertheless, our experimental verification of the existence of Giffen goods is important theoretically since their existence is incompatible with a number of competing explanations of consumer-choice behavior.

The problems inherent in identifying Giffen goods in market data from national economies (Dougan, 1982; Dwyer and Lindsay, 1984), can be overcome in a laboratory environment. The experimenter can control supplies of the commodity in question and can structure the environment in an effort to induce the commonly cited precondition for observing Giffen goods – namely, inferior goods should take up a sizable portion of a consumer's expenditures. And searches for the existence of Giffen goods in animal laboratories have been successful, at least at the level of individual subject demand (Battalio, Kagel, and Kogut, 1991; Hastjarjo, Silberberg, and Hursh, 1990).

In our experiment, rats chose between two liquids, root beer and a quinine solution, with ad lib access to food in their home cages. We used a quinine solution because its bitter taste meant that rats would not particularly care for it but would nevertheless consume it rather than go thirsty. To induce consumption of the quinine solution, the baseline price of quinine was half the price of root beer (two cups of quinine per lever press to one cup of root beer).

There were two parts to the study. In the first part, we changed income levels while holding prices constant, in order to determine if quinine was indeed inferior, as theory requires if it is to be a Giffen good. If quinine is an inferior good, its consumption should decrease as income increases, and increase as income decreases. For three of the six rats studied, quinine proved to be strongly inferior. Data for these three rats are shown in Figure 2.5. The income elasticity of demand for quinine (ξ_m) is shown in each case (income elasticities are measured as the percentage change in quantity consumed divided by the percentage change in income). The negative sign of the income elasticity of demand for quinine indicates that it was inferior, and its size indicates that it was strongly inferior for all three of these rats (quinine consumption increased by 50% or more following reductions in income of 20–30%).

The second step of the study involved changing prices. Demand curves resulting from these price changes are shown in Figure 2.5. If quinine is a Giffen good, the demand curve must be positively sloped. This is indeed the case for the three rats in Figure 2.5. For two of the rats, 532 and 543, we observe a reversible sequence of data points. That is, quinine consumption moved in the same direction as the change in relative prices for both the initial price decrease and the price increase when baseline conditions were replicated. For the third rat, 542, the first price decrease resulted in a sharp reduction in quinine con-

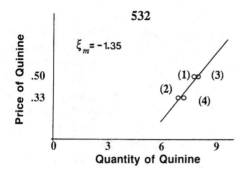

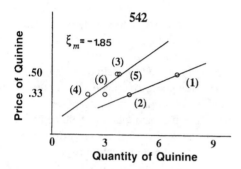

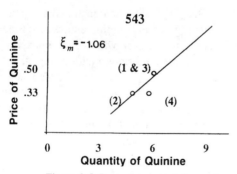

Figure 2.5 Income-constant demand curves for rats showing strong inferiority in quinine consumption. Numbers indicate the sequence in which price changes were studied. Income elasticity of demand (ξ_m) shown next to the demand curve.

sumption, but with the return to baseline prices in condition 3, there was a marked decrease in quinine consumption in relation to baseline (compare points 1 and 3). Subsequent price changes produced results (relative to the subject's new reduced level of quinine consumption) similar to those obtained for the other two rats.

Demand curves for the three rats for which quinine was not strongly inferior are reported in Figure 2.6, along with the corresponding income elasticity measures (ξ_m). For two of these three rats (531 and 533), there were no significant changes in quinine consumption following reductions in income, whereas the relatively large positive income elasticity reported for the third rat, 541, indicates that quinine was a normal good, at least over this income range. For each of these rats, the price changes yield standard negatively sloped demand curves that are in marked contrast to those in Figure 2.5. The contrasting results between these two cases provide added support for the theory, which states that a necessary condition for the existence of a Giffen good is strong inferiority.[9]

One interesting postscript to this study is that aggregate per capita demand for quinine, a standard measure of demand reported for field data, fails to provide strong evidence that quinine is a Giffen good. Averaged across rats, consumption was 6.09 cc per capita under the original baseline prices, with a modest, statistically insignificant, decrease in consumption to 5.90 cc following the first price decrease. Thus, at the market level, the rats' differences in consumption patterns resulted in a negligible, and statistically insignificant, reduction in quinine consumption in response to the reduction in its price. These differences in consumption patterns among individuals may be another reason, previously unrecognized in the literature, why Giffen goods are so difficult to identify in market data.

Hastjarjo, Silberberg, and Hursh (1990) have also demonstrated the existence of a Giffen good, in this case using regular and quinine-adulterated food pellets with rats. They examined the consumption path within a given experimental session. They observed that the entire consumption path changed, not just the final choice ratios, following income and price changes. These results suggest that changes in consumption patterns are based on anticipated daily income from a session (more on this point in Section 3.2C). Using somewhat different procedures, Silberberg, Warren-Boulton, and Asano (1987) arrived at similar results with two monkeys choosing between regular and quinine-adulterated food pellets.

2.5 The relationship of economic demand theory to optimal foraging theory

Rapport (1971) developed a simple geometric model, based on consumer-choice theory, to analyze optimal choice for predators possessing food preferences. A specialized version of the model produces the marginal

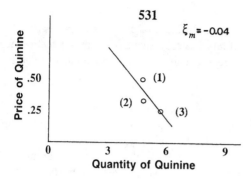

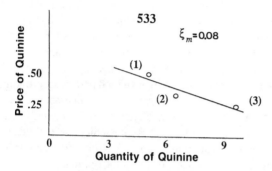

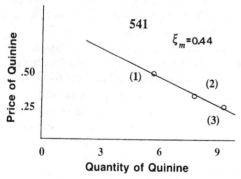

Figure 2.6 Income-constant demand curves for rats showing weak inferiority or normalcy in quinine consumption. Numbers indicate chronological sequence of price changes. Income elasticity of demand (ξ_m) shown next to the demand curve.

value theorem (Charnov, 1976; Parker and Stuart, 1976), which is widely used to analyze foraging behavior between different patch types (foragers are predicted to equate marginal rates of return across patch types). In this section, we review Rapport's model and the relationship between demand theory and the marginal value theorem.

2.5a Predators' choice with food preferences

Time serves as the medium of exchange in Rapport's model; predators have a limited amount of time at their disposal in which to capture prey. The prices of alternative prey are measured in terms of the time-cost of capture and handling. The budget constraint may be linear, which indicates constant capture and handling costs per unit of time, or concave (to the origin), which indicates increased capture and handling costs as prey become scarcer. Uniform changes in prey availability result in parallel shifts in the budget constraint and correspond to changes in the predator's income, whereas increased availability of a given prey type corresponds to an income-constant price change, and thereby alters the slope of the budget constraint (and one of the intercepts as well).

In Rapport's model, the predator is assumed to have food preferences among the different prey types, either because the prey satisfy different essential food requirements or because certain prey types taste better. Preference yields convex indifference curves, with the degree of convexity indicating the substitutability of the different prey in satisfying nutritive requirements or taste tradeoffs. Figure 2.7a illustrates the model and shows the optimal prey choice for the case of increasing marginal cost of prey capture.

In Rapport's model, if nature is ruthlessly efficient in "weeding out" individuals that fail to make optimal food choices, then the optimal choice point (point X in Figure 2.7a) is one that will yield the maximum inclusive fitness to the animal in relation to any other point on the budget constraint. This notion of optimality, common in the biology literature, is quite different from the economist's, for whom tastes are regarded as given, even if they are detrimental to the consumer's health (*de gustibus non est disputandum*; see, for example, Stigler and Becker, 1977). For the economist, on one hand, the question is simply whether the marginal return per unit price is the same across commodities. If so, no reallocation of expenditures (in this case time) will make the consumer better off, *as defined by his/her own preferences*. For the biologist, on the other hand, inclusive fitness relates to the ability of individuals to replicate, although once one allows for uncertainty (Chapter 6) or distinctions between long- versus short-run survival requirements (Chapter 7), it can become difficult to specify unambiguously those behaviors that maximize fitness. Finally, most biologists are keenly aware that evolutionary processes respond neither so finely nor so rapidly to environmental shifts that inclusive fitness is ever likely to be fully maximized.[10]

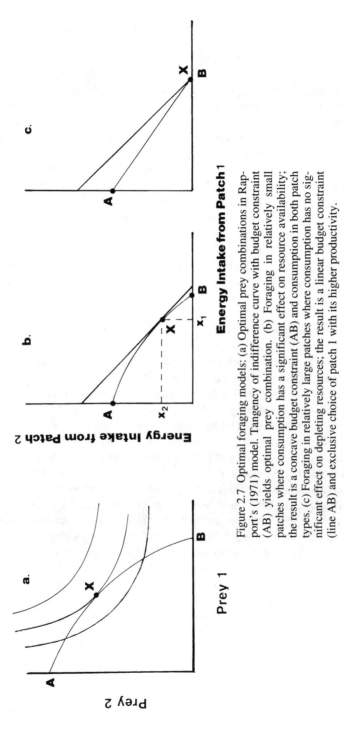

Figure 2.7 Optimal foraging models: (a) Optimal prey combinations in Rapport's (1971) model. Tangency of indifference curve with budget constraint (AB) yields optimal prey combination. (b) Foraging in relatively small patches where consumption has a significant effect on resource availability; the result is a concave budget constraint (AB) and consumption in both patch types. (c) Foraging in relatively large patches where consumption has no significant effect on depleting resources; the result is a linear budget constraint (line AB) and exclusive choice of patch 1 with its higher productivity.

Rapport employs this model to analyze the phenomenon known as "predator switching" (Murdoch, 1969). "Predator switching" is defined by Murdoch as a predator's consumption of alternative species that is more than proportionate to the change in relative abundance of the prey (so that the prey in question are gross substitutes). Rapport notes that within the framework of his model, diet changes result from a shift in the budget constraint (line AB in Figure 2.7a) rather than from any change in "preferences," as Murdoch suggests.

Stephens and Krebs (1986, chap. 5) note that while this sort of time-constrained choice model is suitable for studying trade-offs between activities such as foraging and territorial defense, or between foraging and vigilance, it has not found wide used in behavioral ecology (an exception is a study of the trade-off between foraging and territorial defense in great tits by Kacelnick, Houston, and Krebs, 1981). One reason for its limited use is that behavioral biologists are more interested in quantitative predictions with regard to survival probabilities than predictions about qualitative trade-offs that are of interest to economists and psychologists (Stephens and Krebs, 1986).

2.5b Predators' choice without food preferences: The marginal value theorem

A question of much broader concern in the optimal foraging literature concerns efficient exploitation of a *single* food type (or food characteristic), given differences in the costs of exploiting scattered resources. The marginal value theorem characterizes a predator's optimal behavior when foraging in such a "patchy habitat." The general problem is stated as follows (Charnov, 1976). Food is found in clumps or patches, and each patch yields a different prey density (food intake) per unit cost of exploiting the resource. (Costs are typically specified in terms of net energy expenditure or time spent in capturing and handling prey.) The predator must make decisions as to which patch types it will visit and when to leave the patch it is presently in. An important assumption of the model is that while the predator is in a patch, capture rates decrease with the time spent there. That is, foraging depresses the availability of prey so that although energy intake increases with time or energy spent in a patch, the rate of increase decreases with time spent in the patch. In effect, the price of additional units of consumption increases as the predator consumes more in any particular patch.

Time is specified as the medium of exchange. The marginal value of time spent foraging in a patch is defined as the *incremental* food return from an additional unit of time spent in a patch. As the marginal value of time decreases, the price of consumption increases.

The concave function AB in Figure 2.7b shows the budget constraint the forager faces in obtaining food from one of two patches under the assumption that the marginal value of time is decreasing as more time is spent in a patch. By definition, the slope of the budget line is (in absolute value) equal to the ratio of marginal prices, in this case the ratio of the marginal (incremental) value of time spent in the two patches. As we have drawn it, if the forager spent all of its time in patch 1 it would obtain a higher total energy intake than if it spent all of its time in patch 2. However, under our construction, the slope of the budget line at point B is such that the predator can increase its total energy intake by leaving patch 1, reallocating some of its time to patch 2. That is, the marginal value of time in patch 2 is greater than in patch 1 at point B. The problem to be solved is how much time to spend in each patch.

The optimal choice point is the point where the budget line (AB) and the indifference curve are tangent. By assumption, there are no qualitative differences in the value of prey items across patches (only capture cost differences), and there are no factors dictating a preference for one patch over another, such as a differential probability of being the prey of some other predator! Consequently, the indifference curves for energy intake from the two patches are linear, with a slope equal to -1.0; energy from patch 1 is a perfect substitute for energy from patch 2. At the point of tangency between the budget line and the indifference curve (point X in Figure 2.7b) the slopes of the two curves are equal, so that in equilibrium choice occurs at a point on the budget line with slope of -1.0. At this point the marginal value of time spent in the two patches must be equal.

The marginal value theorem has been the subject of a number of investigations in field settings, seminaturalistic settings, and in the laboratory. The two primary means of testing the model have consisted of (1) manipulating travel times between patches while measuring the time spent in each patch, and (2) presenting the predator with a number of patches of different quality and comparing marginal encounter rates at the time of departure by patch type. These studies provide strong qualitative support for the model. Cowie (1977), for example, found that birds spent substantially more time in patches when travel time was increased between identical patches; this result satisfies the theory. Hubbard and Cook (1978) looked at wasps' strategies for laying eggs. Although not strictly a foraging problem, it is similar, in that the wasp should try to maximize its encounter rate with suitable hosts. In this study, the wasps' behavior was close to optimal except for the fact that they spent more time than predicted in the patches with the lowest density. This observation was attributed to the wasp's need to sample patches before deciding if they were worth exploiting, a feature omitted from the marginal value formulation that assumes predators know the encounter rates of different patch types. Results similar to Hubbard and Cook's have been reported for different species of birds (for reviews of these studies, see Cowie and Krebs, 1979).

In addition to equating marginal rates of return across patches, the marginal value theorem predicts that this marginal rate of return will equal the average rate of return for the habitat as a whole. As the appendix to this chapter shows, the latter prediction fails to hold when there is a binding constraint on the time available for foraging, as will typically be the case. With a binding time constraint, optimality requires that the marginal return for foraging in each patch be greater than the average rate of return from foraging in the habitat as a whole. This has the observable implication that foragers will leave patches earlier than they would in the absence of a time constraint (or earlier than they should, according to the marginal value theorem). This fact appears to have gone unrecognized in the literature, although it will have an effect on some quantitative tests of the theory (see the appendix).[11]

2.5c Predators' choices without food preferences: Choosing between ratio schedules of reinforcement

Consider the case in which patch sizes are large enough, in relation to a particular predator's activities, that energy intake in a patch is not diminished with increased time spent foraging there. This results in a linearization of the budget constraint, as in Figure 2.7c. Optimality now requires the predator to spend all of its time in the higher-yielding patch.

Psychologists have, in fact, conducted experiments of this sort, using concurrently available fixed-ratio (FR) or variable-ratio (VR) schedules of reinforcement. On an FR schedule, the animal must respond a fixed number of times, say 10 responses (FR10), to receive a reinforcement; but the reinforcement rate does not diminish with increased responding. A VR schedule is similar to an FR schedule except that the experimenter programs a mean number of required responses per payoff, plus a stochastic term whose mean value is zero, which results in variability in the response requirement. Where FR or VR schedules are concurrently available and the same amount and type of reinforcer is present on all schedules, the animal faces a linear budget constraint whereby the relative "prey" densities are equal to the inverse of the response requirement (that is, the higher the ratio value, the lower the density.)

Under these conditions, the main effect is maximization. That is to say, pigeons come close to exclusive preference for the smaller of the pair of ratio schedules (Green, Rachlin, and Hanson, 1983; Herrnstein and Loveland, 1975). For example, the average deviation from exclusive choice of the smaller VR exceeded 5% of total responses in only 1 of 12 treatment conditions in Herrnstein and Loveland. Exclusive choice often occurred when the ratio values studied were maximally different, with the largest deviations from exclusive choice occurring when the ratio values differed the least. Deviations from full maximization suggest some sort of threshold effect before differences between the two schedules are fully recognized and acted upon, an effect that is likely to be exacerbated by the stochastic nature of the two schedules (see Section 6.6).

From a broader biological perspective, this residual variability may be adaptive; nonexclusive choice increases the likelihood that the organism will adapt to unstable environmental circumstances. In either case, the results clearly differ from probability matching (Brunswik, 1939; Estes, 1964; see Section 3.2b of this volume) in favor of maximizing, as both consumer-demand theory and the marginal value theorem require.

2.6 Summing up

The results reported in this section provide overwhelming support for the fundamental law of demand (consistent responses to income-compensated price changes) and for negatively sloped income-constant demand curves in the case of normal goods. Having confirmed the most basic propositions of the theory, we have the foundations needed to begin an experimental analysis of the economic behavior of animals. There are two purposes behind our initially studying such "well-known" phenomena (meaning that most economists are already convinced of these phenomena in wider market environments). First, as an exchange in the *American Economic Review* points out, even the most basic phenomena require more adequate documentation:

Laboratory experiments [of market and small group behavior] in economics have been structured around the assumption of fully determinate preference orderings, usually in the form of prespecified demand and supply value schedules. This assumption is basic to standard choice theory, but it is nevertheless a theoretically created rather than an empirically discovered feature. (Heiner, 1985, p. 263)

The evidence for a bedrock assumption of economic theory – the existence of well-defined individual preferences – is not very compelling in nonexperimental market settings. (Friedman, 1985, p. 264)

It is useful to examine such basic phenomena as part of the basic reevaluation of the discipline in which experimentalists are engaged (Smith, 1982). The second objective of our reestablishing "well-known" phenomena is strictly practical. It provides a starting point for attacking other more complex and controversial issues.

Experimental verification of the existence of Giffen goods is important, not because these goods are likely to be observed in market data, but because verification of their existence validates one of the few counterintuitive predictions of demand theory. Although the Giffen response, under conditions designed to produce it, was far from universal (it occurred in only three of our six rats), it was found to be reliably associated with conditions of strong inferiority for the commodity in question. Equally important, standard negatively sloped demand curves occurred for rats for whom quinine consumption was normal or only mildly inferior. The implication is that it is not so much the Giffen phenomenon per se that is difficult to generate, as much as it is the initial condition of strong inferiority that the theory calls for.

There have been earlier direct tests for transitivity of preferences and efforts to construct indifference curves for pigeons and rats.[12] For example, Logan (1965) constructed indifference curves and tested for transitivity between the amount of and delay to reinforcement using different groups of rats. He reported that transitivity predictions yield "tolerably good results" (p. 8). Navarick and Fantino (1972, 1974) report intransitive choices, but they employ a utility model that makes stronger assumptions about preferences than the ordinal utility model developed here, and their transitivity tests depend critically on these stronger assumptions.[13] In our discussion of choice under uncertainty (Chapter 6) and time preferences (Chapter 7), we specify particular utility functions with stronger assumptions (and more precise predictions) than the general, ordinal utility theory that applies to choice under uncertainty and time preferences, and we find violations of these models as well.

A number of the results of this chapter, and those of Chapter 4 concerning the labor-supply behavior of pigeons, have found their way into introductory texts in economics. In addition to being "cute" (which they are), the results serve to support the basic notion of maximizing behavior underlying much of economic analysis. As Paul Samuelson notes,

It is possible to formulate our conditions of equilibrium as those of an extreme problem, even though it is admittedly not a case of an individual's behaving in a maximizing manner, just as it is often possible in classical dynamics to express the path of a particle as one which maximizes (minimizes) some quantity despite the fact that the particle is obviously not acting consciously or purposively. (Samuelson, 1974, p. 23)

Hence, in the studies we have described, the animal subjects may be viewed "as if" they were maximizing, while yet remaining intrinsically passive reactors to conditions and constraints, reflecting generations of natural selection and the fact that our experimental procedures have not strayed too far from the animals' natural ecology. Alternatively, it may be that animals are capable of acting on the basis of conscious forethought in relatively simple situations such as those explored here. Under either interpretation, a better understanding of adaptive principles may suggest domains in which "optimizing" behavior breaks down and poor performance results.

Traditionally, economic analysis has been applied to goods and services traded in the marketplace. But over the past 30 years, economic principles have been applied to a wide range of activities, both in and out of the marketplace. Economists study love and marriage (Becker, 1981; Manser and Brown, 1980), medieval agriculture (McCloskey, 1989), crime and punishment (Becker, 1968; Ehrlich, 1973), and even the demand for sleep (Biddle and Hamermesh, 1990).

A common complaint about such extensions is that these are situations in which individuals are acting nonrationally. However, if one were to suggest that our animal subjects are nonrational (after all, they are pigeons and rats), then results such as ours strongly suggest that basic economic principles, such as income and substitution effects, are indeed applicable to these areas.[14] At the same time, there are rival explanations for the behavior we have reported. These are discussed in Chapter 3.

Appendix: The marginal value theorem with a time constraint

This appendix has two purposes: (1) to formally relate the consumer-choice problem specified in the text to the marginal value theorem, and (2) to show the effects of introducing a time constraint into the optimal foraging problem specified in Charnov (1976) and Parker and Stuart (1976).[15] We proceed as follows. First, we develop a generalized version of Charnov's optimal foraging problem using notation and terminology commonly employed in the economics literature, and we establish the optimality conditions for this model. We then relate these optimality conditions to the typical specification of the optimal foraging problem in the behavioral biology literature, which is directly related to our specification, except that in the behavioral biology literature there is no time budget to constrain choices. We characterize the bias resulting from failure to account for the time constraint when it is binding and relate this bias to a well-known test of the marginal value theorem.

The marginal value theorem argues that the forager equates marginal capture rates across patches within a habitat and that the marginal capture rate in each patch equals the average capture rate for the habitat as a whole. With the introduction of a time constraint, an optimal forager will equate marginal capture rates across patches, but the marginal capture rate will be greater than the average capture rate for the habitat. Time-constrained choice is more relevant than unconstrained choice, except in cases where the marginal return from additional foraging is zero – that is, except when there is an unlimited amount of time for foraging, or the animal is satiated. The distinction between time-constrained and unconstrained choices has important implications for evaluating tests of the theory, which are briefly developed.

2A.1. The basic model

We assume that there are n commodities available for consumption, $x_1, x_2, \ldots, x_n$, which must be obtained by the decision maker (forager) using time, energy and, possibly, other inputs. For example, a fox must hunt to obtain food, and hunting requires a time input on the animal's part. Or a member of a primitive tribe must gather berries, which requires a time input, the effort in gathering the berries, and also a basket to hold the berries. Since we are interested primarily in the marginal value theorem, we will concentrate only on the time input. The extension to other types of inputs is straightforward.

We next specify a production function that determines the relation between the time spent in the ith activity, t_i, and the amount of the ith commodity produced. We assume that

$$x_i = g_i (t_i) \tag{2A.1}$$

where g_i is twice differentiable, increasing, and concave. In the Charnov model, g_i represents the assimilated energy from hunting for t_i units of time in a patch of type i, corrected for the cost of searching.

Finally, we assume that the utility function depends on the commodities available for consumption, the x_i's. The objective of the decision maker is to choose the amount of time to be allocated to each activity such that utility is maximized subject to the production constraints facing the decision maker, given by equation (2A.1), and the constraint on the total amount of time available to the decision maker. Formally, the decision maker must choose $t_1, \ldots, t_n$ to maximize

$$\begin{aligned} U &= F(x_1, \ldots, x_n) = F[g_1(t_1), \ldots, g_n(t_n)] \\ &= \phi (t_1, \ldots, t_n) \end{aligned} \tag{2A.2}$$

subject to (2A.1) and

$$T = TR + \sum_{i=1}^{n} t_i \tag{2A.3}$$

where T is the total amount of time available and TR is total travel time, for example, the time it takes to move from one activity to another. $F(\cdot)$ is assumed to be twice differentiable and increasing in the x_i's.

As formulated above, the optimization problem is a standard classical programming problem. Define the Lagrangian as

$$L = \phi(t_1, \ldots, t_n) + \lambda\left(T - TR - \sum_{i=1}^{n} t_i\right)$$

where λ is the associated Lagrange multiplier. The necessary and sufficient conditions for a maximum are:

$$L_i = \phi_i - \lambda = \left(\frac{\partial F}{\partial x_i}\right)g_i' - \lambda = 0 \qquad i = 1, \ldots, n \tag{2A.4}$$

$$L_\lambda = T - TR - \sum_{i=1}^{n} t_i = 0 \tag{2A.5}$$

the border-preserving principle minors of

$$J = \begin{vmatrix} L_{11} & L_{12} & \cdots & L_{1n} & L_{1\lambda} \\ \cdot & \cdot & \cdots & \cdot & \cdot \\ L_{n1} & L_{n2} & \cdots & L_{nn} & L_{n\lambda} \\ L_{\lambda 1} & L_{\lambda 2} & \cdots & L_{\lambda 1 n} & 0 \end{vmatrix} \tag{2A.6}$$

alternate in sign beginning with plus,

$$\text{where } L_i \equiv \frac{\partial L}{\partial t_i}, \qquad L_{ij} \equiv \frac{\partial^2 L}{\partial t_i \partial t_j}, \qquad \phi_i \equiv \frac{\partial \phi}{\partial t_i} \qquad \text{and } g_r' \equiv \frac{\partial x_i}{\partial t_i}$$

Rearranging the equations given in (2A.4), we have that

$$\phi_i = \phi_j = \lambda, \qquad \text{for all } i, j.$$

This last equation implies that time should be allocated across activities such that the marginal value of time is equal across all activities, provided the decision maker does not violate the time constraint.

2A.2 *Relation to the marginal value theorem*

In order to illustrate the relation between our first-order conditions and the marginal value theorem, we will use the original Charnov model (Charnov, 1976) for comparison. Charnov assumes that $g_i(t_i) = h_i(t_i) - E_{si}t_i$ where $h_i(t_i)$ is the assimilated energy from hunting for t_i units of time in patch i, and E_{si} is the energy cost per unit of time spent searching in the ith patch.

In deriving the marginal value theorem, Charnov further assumes that the utility function takes the form:

$$F = \frac{\displaystyle\sum_{i=1}^{n} g_i(t)_i - TR \cdot E_{TR}}{\displaystyle TR + \sum_{i=1}^{n} t_i} \tag{2A.7}$$

where E_{TR} is the energy cost per unit of time spent traveling between patches. In this instance, the utility function is interpreted as the net rate of energy intake. The utility function embodies the assumption that the forager does not possess food preferences, or that foodstuffs are identical across patches, so that the sole objective is to maximize net energy intake.

Notice that, given this objective function, the forager does not face a constraint on the amount of time available for hunting. The forager is free to choose any values for the t_i's that maximize net energy intake. That is, unlike the model formulation in Section 2A.1, the objective function (equation 2A.7) is maximized with no consideration for equation (2A.3), the time constraint.

The first-order conditions for this optimization problem yield the marginal value theorem. In particular, the forager should choose the t_i's such that

$$\phi_i = \frac{\left(TR + \displaystyle\sum_{i=1}^{n} t_i\right) g_i' - \left(\displaystyle\sum_{i=1}^{n} g_i - TR \cdot E_{TR}\right)}{\left(TR + \displaystyle\sum_{i=1}^{n} t_i\right)^2} \qquad i = 1, \ldots, n. \tag{2A.8}$$

Rearranging the first-order condition (2A.8) and evaluating at the optimum point gives the marginal value theorem:

$$g_i'(t_i^*) = F^*, \qquad i = 1, \ldots, n$$

where t_i^* is the optimal amount of time to spend in the ith patch and F^* is the maximized value of the objective function. This equation implies that, at the optimum, the marginal capture rate is equal across patches and is equal to the average capture rate for the habitat as a whole.

If there are only two patches, we can illustrate this optimization problem graphically. In Figure 2A.1a, we have drawn two curves associated with the objective function given in equation (2A.7). Each level curve shows the different combinations of hunting times that yield the same net energy intake. The optimal amount of time to spend in the two patches is given by point A in the diagram. Here the forager is satiated.

In Figure 2A.1a, the time constraint is depicted as a straight line with a slope of minus one. Note that in this figure, the satiation point (A) is inside the time constraint, so that the forager can hunt until satiation is attained. In this instance, the marginal value theorem as specified by Charnov (1976) and Parker and Stuart (1976) holds. However, also notice that in this case, the hunter-gatherer has excess time, which means that foraging in one patch imposes no costs in terms of forgone opportunities for prey capture in another patch.

The problem solved by Charnov is fundamentally different from the one discussed in Section 2A.1 since there is no binding time constraint (equation (2A.3) is not accounted for). The importance of this observation is illustrated by comparing Figure 2A.1a with 2A.1b. In Figure 2A.1b, the satiation point is outside the time constraint; that is, the forager does not have enough time to hunt and capture enough prey to become satiated, which means that time spent in patch one is costly in terms of forgone opportunities for foraging in patch j. In this instance, the marginal value theorem does not hold.

We can quantify the graphical analysis by using the model discussed in Section 2A.1. Given Charnov's objective function, optimality conditions (2A.4) become

$$g_i' = F + \lambda T, \qquad i = 1, \ldots, n. \tag{2A.9}$$

Now, using the envelope theorem (see Silberberg 1978, pp. 170–1, for example), we have that

$$\lambda = \frac{\partial F^*}{\partial T} \tag{2A.10}$$

Substituting (2A.10) into (2A.9) gives

$$g_i' = F^* + \left(T \cdot \frac{\partial F^*}{\partial T} \right), \qquad i = 1, \ldots, n \tag{2A.11}$$

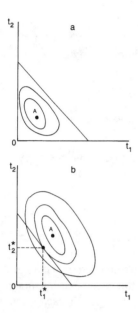

Figure 2A.1 (a) If the satiation point (point A) is inside the time constraint, the marginal value theorem does hold. (b) If the satiation point (point A) is outside the time constraint, the marginal value theorem does not hold.

The marginal value theorem implies that when time is allocated optimally, $g'_i = F^*$. From equation (2A.11) it is clear that the marginal value theorem holds only if $\partial F^*/\partial T = 0$; in other words, the marginal value theorem holds only if an exogenous change in the time constraint has no impact on the maximized value of the average capture rate for the habitat as a whole (this corresponds to the situation shown in panel (a) of Figure 2A.1). This condition is unlikely to be satisfied in practice. Rather, with a binding time constraint (panel (b) in Figure 2A.1), $\partial F^*/\partial T > 0$ so that from equation (2A.11) $g'_i > F^*$, the marginal capture rate will exceed the average capture rate for the habitat as a whole.

These results have important implications for what constitutes appropriate quantitative applications of the theory; that is, applications relying on $g'_i = F^*$ are incorrectly specified when there is a binding time constraint. Further, our theoretical analysis allows us to *measure* the magnitude of the error for given energy intake functions. The error is simply $T(\partial F^*/\partial T)$.

2A.3. *An application*

To illustrate our results, consider the case in which there are n identical patches, and the forager's production function (the assimilated energy from hunting corrected for the cost of searching) is given by

$$g(t_i) = Q[1 - \exp(-mt_i)] - E_s t_i, \qquad i = 1, \ldots, n \qquad (2A.12)$$

where m and Q are positive constants.

Using equation (2A.12), the first order-conditions imply that

$$t_i^* = t^* = \left(\frac{T - TR}{n} \right), \qquad i = 1, \ldots, n$$

Substituting these optimal values into the objective function, we have

$$F^* = (1/T) [ng(t^*) - E_{TR} \cdot TR]$$

Differentiating F^* with respect to T and multiplying the result by T gives the error

$$\left(T \frac{\partial F^*}{\partial T} \right) = [g'(t^*) - F^*]$$

where $g'(t^*) = m \cdot Q \cdot \exp[-m(T - TR)/n] - E_s$. Note that if $g'(t^*) > F^*$, then the error term is positive, and the forager will spend less time in each patch then is indicated by the marginal value theorem. This result is shown in Figure 2A.2. When there is no constraint on the amount of time available for foraging, net energy intake is maximized when $\hat{t}$ units of time are spent in each patch. When there is a binding time constraint, net energy intake is maximized when t^* units of time are spent in each patch. In this case, if one is relying on the marginal value theorem to test behavior, the forager will appear to spend too little time in each patch.

In Cowie's test (1977) of the marginal value theorem, a study that is sometimes cited as one of the most precise tests of the model (Krebs, Houston, and Charnov, 1981), equation (2A.12) was used to estimate the net rate of energy intake, with mean values of $Q = 6.36, m = 0.0081$ and $E_s = 0.155$. In Cowie's (1977) experiment, six wild great tits (*Parus major*) were studied in two environments, one with high "travel costs" and one with low "travel costs." (Patches could not be separated far enough apart within the confines of the aviary, so Cowie covered each patch with a cardboard lid to influence the "travel cost." The lid was hard to remove in the case of high travel cost and easy to remove in the case of low cost.) Six trials were conducted on each of six birds. Each trial was preceded by 2 hours of food deprivation and lasted 10 minutes. Cowie (1977) notes that satiation and overall depletion of the environment had no observable effect within the 10-minute foraging period allotted.

Assuming a common production technology for all birds, Cowie (1977) determined the "optimal" relationship between travel time and time in the patch, using parameter values for equation (2A.12) based on mean values for all six birds, and equating the marginal capture rate with the average capture rate for the habitat as a whole, as the marginal value theorem requires. He then compared the "optimal" relationship with the actual relationship between mean

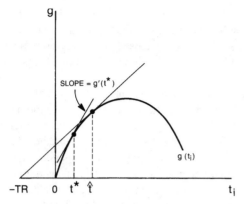

Figure 2A.2 Optimal foraging time with identical patches; $\hat{t}$ is the optimal amount of time to spend in each patch according to the marginal value theorem and the optimal patch time in the absence of a time constraint on foraging; t^* is the optimal amount of time to spend in each patch when the forager faces a binding time constraint, the case most likely to be encountered in practice.

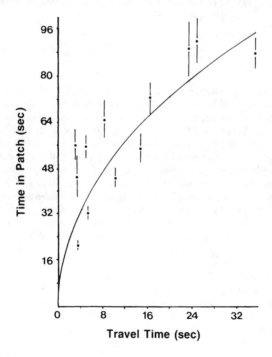

Figure 2A.3 Results from Cowie's (1977) experiment. Solid line is optimal solution if it is assumed that the marginal value theorem holds (no time constraint). Closed circles are average values for individual birds, with bars showing standard error of the mean.

travel time and mean time for each bird in both environments. Figure 2A.3 shows Cowie's (1977) data; the solid line represents the "optimal" relationship between travel time and time in a patch, and the closed circles represent average values for each of the birds under both environments, with vertical bars representing the standard error of the mean.

Approximately half the data points lie below the predicted "optimal" solution line; these birds spent too little time in each patch in relation to the marginal value theorem's prediction. This is consistent with the positive error term that our analysis predicts. The other half of the data lie above the predicted solution based on the marginal value theorem, with these birds spending more time in each patch than the marginal value theorem predicts. This is not consistent with the positive error term predicted. Taken literally, these data points imply $\partial F^*/\partial T < 0$, so that the birds would prefer to spend less time foraging, as they are operating beyond the satiation point in Figure 2A.1a. However, since the birds were free to stop foraging but did not do so, this cannot possibly be the case. Rather, the data points above the predicted optimal solution line must mean either an error in Cowie's (1977) empirical specification, a failure on the birds' part to respond to the time constraint, or some other deviation from the foraging model formulated, such as might result from imperfect information and search costs.

Notes

1 Lever-pressing requirements are trivial here in comparison with what a rat can perform – see Chapters 4 and 5 – and are ignored. For further discussion of this issue, see Section 2.2.

2 For example, consider a rat obtaining food and water at a cost of 1 lever press per payoff with an income of 100 lever presses versus the same rat obtaining the same payoffs at a cost of 10 lever presses per payoff and with an income of 1,000 lever presses. Weak separability of consumption from leisure requires that *if* all of the income is used up in both cases, then the composition of consumption will be the same. However, weak separability does not require the rat to use up its allotted income in both cases, in which case the total composition of consumption cannot be compared across conditions.

3 Price elasticity of substitution ξ_p is defined as $(\partial x_{it}/\partial p_{it})(p_{it}/x_{it})$. Normalizing the price of the other commodity, p_{jt}, to 1 and differentiating equation (2.1) with respect to p_{it} yields $\partial x_{it}/\partial p_{it} = a_i (x_{it}/p_{it})$ so that $\xi_p = a_i$. The choice of which commodity to employ in the own-price regression is arbitrary. We used food in the essential commodity studies and root beer in the nonessential commodity studies.

4 Battalio et al. (1981) also noted a tendency for inconsistencies to result from compensated price changes that did not originate from the baseline budget line. Follow-up experiments were conducted on four rats in an attempt to determine the generality of this phenomenon but failed to replicate it; of eleven compensated price changes that did not originate from the baseline, only one resulted in an inconsistent choice.

5 This measure is invariant to the commodity we chose to measure and controls for the fact that at higher incomes subjects can vary the absolute amount of a commodity consumed more than at lower income levels.

6 Applying a two-sample *t* test to these data, we can reject the hypothesis that consumption patterns are equally variable between the essential and nonessential commodity conditions ($p < .01$).

7 Strictly speaking, the logic underlying this argument calls for a one-way relationship, whereby large day-to-day variability implies large substitution effects, and whereby one can observe relatively large substitution effects in the absence of relatively large, day-to-day variability in choices. The latter might arise in cases of exclusive, or near-exclusive, choice of a given commodity, as might happen, for example, with nearly perfect substitutes (nearly linear indifference curves), given a linear budget constraint. The interesting thing here, however, is that we observe considerable variability in choice even with the same, equally priced commodities behind both levers before the pattern settles down to near-exclusive choice.

8 More generally, the less substitutable two goods are, holding income effects constant, the smaller the cross-price elasticity of demand $(\partial x_{it}/\partial p_{jt})(p_{jt}/x_{it})$.

9 Income-compensated price changes were implemented for rats 532, 542, and 543 following the income-constant price change reported in Figure 2.5. Rats 542 and 543 showed a small (statistically insignificant) decrease in quinine consumption in response to an increase in its relative price (as demand theory requires), whereas rat 532 showed a small, statistically insignificant increase in quinine consumption. However, a further increase in the relative price of quinine, directed through this new choice point, produced a statistically significant reduction in quinine consumption ($t = 4.23$, $p < .01$, 2-tailed *t* test, d.f. $= 8$). This provides additional evidence that the positively sloped demand curves reported result from the mechanism specified within the theory.

10 In the behavioral ecology literature, methodological discussions of optimality theory can be found in Maynard Smith (1978) and Stephens and Krebs (1986).

11 Brown (1988) uses constrained optimization techniques from economics to extend Charnov's (1976) marginal value theorem to include the effects of predation risk and alternative activities on patch use. Thus, he introduces a time constraint on choice, as we do. However, he does not determine the bias resulting from the failure to account for the time constraint when it is binding, as we do. This is required to assess the bias associated with ignoring the time constraint, a bias that has been ignored in a number of empirical studies (see the appendix to this chapter).

12 Interestingly, the psychologist Thurstone (1931) initiated the first study along these lines using human subjects. Roth (in press) offers a brief history of the work done with human subjects. Also see Battalio et al. (1973).

13 Navarick and Fantino (1972, 1974) test a strengthened version of strong stochastic transitivity called functional equivalence. Let $P(X,Y)$ represent the frequency of choosing X over Y in a series of pairwise comparisons. Then functional equivalence requires that if $P(X,Y) = 0.5$ then $P(X,Z) = P(Y,Z)$. In terms of pairwise choices, ordinal utility theory only requires weak stochastic transitivity: if $P(X,Y) \geq 0.5$ and $P(Y,Z) \geq 0.5$, then $P(X,Z) \geq 0.5$. This is a considerably weaker requirement than functional equivalence (see Navarick and Fantino, 1974, and the references cited therein). Functional equivalence is similar to the independence axiom of expected utility theory, which we show to be violated, while choices still satisfy weak stochastic transitivity (Chapter 6).

14 In applying economic choice theory to these different areas, crucial supplemental assumptions are made regarding the sign of the income effect (whether the commodities in question are normal or inferior goods), the relative strength of income effects compared to the substitution effects, and the like. Needless to say, our experiments rarely

have anything to say about these crucial supplemental assumptions. Rather, what they do indicate is that objections to these applications of economic reasoning based on the argument that behavior outside market situations is likely to be nonrational is probably misplaced.

15 This appendix was written in collaboration with Michael B. Ormiston of the Department of Economics, Arizona State University.

3

Commodity-choice behavior II: Tests of
competing motivational processes and the
representative consumer hypothesis

> What the empirical data do confirm is that demand curves generally have neg-
> ative slopes. . . . But negatively sloping demand curves could result from a
> wide range of behaviors.
>
> (Simon, 1979, p. 496)

As the experiments reported in Chapter 2 demonstrate, income-compensated
price changes reliably result in reduced consumption of goods whose price has
increased. Further, in the case of normal goods, income-constant demand
curves are negatively sloped. Although these studies provide new evidence to
support some of the standard operating principles of economic analysis, the
question remains, what decision rule, or behavioral process, underlies these
outcomes? In this chapter, we examine competing behavioral allocation rules
to determine which ones best organize the data. We consider random behavior
models, psychological/biological models of choice, and utility function formulations commonly employed in the economics literature.

We consider four competing behavioral allocation rules. The first is Becker's
(1962) *irrational choice model,* in which essentially random behavior controls
choices. That is to say, negatively sloped demand curves do not result from any
explicit utility-maximizing process but are incidental to random behavior in
conjunction with changes in the budget constraint. The second rule is the
matching law (Herrnstein, 1961, 1970), which is prominent in the psychology
literature. Under some conditions, the matching law produces optimizing outcomes. Under others, it results in suboptimal behavior. The last two rules considered are explicit utility-maximizing formulations. The first of these,
proposed by a number of biologists and psychologists, is that behavior is motivated by attempts to minimize deviations from some optimal-state values
(Houston and McFarland, 1980; Staddon, 1979a). We consider a generalized
version of this model, known as the *generalized minimum distance (MD) hy-*

47

pothesis, the most familiar example of which is the quadratic utility function. The fourth rule is an alternative to the MD hypothesis; it is one in which consumers attempt to meet "minimum" survival requirements first, after which they are free to allocate expenditure in any fashion. This *generalized minimum needs (MN) hypothesis* is adopted in many applications of consumer-demand theory (see, for example, Pollak and Wales, 1980), and is characterized, at a first approximation, by the generalized constant-elasticity-of-substitution utility function. Each of these four motivational processes has distinctly different implications for consumer preferences and responses to variations in prices and income. These various implications are reflected in the tests we report in Sections 3.1–3.3.

The remainder of the chapter deals with two related issues. Section 3.4 examines the degree to which the "representative consumer" hypothesis holds for our data; that is, the degree to which aggregate per capita data, of the sort usually available to economists, reflect individual choices within the aggregate. Finally, Section 3.5 uses consumer-demand theory to investigate the incentive effects of different reinforcers, notably, brain stimulation and food, an area of investigation usually considered the province of physiological psychology.

3.1 Random behavior models

Negatively sloped demand curves need not result from any explicit "rational" choice process. Simon (1979), in advocating this position, cites Becker's (1962) finding that nonrational choices are capable of producing negatively sloped demand curves in the absence of any explicit maximization process. Becker (see also Chant, 1963) shows that random behavior by a collection of individuals, in conjunction with changes in the budget set, can result in negatively sloped aggregate demand curves. This formulation can be adapted and applied to the behavior of individual subjects. The resulting model implies restrictions on a system of demand equations identical to those derived from individuals maximizing a particular utility function. Consequently, if individual choices are found to be consistent with a random behavior model, then we must look for additional implications of the model that differ from the corresponding utility maximization formulation or accept the apparent equivalence of the two representations and choose between them on other grounds. Random behavior models seem a particularly appropriate null hypothesis for studies of choice with animals, given their limited cognitive capacities. Three types of random choice models are considered in this chapter: random money deciders, random goods deciders, and a mixed model comprising a weighted average of the first two.

3.1a Model specification

Random money deciders randomly allocate expenditures across commodities. In our experiments, this would involve, for example, rats randomly allocating lever presses between two commodities such as food and liquid. Now suppose, as is typically the case, that price changes occur because of a change in the payoffs for responding – say, the food payoff is increased and the liquid payoff decreased in an essential-commodity experiment. The consumer, in continuing to randomly allocate lever presses between commodities, will naturally end up consuming more of the cheaper food and less of the expensive fluid. This will happen for both income-constant and income-compensated price changes, so that consumer-demand theory is fortuitously satisfied.

As an example, consider a consumer with 100 lever presses. Each press on one lever delivers one pellet of food, and each press on the other lever delivers 0.1cc of water. Assume that the consumer randomly allocates its responses, 40% to the food lever and 60% to the water lever, and thereby obtains 40 food pellets and 6 cc of water. If we were then to institute an income-compensated price change by halving the price of food (2 pellets of food per payoff instead of 1) and doubling the price of water (0.05 cc of water delivered in place of 0.1 cc), income would need to be increased to 140 lever presses. It follows that continued random allocation of responses, 40% to the food lever and 60% to the water lever, must result in increased consumption of the now cheaper food (112 food pellets) and reduced consumption of water (4.2 cc of water).

To determine whether a random money rule actually underlies animals' choices, we compare the expenditure patterns predicted by this model with actual expenditure patterns. Let e_i be expenditure on commodity i; $e_i = p_i x_i$ where p_i is the price of good i and x_i is the amount of good i purchased. Random money deciders have expenditure functions of the form

$$e_i = \beta_i m, \qquad \beta_i > 0, \qquad \sum_i \beta_i = 1, \qquad i = 1, \ldots, n \qquad (3.1a)$$

where m is total expenditure on the n goods and β_i is the share of money income devoted to good i. Solving equation (3.1a) for x_i yields the demand function for commodity i:

$$x_i = \beta_i \frac{m}{p_i}, \qquad \beta_i > 0, \qquad \sum_i \beta_i = 1, \qquad i = 1, \ldots, n \qquad (3.1b)$$

The choice functions (3.1a-b) may also be derived from the following utility function

$$U = \sum_i \beta_i \log(x_i), \qquad \beta_i > 0, \qquad \sum_i \beta_i = 1, \qquad i = 1, \ldots, n \quad (3.2)$$

under a maximization hypothesis. (A *utility function* provides a mathematical characterization of the preference structure, so that for any given level of utility, U, the set of commodity bundles $\{x_1, x_2, \ldots, x_n\}$ satisfying (3.2) defines an indifference curve. The utility function (3.1b) is called a Cobb–Douglas utility function in economics.) Maximizing (3.2) subject to a linear budget constraint yields equations (3.1a-b).

Random goods deciders are similar to random money deciders, except that their decisions are based on goods rather than money. Under this model, a consumer will randomly choose a collection of goods from those obtainable. If the consumer spends all of his income on the goods available and applies the same allocation rule independent of income level, then there should be no systematic response to income-compensated price changes since these price changes always permit consumption of the original commodity bundle. However, if income-constant price changes were to occur under a random goods rule, consumption would automatically satisfy the law of demand, since the income effect of the price change would serve to guide consumption in the "right" direction.

Demand functions consistent with these expenditure patterns are of the form

$$x_i = \frac{\beta_i m}{\sum_k \beta_k p_k}, \qquad \beta_i > 0, \qquad \sum_i \beta = 1, \qquad i = 1, \ldots, n \qquad (3.3)$$

and may also be derived from a fixed coefficient utility function

$$U = \min_i \left[\frac{x_i}{\beta_i} \right], \qquad \beta_i > 0, \qquad \sum_i \beta_i = 1 \qquad (3.4)$$

Pure random goods deciders and pure random money deciders are polar models. Becker (1962) suggests extending the framework by taking weighted averages of the two behavior classes; individuals might obtain part of their consumption by randomly purchasing goods, while any remaining income is allocated according to a random money deciders rule. A demand function that captures this kind of behavior is

$$x_i = \gamma_i + \frac{\beta_i}{p_i} \left(m - \sum_k \gamma_k p_k \right), \qquad \beta_i, \gamma_i > 0, \qquad \sum_i \beta_i = 1 \qquad (3.5)$$

Within the random choice framework, the γ_i represent random purchases of goods (provided income is sufficient to cover expenses $(m - \sum \gamma_k p_k) \geq 0$), with remaining purchases following a random money deciders rule. Demand functions of the form (3.5) are a special case of the linear expenditure model (Stone, 1954) in that the γ_i are constrained to be positive. If one or more of the γ_i terms is negative, the linear expenditure model still constitutes a valid system of demand equations. A negative γ_i, however, is incompatible with the present interpretation.[1] The system of demand equations (3.5) can be derived under a maximization hypothesis from a utility function of the form

$$U = \sum_i \beta_i \log(x_i - \gamma_i), \qquad \beta_i, \gamma_i > 0, \qquad (x_i - \gamma_i) > 0, \qquad \sum_i \beta_i = 1 \quad (3.6)$$

The mixed random choice model describes more adaptive behavior in response to changes in prices and income than either of the pure random choice strategies.

3.1b   *Initial test results*

We can reject the pure form of the random goods decider model on the basis of the experimental evidence reported in Chapter 2. Random goods deciders do not change consumption in response to income-compensated price changes. However, 86% of the compensated price changes for essential commodities, and 100% of those for nonessential commodities, resulted in reduced consumption of the commodity whose price increased. This systematic response pattern is consistent with consumer-demand theory and involves far too many changes in one direction to be explained on the basis of chance factors alone.

A key implication of the pure random money deciders model is that the ratio of expenditures between different commodities remains constant, regardless of changes in relative prices or income. That is, dividing e_i by e_j using equation (3.1a),

$$\frac{e_i}{e_j} = \frac{\beta_i}{\beta_j} \tag{3.7}$$

where β_i/β_j is a constant. Figure 3.1 graphs the relative expenditure on food and water by a group of rats, in response to a series of income-compensated price changes. According to equation (3.7), the expenditure ratio should not vary with relative prices; that is, the data should lie on a straight line *parallel* to the horizontal (price) axis. Instead, the data show a clear positive slope; the expenditure ratios vary directly with relative prices, contrary to the pure random money deciders model.[2] The problem with the random money model is that the demand for food and fluid is price inelastic, so that even though the quantity of food consumed increases following a price decrease, the increase is small enough that total expenditure on food decreases.

We report tests of the more flexible mixed random choice model, equation (3.5), in Section 3.3.

3.2   **Matching law**

In this section we first present a thorough specification of the model and then discuss its ability to organize our data. We show how both consumer-demand theory and the matching law organize choices on concurrent schedules of reinforcement. These schedules have been extensively studied by psychologists and have provided the empirical basis for the development of the matching law. We also show how direct extensions of the matching law to consumer-demand studies, like those reported in Chapter 2, fail to organize the data.

3.2a   *Model specification*

The matching law is an effort to quantify the "law of effect," a first principle of behavioral psychology stating that greater reinforcement produces

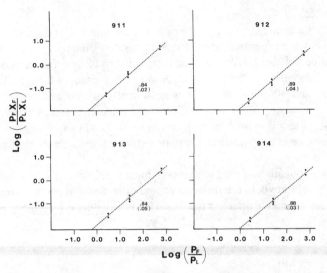

Figure 3.1 Graph of the log of the expenditure ratio (on the vertical axis) as a function of the log of the relative price ratio (on the horizontal axis) for income-compensated price changes. Straight lines determined by method of least squares with slope estimate shown directly below each line (standard error of the estimate in parentheses).

greater response strength (Hull, 1942; Skinner, 1938; Thorndike, 1911). The question of concern here is how to sensibly quantify this principle of behavioral psychology? The answer offered by Herrnstein (1961, 1970) is to use the relative frequency of response as the measure of response strength. In its simplest form, the matching law states that given two response alternatives, 1 and 2:

$$\frac{C_i}{C_1 + C_2} = \frac{R_i}{R_1 + R_2}, \qquad i = 1,2 \tag{3.8a}$$

or

$$\frac{C_1}{C_2} = \frac{R_1}{R_2} \tag{3.8b}$$

where C_1 and C_2 are choice frequencies (the amount of time or the number of responses allocated to the two alternatives), and R_1 and R_2 are *obtained* rates of reinforcement from these choices.

Equation (3.8b) bears a superficial resemblance to the first-order condition for a consumer maximizing a utility function subject to a budget constraint

$$\frac{p_1}{p_2} = \frac{MU_1}{MU_2} \tag{3.9}$$

where MU_1 and MU_2 measure the *marginal utilities* of the two goods (the *increase* in value from the *last* unit of a good consumed) and p_1 and p_2 measure the prices of the two goods. However, the C_1 and C_2 in equation (3.8) do not measure prices, but rather response rates that, as we will show, are only indirectly related to prices, and then only under special circumstances. Further, the R_i in (3.8) represent average reinforcement rates, the average value of consumption, in contrast to the marginal reinforcement rates in (3.9). Progressive ratio schedule procedures, discussed in Section 5.2d, provide a direct test of this difference between the two formulations.

The matching law has been successfully applied to concurrent ratio and variable-interval schedules of reinforcement when both alternatives deliver the *same* commodity such as food or water or money (typical examples of procedures producing matching are provided in Section 3.2b). In this respect, it has been validated across a variety of species, including rats, pigeons, and humans (for reviews, see Davison and McCarthy, 1988; and de Villiers, 1977). According to its proponents, the matching law is a biologically based rule that maximizes reinforcement rates in situations commonly encountered in nature but is likely to result in suboptimal behavior in less common or artificial situations that can be constructed in the laboratory.

Melioration theory (Herrnstein and Prelec, 1991; Herrnstein and Vaughan, 1980; Vaughan, 1985) is a quasi-dynamic model whose equilibrium predictions yield matching under a number of common experimental procedures. Melioration theory provides a mechanism that explains matching under a number of common experimental procedures. According to melioration theory, organisms allocate behavior on the basis of the difference, D, between local reinforcement rates

$$dF/dt = f(D) = f(N_1/C_1 - N_2/C_2) \qquad (3.10)$$

where F is preference for the alternative whose current local rate of reinforcement is N_1/C_1 (where N_1 is the number of reinforcers *obtained* from alternative 1), and $f(D)$ is any increasing function such that $f(0) = 0$.[3] At equilibrium $N_1/C_1 - N_2/C_2 = 0$, so that rearranging yields $C_1/C_2 = N_1/N_2$. Dividing the numerator and denominator of the right-hand fraction by $C_1 + C_2$ converts this fraction to the ratio of the overall rate of reinforcement, R_1/R_2, which equals (matches) the choice ratio (equation 3.8a). In what followes we restrict our attention to comparing equilibrium predictions of the matching law with the equilibrium predictions of consumer-demand theory, since our applications of demand theory to animal choice behavior have focused on these predictions and have by and large ignored dynamic adjustment paths (however, see Section 7.4 for some discussion of this topic).[4]

When applying equation 3.8b to data, one typically employs Baum's (1974) generalization of the matching law

$$\frac{C_1}{C_2} = h \left[\frac{R_1}{R_2} \right]^y \tag{3.11}$$

where h and y are constants to be estimated from the data. The coefficient h represents bias, a systematic asymmetry, often of unknown origin, between the alternatives. A complete lack of bias would be the case in which $h = 1$. Rats frequently display a position bias in choosing between alternative levers, and pigeons sometimes show a color bias in choosing between alternatives signaled by color coding of the response keys. Such biases are readily measured experimentally by switching the reinforcement schedules between levers and by switching colors. When the value of the exponent $y > 1$, the behavior is called overmatching; the subject overvalues the richer schedule of reinforcement. When $y < 1$, the behavior is called undermatching; the subject overvalues the leaner schedule of reinforcement. When the constants h and y both equal 1, the generalized matching equation (3.11) reduces to equation (3.8b).

Values of y less than 1 (undermatching) are frequent (Baum, 1974; Myers and Myers, 1977). For example, in data reviewed by de Villiers (1977) y varied from 0.6 to 1.29 for 34 individual subjects from seven separate experiments, its median value being 0.94. Undermatching represents a "systematic deviation from the matching relation . . . in the direction of indifference" (Baum, 1974, p. 232). Procedural variations among experiments that may lead to undermatching have been discussed by Baum (1974, pp. 277–9). In addition, undermatching may be due to the subject's inability to discriminate completely between the choice alternatives (Baum, 1974), particularly when both alternatives produce the same type and quantity of reinforcement, the common practice in studies of matching (see Section 3.2b).[5] In contrast, a discrimination-problem account of undermatching does not seem compelling in the case of qualitatively different reinforcers (for a discussion of this issue, see Green and Freed, 1993).

3.2b Successful applications of the matching law and related predictions from consumer-demand theory

As mentioned earlier, the matching law has successfully explained behavior under concurrent ratio and concurrent variable-interval schedules of reinforcement, when the *same* commodity is delivered from both alternatives. We shall briefly describe the procedures underlying these experiments, present typical experimental outcomes, and point out the similarity of predictions offered by consumer-demand theory and melioration theory regarding these results.

With respect to concurrent ratio schedules of reinforcement, our discussion of the relationship between the marginal value theorem and consumer-demand theory explained how the latter predicts exclusive allocation of time to the schedule with the higher payoff (lower ratio value) (recall Section 2.5c). The matching law (equation (3.8a)) is trivially consistent with exclusive choice of either one of the alternatives: when all choices are allocated to one alternative, all reinforcement is obtained from that alternative, and thus matching obtains. Melioration theory (equation (3.10)) bolsters the matching law because it predicts that equilibrium choices will be exclusively confined to the higher-valued alternative. Imagine two independent slot machines, one paying off twice as often as the other, at even money. If a man played the machines equally, he would receive twice as many coins per response (twice the rate of reinforcement) from the better machine. Melioration theory predicts that play will shift steadily toward the higher payoff machine until that machine is played exclusively. The fact that responding on the richer ratio schedule does not reduce the average rate of reinforcement on that schedule generates exclusive choice for the richer schedule.

This prediction of exclusive choice under ratio schedules of reinforcement is not trivial or degenerate; in cases with stochastic payoffs (as with variable-ratio schedules), it goes against the "probability matching" hypothesis, sometimes advanced to describe gambling behavior (Brunswik, 1939). According to probability matching, responses are allocated among alternatives so that choice frequencies equal the probability of reinforcement: $C_1/(C_1 + C_2) = \rho_1/(\rho_1 + \rho_2)$ where ρ_1 is the probability of reinforcement on schedule 1 (the inverse of the average response requirement on a variable-ratio schedule of reinforcement). Depending on the probability of reinforcement on the two schedules, probability matching can imply relatively large deviations from exclusive, or near-exclusive, choice. However, in cases where subjects receive actual (as opposed to hypothetical) payoffs, in which instructions to humans do not imply that the subject will be successful only if all payoffs are received, and in which the contingencies are clearly presented, subjects respond nearly exclusively to the higher-value alternative, consistent with the matching law and consumer-demand theory (Bruner, Goodnow, and Austin, 1956; Green, Rachlin, and Hanson, 1983; Herrnstein and Loveland, 1975; Siegel, 1961; also, recall the discussion in Section 2.5c).

On variable-interval (VI) schedules, subjects, on average, receive reinforcement for the first response made after a prescribed period of time has elapsed; for example, a VI two-minute schedule will deliver one unit of reinforcement for the first response after two minutes, on average. The times between reinforcement availability are stochastically determined. Under typical procedures, once a reinforcer is set up, it is held until collected and the time clock setting up delivery of additional reinforcers is stopped and begins running again only after the reinforcer is collected.[6] The uncertain time between reward availability, in conjunction with the deprivation period that typically precedes an ex-

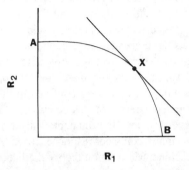

Figure 3.2 Curve AB shows how reinforcement rates vary as time devoted to responding to each schedule varies under conc VI–VI procedures. Allocating time exclusively to either one of the VI schedules eliminates reinforcement from the other schedule and reduces the overall rate of reinforcement. With a straight line indifference curve, the equilibrium choice point is at X.

perimental session, is usually sufficient to induce a moderate, but steady, response rate under VI schedules.

Under typical concurrent variable-interval schedules (conc VI–VI schedules), two independently programmed VI schedules run simultaneously.[7] Further, there is usually a fixed cost in terms of a changeover delay (COD) for switching between schedules, a period of a few seconds during which responses cannot produce reinforcement. (The COD is designed to help the subject distinguish between reinforcement contingencies on the two alternatives. In the absence of a COD, there is rapid switching back and forth between response alternatives.) Although psychologists disagree as to the exact nature of the constraint faced under conc VI–VI procedures, there is general agreement that the response rates generated are sufficiently high and invariant between the two alternatives so that increasing the time spent on one alternative reduces the realized reinforcement rate on that alternative. This produces a concave constraint like AB in Figure 3.2. If the rat devotes all of its time to the richer VI schedule, it fails to collect any reinforcers from the leaner schedule. Given this budget constraint, it is necessary to specify the rat's preferences in order to identify the most preferred consumption point. With identical reinforcers, and no position bias, preferences between payoffs on the two schedules must be represented by a straight-line indifference curve. This indifference curve is tangent to the budget constraint at a point where the marginal rate of reinforcement is the same for each alternative (point X in Figure 3.2). Further, as has been demonstrated under a variety of assumptions regarding the exact nature of the budget constraint for conc VI–VI schedules, matching and maximizing produce essentially the same outcome (Morgan and Tustin, 1992; Rachlin 1978; Rachlin et al. 1976; Rachlin, Kagel, and Battalio, 1980; Staddon, 1980; Staddon and Motheral, 1978). A brief demonstration follows.

The peculiar coincidence of matching and maximization under conc VI–VI schedules follows from the structure of the constraint embodied in VI schedules. This can be approximated by a power function

$$R_i = a_i C_i^b, \quad b < 1 \tag{3.12}$$

where a_i is equal to the average time interval between reinforcer setups plus the average time between responses. Taking the derivative of (3.12): $dR_i/dC_i = ba_i C_i^{b-1}$, and equating marginal rates of reinforcement across schedules, as required by consumer-demand theory and the marginal value theorem, yields

$$ba_i C_i^{b-1} = ba_j C_j^{b-1}$$

Substituting from (3.12) gives

$$\frac{bR_i}{C_i} = \frac{bR_j}{C_j}$$

or

$$\frac{C_i}{C_j} = \frac{R_i}{R_j}$$

Even proponents of the matching law agree that differences between the matching and maximizing predictions are sufficiently small under conc VI–VI procedures to yield observationally distinguishable results (Herrnstein and Vaughan, 1980; Prelec, 1982). As a result, testing between the two models has shifted to other procedures, as discussed in Sections 3.2c and 5.2.

3.2c Extensions of matching to qualitatively different reinforcers

Direct extensions of the matching law generally fail to explain choice behavior when different commodities, such as food and water or root beer and Tom Collins mix are the alternatives. This is hardly surprising given that the theory was not set up to explain such choices. In what follows we show two important ways in which commodity behavior deviates from matching and explain when, and why, such deviations may be expected. We also discuss some of the proposals adherents of the matching law have offered to modify the theory in attempts to explain these outcomes.

Antimatching: choices between gross complements.

When commodities are gross complements, so that they have price-inelastic demand curves, as is the case with essential commodities such as food and water, the choice ratio moves inversely to the reinforcement ratio; that is, $y < 0$ in Baum's generalized matching formulation, a situation we call *antimatching*. Figure 3.3 graphs the data for food and water consumption in terms of the matching law (equation (3.8b)), for the rats reported on in Figure 3.1. Least-squares estimates of the slope coefficient in Baum's generalized matching for-

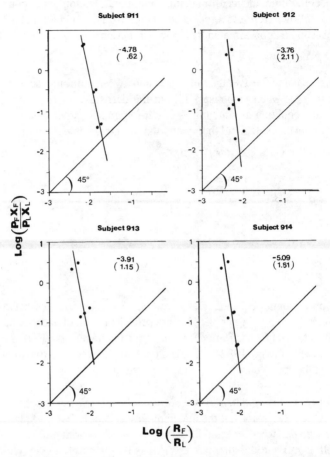

Figure 3.3 Graph of log of expenditure ratio (on the vertical axis) as a function of the log of the relative reinforcement ratio (on the horizontal axis) for income-compensated price changes. Straight lines determined by method of least squares, with slope estimate shown directly above each line (standard error of the estimate in parentheses). Solid 45° line represents perfect matching.

mulation (parameter y in equation (3.11)) are reported, along with standard errors of the estimates in parentheses below the coefficient values.[8] The solid 45-degree line represents perfect matching (equation (3.8b)). Baum's generalized matching law requires a positive slope coefficient. All of the estimated slope coefficients are negative and are significantly below zero at better than the 5% level for three of the four rats. Response ratios move *inversely* to reinforcement ratios for these rats, so that the *greater* the amount of food delivered, the *fewer* the number of responses allocated to the food lever. This is the exact opposite of the matching prediction for which the greater the amount of food, the greater the number of responses that should be allocated to the food lever – thus the origin of our term antimatching. Antimatching has also been found on conc VI–VI schedules with monkeys choosing between food and water (Hursh, 1978, 1980), and with pigeons choosing between food and water (Baum, unpublished data). Thus, antimatching is not peculiar to concurrent ratio schedules or to rats.

The antimatching found with food and water follows directly from the relatively inelastic demand for these commodities (which in turn results from their relatively low degree of substitutability). With inelastic demand, a reduction in price (increases in the reinforcement rate) is followed by a reduction in total expenditure (reduced responding) for the good that decreased in price, and increased expenditure (increased responding) for the other good. The net result is antimatching.[9]

In contrast, heterogeneous reinforcers that are relatively substitutable and exhibit elastic demands will tend to satisfy the generalized matching law (3.11), or at least not exhibit antimatching. With an elastic demand curve, reductions in price (increases in the reinforcement rate) result in increased total expenditure (increased responding) for that commodity. With a limited income (limited total number of responses), this results in reduced responding for the alternative good, hence matching.

Herrnstein (1970) recognized that matching would not be expected with qualitatively different reinforcers or with qualitatively different response requirements. In fact, he proposed to use the matching relation "to construct equivalences between qualitatively different responses or reinforcers, although no such undertaking has come to the author's attention. It should, however, be possible to scale reinforcers against each other or responses against each other assuming that the subject must be conforming to the matching relation whenever it is in a choice situation of the general type employed in these experiments, and by adjusting the measures of response accordingly" (Herrnstein, 1970, p. 247).[10]

One concrete application along these lines was proposed by Rachlin, Kagel, and Battalio (1980). They suggested that the value of the exponent y obtained in Baum's generalized matching law when studying choices of different commodities could serve as an index of commodity substitutability. For example, experiments in our laboratories with ratio schedules indicated that milk and sucrose solution are not perfect substitutes for rats. With these commodities as reinforcers, Hamblin and Miller (1977) did find consistent undermatching (y well below 1). In contrast, Miller (1976), who studied pigeons choosing between different types of grain comprising their normal diet, found little undermatching ($y \approx 1$). Since taste has little effect on preference among pigeons, and among birds in general (Gustavson, 1977), various grains may be expected to be close to perfect substitutes. Section 3.5 extends this analysis to evaluate the incentive effects of brain stimulation in comparison with other reinforcers.

Rachlin et al. (1980) also provided a formal model specifying the conditions under which the coefficient *y* in (3.11) would reflect the substitutability of commodities. The model requires a homothetic constant elasticity of substitution utility function (the CES formulation, equation (3.15), with the γs = 0). Although these conditions are unlikely to be satisfied exactly with heterogeneous reinforcers (see Section 3.3d), it is clear that the exponent *y* can provide a reasonably good measure of substitutability between alternatives over a limited area of the choice space. Proponents of the matching law have never completely warmed to this suggestion, in part because of their distaste for the maximizing assumptions that commonly (but not necessarily) go along with utility functions in economics. However, Herrnstein and Prelec (1989) present a melioration model that introduces income and substitution effects while preserving the notion that subjects equate *average* local rates of reinforcement.

Income Effects

With animals choosing between qualitatively different reinforcers, there is ample evidence that changes in income produce rather strong changes in consumption patterns. For those rats for which quinine water was strongly inferior (Section 2.4b), the overwhelming majority of responses were allocated to quinine at the low-income level, whereas a majority of responses were allocated to root beer at the high-income level. Similar variations in response ratios under changing income levels, with all else constant, have been reported by other investigators using different species and a variety of consumption goods and experimental procedures: Hursh and Natelson (1981) with rats choosing between electrical brain stimulation and food under concurrent variable-interval schedules; Elsmore et al. (1980) with baboons choosing between heroin and food under concurrent ratio schedules; and Silberberg and his associates (Hastjarjo, Silberberg, and Hursh, 1990; Silberberg, Warren-Boulton, and Asano, 1987) with monkeys and rats choosing between large, bitter food pellets and small, standard food pellets under concurrent ratio schedules.

These income effects are anticipated within consumer-choice theory through the explicit inclusion of income into the budget constraint, with its resultant effects on choice (recall Section 2.1d). Under the matching law, the local average rate of reinforcement alone guides behavior. Changes in overall levels of reinforcement have no effect, except to the extent that there are within-session changes in reinforcer value such as might result from changes in deprivation levels. However, to uphold the matching law's notion that average local rates of reinforcement guide behavior, changes in the overall consumption patterns should be reflected in the pattern obtained within experimental sessions. For example, in the case of inferior goods, the consumption pattern should vary dramatically during the course of a high-income session. That is, the initial responses should be allocated almost exclusively to the inferior good, because of its relatively high value under low-income conditions, followed by excessive consumption of the normal good at the end of the experimental session.

Using detailed sequential choice data, Silberberg and his associates have been particularly keen to investigate this issue. They find cases in which the matching hypothesis holds: rats choosing between food and saccharin water while also having ad lib access to tap water (Shurtleff, Warren-Boulton, and Silberberg, 1987). But they also report cases in which the matching hypothesis clearly fails: rats choosing between regular food pellets and quinine-adulterated food pellets (Hastjarjo et al., 1990) and monkeys choosing between regular food pellets and bitter food pellets (Silberberg et al., 1987).

3.3 Bliss points versus minimum needs

This section compares two competing static choice models that are substantially more complicated than those considered thus far. The first is a generalized version of Staddon's (1979a) minimum-distance hypothesis (MD), which argues that behavior is motivated by attempts to minimize deviations from some optimal state values. An alternative to this motivational process is one in which subjects attempt to meet "minimum" survival requirements first, after which they are free to allocate expenditure in any fashion. The latter hypothesis is common in applied consumer-demand analysis in economics (Pollak and Wales, 1980). We refer to this model as the generalized minimum-needs hypothesis (MN), and use a generalized constant-elasticity-of-substitution utility function as a convenient first approximation in characterizing it.

The basic structure of the two models is the same: the utility function and associated demand equations have the same functional form, the number of free parameters is the same, and both models postulate a fixed point in the choice space at which substitution effects are zero. However, there are key differences in the assumed ranges of parameter values and the position and interpretation of the fixed choice point. The net outcome of these differences is that the MD hypothesis predicts less substitutability between activities as the consumer becomes better off, whereas the MN hypothesis predicts relatively greater substitutability. We test the two models using data from rats choosing between food and fluid in a "closed" economy and find that these data more closely fit the generalized minimum-needs hypothesis.

3.3a The generalized minimum-distance hypothesis

A number of psychologists and biologists have argued that animals have a preferred distribution of activities, and that when faced with constraints they seek a distribution as near as possible to the preferred distribution (Houston and McFarland, 1980; Staddon, 1979a; Timberlake, 1980). Staddon (1979) casts this concept in the form of a quadratic utility function

$$U = -\sum_i \frac{\beta_i}{2} \left[\frac{\gamma_i - x_i}{\beta_i}\right]^2,$$ (3.13)

$$\gamma_i, \beta_i > 0, \qquad (\gamma_i - x_i) > 0, \qquad \sum_i \beta_i = 1$$

where x_i, $i = 1, 2, \ldots, n$, represent the set of commodities in the environment, such as eating, drinking, instrumental responding, and so on; the γs represent the most preferred set of commodities, sometimes referred to as the "bliss" point; and the β_i are constants that vary with the units of measurement employed and the relative value of x_i to the consumer. The model is based on the concept of a homeostatic control mechanism, developed to characterize physiological functions – a set point from which organisms attempt to minimize deviations.

The minimum-distance hypothesis is an attractively simple concept capable of organizing a good deal of data. In an experimental environment, the premise of a stable "bliss" point is plausible since the commodity choice set is fixed and stable, which is not the case in market economies. Further, the impact on behavior of variations in background conditions, such as the severity of subjects' deprivation level, can be represented in terms of shifts in the bliss point. The bliss point is also subject to verification by simply eliminating the experimenter-induced constraints on choice and observing the behavior that results.

The quadratic utility function is a special case of the more general function

$$U = -\sum_i \frac{\beta_i}{v} \left[\frac{\gamma_i - x_i}{\beta_i}\right]^v$$ (3.14)

where

$$v > 1, \quad \beta, \gamma_i > 0, \qquad (\gamma_i - x_i) > 0, \qquad \sum_i \beta_i = 1$$

This generalized minimum-distance hypothesis permits greater flexibility in the metric used to measure deviations from the bliss point, while still maintaining all the essential characteristics of the simpler alternative (3.13). Under (3.13), the subject is required to minimize the squared deviations from the bliss point. Under (3.14), this requirement is relaxed so that, for example, the consumer can minimize the cubed deviations ($v = 3$) or any other metric, provided $v > 1$.

Figure 3.4a illustrates how commodity choices vary under the generalized MD hypothesis for the case of two goods. The negatively sloped, curved lines are indifference curves. (Indifference curves are closed ellipses under the generalized MD hypothesis. Our attention is confined to the negatively sloped segments, because these constitute the area of the choice space in which more of both goods is preferred: and these are the relevant segments, given the structure

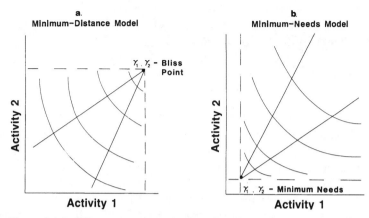

Figure 3.4 Indifference curves under (a) generalized minimum-distance hypothesis and (b) generalized minimum-needs hypothesis. Straight lines show optimal activity combinations (expansion paths) under different relative prices as income varies.

of our experiments.) Each of the two straight lines shows how the optimal activity level varies as income changes, with relative prices held constant. These straight lines are referred to as *expansion paths* in the economics literature. Prices vary between expansion paths, with the cost of activity 1 being relatively less for the steeper of the two lines in Figure 3.4a. (The point where the straight line intersects an indifference curve represents a point of tangency between a budget line – which is not shown – and that indifference curve. The budget lines associated with a given expansion path are all parallel to each other since relative prices are constant and only income changes along an expansion path.)

Most important, under the generalized MD hypothesis, the farther a consumer is from the bliss point (the poorer she is), the more her consumption pattern will change for any change in prices if she were to be kept on a given indifference curve. In this respect, commodities are relatively more substitutable the poorer the consumer is, and as a result the expansion paths (the straight lines in Figure 3.4a) fan out and down in relation to the bliss point. At the bliss point itself, an income-compensated price change has no effect on consumption because the indifference curve is a single point.[11]

3.3b The generalized minimum-needs hypothesis

An alternative to the generalized MD hypothesis is a motivational process in which individuals have minimum consumption requirements, either biologically or psychologically determined, which must be met before any discretionary choice over expenditure is possible. This concept of choice, prevalent in much of the applied choice literature in economics, may be stated, as a convenient first approximation, in terms of a generalized constant-elasticity-of-substitution (CES) utility function.

$$U = \sum_i \frac{\beta_i}{v} \left[\frac{x_i - \gamma_i}{\beta_i} \right]^v \tag{3.15}$$

$$v < 1, \qquad \beta_i > 0, \qquad (x_i - \gamma_i) > 0, \qquad \sum \beta_i = 1$$

In cases where $\gamma_i > 0$ for all i, they represent "minimum consumption requirements" or "minimum-needs." A CES rule holds for purchases beyond the minimum needs, $(x_i - \gamma_i) > 0$, where $\sigma = 1/(1 - v)$ is the elasticity of substitution. Note that under the minimum-needs hypothesis $v < 1$ and $(x_i - \gamma_i) > 0$, whereas $v > 1$ and $(x_i - \gamma_i) < 0$ for the MD hypothesis. These differences result in significantly different behavioral implications for the two models. In particular, MN predicts that the richer a consumer is, the greater the change in her consumption pattern for any given change in relative prices, if she is kept on a given indifference curve. In this respect, commodities are relatively more substitutable the richer the consumer is, so that the expansion paths fan up and out in relation to the minimum needs point, which is located close to the origin (see Figure 3.4b). This is exactly opposite to the response pattern predicted under the generalized MD hypothesis.

At the minimum-needs point itself, the response to a small income-compensated price change is zero, since the indifference curves collapse to a single point here. Behavior below the minimum needs point is not defined.

The minimum-needs interpretation of the CES utility function requires independent evaluation of the estimated γ coefficients. In an experiment in which the commodities are necessary for survival, the γs should all be positive, and equal in size to plausible minimum consumption requirements. If the commodities are not needed for survival, the γs may have any value. In this case, a positive γ might be suggestive of minimum "psychological" needs or suggest some previously unknown physiological requirement. A zero γ indicates that the minimum consumption requirement of a good is zero, and the consumer can survive quite well without it. A negative γ value might be found in cases where consumption opportunities outside the experimental session were more than sufficient to meet minimum requirements, and this outside consumption affected choices within the session.[12] Whether γ is positive or negative, the MN model implies greater substitutability of activities at higher income levels, in direct contrast to the generalized MD hypothesis. Our experiments were designed to test these opposing predictions.

Of particular interest is the special case of (3.15) in which the coefficient v equals 0, since this reduces to the linear expenditure model, equation (3.6) without any restrictions on the γ_i (Pollack, 1971).[13] Numerous studies have applied the linear expenditure model to aggregate per capita data from market

economies because of the ease of statistical estimation. We thought it would
be interesting to ask how well this model fits individual subject data. In addition, the linear expenditure model with the γ_i restricted to nonnegative values
provides a means of testing the mixed random choice model specified in Section 3.1.

3.3c   Test procedures

Maximization of (3.14) or (3.15) subject to a linear budget constraint,

$$m = \sum_i p_i x_i \tag{3.16}$$

where m defines the consumer's income level, results in demand functions with
the common functional form

$$x_i = \gamma_i + \frac{\beta_i p_i^{-\sigma}}{\sum_k \beta_k p_k^{1-\sigma}} \left(m - \sum_k \gamma_k p_k \right) \tag{3.17}$$

where $\sigma = 1/(1 - v)$. Restrictions on the parameters σ, $(\gamma_1, \ldots, \gamma_n)$ and

$$\left(m - \sum_k \gamma_k p_k \right)$$

result in special cases corresponding to the motivational processes of interest. The models and their associated parameter restrictions are summarized in
Table 3.1.

For our tests of these competing hypotheses, we limit our procedures to
choice between two goods. Economists sometimes express concern about this
limitation because they consider (3.14) and (3.15) far too simple to character-

Table 3.1. *Parameter restrictions associated with different models*

Model	Parameter restrictions		
	σ	γ_k	$(m - \sum_k \gamma_k p_k)$
Mixed random behavior	1	> 0	> 0
Linear expenditure	1	None	> 0
Generalized minimum distance hypothesis[a]	< 0	> 0	< 0
Generalized minimum needs hypothesis[a]	> 0	See text	> 0

[a]$\sigma = 1/(1 - v)$ for both the generalized minimum distance and the generalized
minimum needs hypotheses.

ize "real world" consumption behavior. Our response to this is that in restricting the analysis to two commodities we provide the most favorable conditions for confirming the model.[14] If we are able to reject either the MN or MD hypothesis with two commodities, there is virtually no chance that it would perform better under the substantially more complicated conditions encountered with larger sets of commodities. However, if the models work well here, we have more flexible functional forms to deal with larger sets of commodities, without sacrificing the essential motivational and behavioral characteristics of either model.

In contrast to economists, experimental psychologists are more concerned with the relatively large number of free parameters in (3.14) and (3.15) and prefer simpler functional forms! We contend that simpler functional forms simply do not work (see Section 3.1 and 3.2), and consequently (3.14) and (3.15) are natural next steps in terms of specifying more complicated functional forms.

To discriminate between the MN and MD hypotheses, it is necessary to obtain relatively large numbers of data points along each of several expansion paths. We obtained three such expansion paths for two rats following the closed economy, essential commodity procedures characterized in Chapter 2.[15]

In the analysis, we are concerned with how food and fluid consumption varied as the level of total available responses (income) was changed at different relative prices. If the generalized MD hypothesis is correct, plots of food and fluid consumed should look like Figure 3.4a, with points under the different cost conditions forming relatively straight lines, clustering together at high income levels and spreading apart at lower incomes. In contrast, if the MN hypothesis is correct, the opposite sort of clustering pattern should emerge, as in Figure 3.4b.

More formal tests of competing hypotheses were obtained by fitting the demand equation (3.17) to the data, using a nonlinear, least-squares technique. In this way we can identify the model (coefficient values in Table 3.1) that best fits the data according to the error-sum-of-squares principle. We then varied the parameter σ in equation (3.17) from -1.3 to 1.3 by increments of .1, while choosing the remaining parameter values to minimize the error sum of squares, and compared these error terms with those of the best-fitting model, using a likelihood-ratio test statistic. In this way, we identify the parameter values (and hence the hypotheses) that are statistically indistinguishable from the best-fitting model. We also checked the plausibility of the resulting parameter estimates, particularly the γ values, against independent information about the rat's minimum-needs or most-preferred consumption levels.

3.3d Test results

Figure 3.5 plots food and fluid consumption for the two rats at each of the three relative cost conditions. The straight lines in the figure show *predicted*

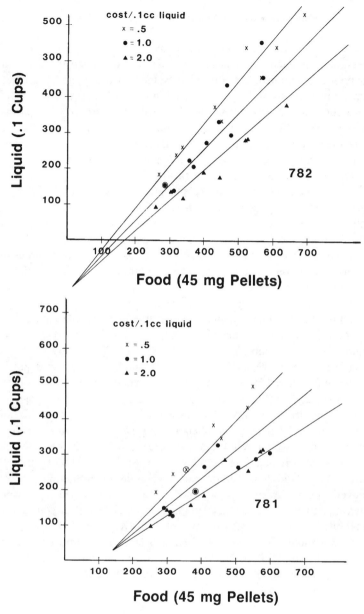

Figure 3.5 Amount of food and fluid consumed as cost of liquid varied for two rats, 781 and 782. Straight lines are predicted consumption of best-fitting model from Table 3.2. Circled points indicate that a replication point is virtually identical to the initial observation. From Kagel, Dwyer, and Battalio (1985).

consumption patterns based on the parameter estimates of the best-fitting model. These parameter estimates are shown in Table 3.2 for each rat separately and with the data pooled. For both subjects, the best-fitting model satisfies the parameter restrictions of the generalized minimum-needs hypothesis. Further, the restriction $(m - \sum_k \gamma_k p_k) > 0$ is satisfied at all points in the choice space: subjects always had sufficient income to cover minimum consumption requirements.

Acceptable values for σ are defined as those for which we cannot reject (at the 5 percent significance level) the null hypothesis that the resulting demand equation fits the data as well as the best-fitting model in Table 3.2, according to a likelihood-ratio test statistic. All acceptable values of σ were positive for both subjects, as required by the MN hypothesis; the generalized MD hypothesis, on the other hand, predicts negative values for σ (see Table 3.1). There seems little justification, therefore, for viewing individuals as tethered to the bliss point in their choices. Instead, the data suggest a more expansive, adventurous motivation to behavior beyond the level at which minimum needs are satisfied.

Although minimum-need food and fluid estimates are positive for subject 781, as we would expect in this experiment since subjects obtained all their food and fluid during experimental sessions, the fluid estimate for subject 782 is negative, and the food estimate is much too small to be treated seriously as a measure of the rat's minimum necessary food intake. As we allow σ to vary for subject 782, however, we obtain positive point estimates for γ values quite similar to those for subject 781, without straying beyond acceptable values for σ – for example, at $\sigma = 0.48$, $\gamma_{LIQ} = 23.4$ and $\gamma_{FOOD} = 172.5$ for subject 782. These γ values translate into minimum-consumption requirements of 2.34 cc of fluid and 172.5 Noyes food pellets (45 mg each), or approximately 7.76 grams of food. If we allow for some variance in these estimates, the values, while low, are still plausible as minimum requirements. For example, our Giffen-study rats did quite well on about 5 cc of liquid. Further, groups of rats employed in experiments reported in Section 6.5 maintained body weights when restricted to 5 cc of liquid or 9 grams of food. The rats even stayed healthy when limited to 3.4 cc of water for over 60 days (Kagel et al., 1986).

Table 3.3 shows the results of likelihood-ratio tests comparing the best-fitting model (the MN hypothesis) with the mixed random choice model and the linear expenditure model. Both of these models are decisively rejected at better than the 1 percent significance level.

3.3e Summary and evaluation of competing motivational hypotheses

We have determined that the generalized minimum-needs hypothesis of all the motivational processes under review provides the best organizing principle for the commodity-choice data. In rejecting the random behavior models proposed by Becker (1962), we have ruled out the possibility that consistent choice may be due to random responses to environmental contingencies.

Table 3.2. *Parameter estimates of best-fitting model*

Subject	σ	γ_{LIQ}	γ_{FOOD}	β_{LIQ}	R^2	N
781	0.357	30.0	143.2	0.445	.907	27
	(0.123)	(69.6)	(97.8)	(0.021)		
782	0.245	− 130.1	17.6	0.504	.908	28
	(0.115)	(155.8)	(169.3)	(0.019)		
781 and	0.348	− 11.0	120.3	0.480	.891	55
782	(0.101)	(70.1)	(57.4)	(0.027)		
combined[a]						

Note: Standard errors of estimates in parentheses. N = number of observations. In fitting to data we transformed the dependent variable in the demand equation (3.17) to budget share form, $p_i x_i / m$.
[a]Likelihood ratio test statistic for pooling observations is $X^2 = 9.6$ with 4 degrees of freedom, which is different from 0 at the .047 significance level.
Source: Battalio, Dwyer, and Kagel (1987).

Table 3.3. *Tests of parameter restrictions of mixed random behavior and linear expenditure models: χ^2 values*

	Subject		
Model[a]	781	782	781 & 782
Mixed random	15.6	27.5	35.6
behavior (d.f = 1)	(< .001)	(< .001)	(< .001)
Linear expenditure	15.6	27.5	35.6
model[b] (d.f. = 1)	(< .001)	(< .001)	(< .001)

[a]Hypothesis is coincident with mixed random behavior choice model in this case.
Source: Battalio, Dwyer, and Kagel (1987).

To be sure, more complicated random behavior models can be invented to explain the data, but we have ruled out some of the more tractable and obvious ones. Likewise, direct extensions of the matching law are unable to account for choice between commodities with inelastic demand. These commodities give rise to antimatching; that is, relative response rate varies inversely with relative reinforcement rate. The matching law often has difficulty accounting for income effects as well. While both the random behavior and matching law formulations operate with fewer free parameters than the MN hypothesis, MN also does substantially better than the generalized MD hypothesis, which has an equal number of free parameters. As we show in Chapter 5, the superiority of the MN hypothesis over these alternatives also extends to choices between consumption and leisure and to open-economy conditions in which body weight is not permitted to fluctuate with choice.

There are important limitations to the generalized MN hypothesis as expressed in the form of the CES utility function of equation (3.15). First, part of the price of its superior fit to the data is its failure to predict response patterns under conditions in which income is too low to meet minimum consumption needs. We need observations in this region of the choice space in order to determine what the animal does under such circumstances.

Second, the model as currently formulated implies that the expansion paths fan up and out continuously; that more is always better. However, in dealing with animals choosing between edibles, or between consumption and leisure, there are upper bounds on consumption beyond which more is aversive. As this boundary is approached, the marginal value of additional consumption is likely to plummet and generate nonlinear consumption patterns at higher income levels with relative prices held constant. Such an outcome would be contrary to the predictions of the CES formulation. The model would have to be modified to account for these effects when they occur (see Section 5.3b, for example). It is of interest to note, however, that goodness-of-fit tests based on the repeat reliability of our data showed that we could *not* reject the hypothesis of linear expansion paths at conventional significance levels (Battalio, Dwyer, and Kagel, 1987), even though income was increased to the point where subjects, apparently sated, consistently failed to use up their daily allotment of lever presses.

Finally, the CES formulation of the MN hypothesis cannot account for Giffen goods as long as the commodities between which the individual is choosing enter directly into the utility function. This same shortcoming applies to the MD hypothesis, as well as to most other systems of demand equations employed in the economics literature. What is needed to accommodate the Giffen good phenomenon is a "commodity characteristics" approach to choice. Under this approach, the consumer is viewed as choosing between commodities with various characteristics, and it is these characteristics, rather than the commodities themselves, that enter into the utility function (Lancaster, 1966). Under this formulation, all commodity characteristics can be normal and satisfy the law of demand, while commodities can be inferior (and thus Giffen goods) because the commodities embody a particular mix of characteristics. For example, in our root beer/quinine experiment, we might postulate that the commodities have two characteristics, H_2O and good taste. Root beer has more of the positive taste characteristic and, under baseline prices, less of the H_2O characteristic than quinine. Quinine, with its higher H_2O content, becomes an inferior and

Giffen good when the income effect of the price change makes the H_2O less important than the taste characteristic.

3.4 The representative consumer hypothesis

Most standard applications of consumer-choice theory employ "aggregate per capita time-series" data: average consumption data for groups of individuals over time. When applying consumer-demand theory (which is a theory of individual behavior) to these aggregate data, economists typically have in mind the notion of a "representative consumer," with demands similar to those reflected in the market data. But the question remains, to what extent do the aggregate data represent those of individual consumers? In this section, we ask to what degree the "representative consumer" hypothesis holds true for our data.

The representative consumer hypothesis has several meanings in the literature. We distinguish between a weak and a strong form of the hypothesis. The weak form, as we define it, holds that different individuals display similar enough taste and choice characteristics that the demand relationships estimated are similar across individuals. Under this formulation, the parameter estimates obtained from pooled time-series data across individuals could be ascribed to a fictitious individual, without implying that consumers are identical or that the parameter estimates obtained apply to any actual individual.

The strong form of the representative consumer hypothesis holds that tastes are sufficiently homogeneous that they satisfy the stringent criteria required to achieve consistent aggregation across individuals. If these stringent criteria (described below) are not satisfied, then consumer-choice theory cannot be applied to aggregate data (Shafer and Sonnenschein, 1982, sec. 4; Sonnenschein, 1973). The strong form with its stringent criteria is important, because a large body of empirical and theoretical research relies on "representative consumer" assumptions to draw powerful implications from consumer-demand theory for aggregate behavior in the fields of labor-supply and "rational expectations" macroeconomy models (Arrow, 1987).

The strong form of the representative consumer hypothesis requires that all expansion paths be linear and that each expansion path have the same slope for all consumers (for an extended discussion of aggregation issues, see Deaton and Muellbauer, 1980, chap. 6). For the MN and MD hypotheses, these requirements imply that the γ values (minimum-needs) can vary for individual consumers, but that all other coefficients in the utility function (equations (3.14) and (3.15)) must be the same. More generally, with income varying and the relative prices of goods held constant, exact aggregation requires that (1) consumption of each good is a linear function of income, and (2) the marginal propensity to consume each good (the slope of the resulting income-consumption relationship) is the same for individual consumers (although it can vary for commodities). When these two criteria are satisfied, there is no need to worry about the effects of changes in the distribution of individual incomes on consumption. Therefore, it would be valid to use the simpler aggregate per capita income (average income) to characterize the impact of income changes on consumption. Deaton and Muellbauer (1980, p. 151) note that the criterion of linearity, while implausible, is not impossible as a reasonable approximation for broad groups of commodities. On the other hand, they offer no opinion as to whether it is plausible for individuals' marginal propensities to consume (MPC) to be identical.

Data from our animal consumers permit us to look at this question. Figure 3.6 shows water consumption at varying income levels for four rats (in a closed economy using the lever pressing procedures outlined in Section 2.2). The MPC, the slope of the straight line fitted to the data by the method of least squares, is reported (with the standard error of the estimate in parentheses). As in our tests of the minimum-needs model, the linearity assumption holds up quite well over a reasonably wide range of income variation, so that the same functional form characterizes the behavior of all the subjects. Since the same functional form organized the behavior of different subjects, the weak form of the representative consumer hypothesis is satisfied. However, the strong form is not, since the MPC is not the same across all rats (the culprit here is quite clearly rat 912, since the MPCs are remarkably similar across the other 3 rats).[16] Similarly, for rats 781 and 782, the weak form of the representative consumer hypothesis is fulfilled, as the MN model fits the data best in both cases (recall Table 3.2). However, tests of the strong form of the hypothesis leave it suspect, since even if the γs are allowed to vary across subjects, we reject the null hypothesis (at the 6% significance leve) that parameters β and σ of the minimum-needs model (equation (3.15)) are the same across subjects.

These results show that tastes are not sufficiently homogeneous, even when linearity holds, to satisfy the criteria for exact aggregation for our simple consumers using such highly standardized and basic consumption goods as food and water. If animals bred for genetic similarity and raised in virtually identical environments fail to satisfy the strong form of the representative consumer hypothesis, it strikes us as highly unlikely that people will, even after allowing for age, education, and other objective differences among them.

Important implications follow from these results. First, tests of consumer-demand theory that employ aggregate per capita income data may be seriously flawed since they do not satisfy the criterion of homogeneity of preferences required for their validity. Second, much empirical and theoretical work in the fields of labor supply and the performance of the macroeconomy – work that relies on the strong form of the hypothesis – is also open to serious question. Although we recognize that the theoretical and empirical problems posed by taste differences of the sort identified here may be small "sins" compared with others committed in applying consumer-demand theory to field data, and that

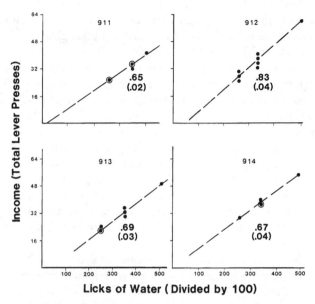

Figure 3.6 Relationship between water consumption and income under constant relative prices. Straight lines fit by method of least squares with slope estimate (marginal propensities to consume) shown directly below each line (standard error of the estimate in parentheses). Circles are used to indicate that replication points and initial observations overlap.

we have no way of empirically evaluating their impact, this should not obscure the fact that these data provide a unique test for such differences in tastes; and the presence of taste differences, under conditions highly conducive to their absence is a result not to be dismissed lightly.

The representative consumer hypothesis, with its criteria, is but one of several approaches to the aggregation problem offered in the literature. Different aggregation criteria involve different specifications for the functional form of the estimating equations and even involve use of different aggregate measures of income. Hence, questions about which aggregation procedures best fit the data, as well as the relative magnitude of the specification error introduced as a consequence of employing aggregate income, are of considerable practical and theoretical importance. We suggest that answers to these questions require individual subject data, generated under laboratory experimental procedures similar to those employed here.

3.5 Incentive mechanisms: The case of brain stimulation

Consumer-choice theory as it is applied to animal behavior is more properly a theory of incentive than of learning. As such, it can be used to evaluate the steady-state efficacy of reinforcers and to describe the interaction between various reinforcers. In psychology, the study of such interactions is usually undertaken on a highly molecular, often physiological, level. Without denying the value of molecular investigation of the mechanisms of interaction among reinforcers, we believe that there is much to be learned about incentive mechanisms from a more molar, behavioral level of analysis. Consumer-demand theory provides a conceptual framework from which insights into such mechanisms might be gained. We explore this possibility for the case of electrical stimulation of the brain (EBS) as a reinforcer.

There is some question among psychologists about whether EBS should be regarded as (a) a general reinforcer that activates neural substrates common to all reinforcers, (b) a reinforcer that shares mechanisms with only some specific reinforcers (e.g., cocaine), or (c) a unique reinforcer. In addition to seeking an explanation of the mechanism underlying EBS reinforcement, researchers have endeavored to establish whether EBS functions like more conventional reinforcers (e.g., food) or whether it has special, unique properties. Evidence has been provided for both points of view, although the tendency in recent years has been to treat brain stimulation as a general reinforcer, much the same as food. As summarized by Mogenson and Cioé (1977): "When appropriate comparisons are made and equivalent conditions established, the two kinds of reinforcers do not differ substantially" (pp. 574–5).

From the perspective of consumer-demand theory, if brain stimulation and food were essentially the same reinforcers, triggering the same incentive mechanisms, then they should be perfect substitutes for each other. We can investigate this question with the the income-compensated price change procedures. If food and EBS are perfect substitutes, then choices between the two reinforcers should change to near-exclusive consumption of the commodity whose relative price is reduced. Similarly, under conc VI–VI schedules of reinforcement, perfect matching should obtain with the exponent y in equation (3.11) approximating 1 if food and brain stimulation are perfect substitutes. Finally, variations in income level should have little effect on choice ratios between perfect substitutes, since income has no role to play when dealing with choice over identical commodities.

The results of several experiments can be used to evaluate these propositions. Hollard and Davison (1971) report pigeons' choices over brain stimulation and food using conc VI–VI schedules in an open economy (the pigeons were maintained at 80% of their free-feeding body weight). The price of food was changed by changing the average time between food presentations while the time-cost of brain stimulation was held constant. When the generalized matching formulation (equation (3.11)) was fitted to the data, the average slope coefficient y was 0.77 and 1.06 using response-based and time-based measures of behavior, respectively. This result suggests strong substitutability.

Green and Rachlin (1991) completed a more extensive study with rats to investigate the degree of substitutability among EBS, food, and water reinforcement. They used an open economy, too, and implemented a series of income-compensated price changes for rats. The procedure used was similar to that described in Section 2.2a: The rats pressed levers to earn the various reinforcers, prices were varied by changing the number of lever presses required per reinforcement, and income was manipulated by changing the total number of lever presses permitted per session. A control condition was also employed in which rats chose between brain stimulation from both levers under changing relative prices. This control provided a measure of the degree of substitutability between presumably identical commodities, and also a means of calibrating for the limits to substitutability and the degree of bias inherent in the procedure. Using a homothetic CES utility function (equation (3.15) with the γs set to 0), Green and Rachlin estimated the elasticity of substitution between brain stimulation delivered from both levers, brain stimulation versus food, brain stimulation versus water, and food versus water. Their estimates indicated that the elasticity of substitution of brain stimulation to food and to water was almost as great as the substitutability of brain stimulation to itself. In contrast, the elasticity of substitution of food to water was substantially less. Although Green and Rachlin cautiously point out that there is not enough evidence to conclude that brain stimulation involves a general "pleasure center" in the brain, they believe that "as an economic good, EBS (like money in the human economy) is highly substitutable for at least two reinforcers that are not substitutable for each other" (Green and Rachlin, 1991, p. 142).

Finally, Hursh and Natelson (1981) studied rats' choices over food and brain stimulation in a closed economy in which income/effort price levels were varied. The rats lived continuously in the experimental chamber and responded on two levers, one of which delivered brain stimulation and the other food. The rats were allowed 24-hour access to the levers in order to earn the commodities whose delivery was scheduled by two equal, variable-interval (VI) timers. The VI timers set the minimum average time that had to elapse between the response-produced delivery of a payoff. As the minimum time between reinforcer delivery was increased equally for both food and brain stimulation, responding for the brain stimulation decreased, and the number of these reinforcers earned decreased sharply, whereas responding for the food increased and food consumption remained relatively constant. Because the amounts of responding increased when the minimum time between reinforcement deliveries increased, Hursh and Natelson interpret their procedure as one in which the effort price of consumption is manipulated (see Section 4.2 for details). They thus argue that food consumption is highly inelastic (unresponsive) to effort price, whereas brain stimulation is quite elastic (responsive) to the same price variations. They conclude that there is a regulatory mechanism for feeding that does not exist with electrical brain stimulation. Consequently, the incentive effects of brain stimulation are not the same as for food. The results also suggest that brain stimulation and food will prove much less substitutable under closed- rather than under open-economy conditions since minimum-consumption requirements for food are essentially zero in an open economy but take on large positive values in a closed economy.

In conclusion, our analysis indicates that economic theory can be applied in comparing the efficacy of different reinforcers and that the economic context in which choice is studied (closed- versus open-economy conditions) has an important role to play in determining the reinforcing value of different commodities. Economic analyses applied in this way could be extremely useful in evaluating the reinforcing properties of drugs such as alcohol, marijuana, and heroin and behavioral economic theory could shed light on drug use and abuse (e.g., Elsmore et al., 1980; Hursh, 1991; also see Green and Kagel, in press, for a collection of papers on this topic). We explore the topic of economic context in regulating the consumption of such commodities in Section 7.6, where we compare outcomes across token economies that were designed to evaluate the effects of marijuana and alcohol use on labor supply.

Notes

1 The more general linear expenditure model emerges as a special case of the minimum-needs hypothesis characterized in this chapter.

2 Similar results have been reported using data from the pigeon experiments as well (Battalio, et al., 1981). One potential generalization of the pure random choice models is to permit the allocation rule to vary with the level of income. However, since compensation was achieved by adjusting the prices of both food and fluid while holding total lever pressing requirements virtually constant, a generalization along these lines would not serve to organize our data.

3 Staddon (1988) calls the model quasi-dynamic because it fails to specify more narrowly the adjustment function, $f(D)$.

4 Myerson and Hale (1988) and Staddon (1988) compare adjustment path predictions of melioration theory with data and predictions from alternative dynamic specifications.

5 When the animal cannot completely discriminate between alternative schedules of reinforcement, some responses will be randomly allocated between the two alternatives. This allocation of responses will result in relatively more responses on the leaner schedule of reinforcement than is predicted. This discrimination problem will be accentuated in concurrent schedules of reinforcement when the same commodity serves as the reinforcer for both schedules and is delivered from a common feeding mechanism (separate feeding mechanisms are required for heterogenous goods).

6 Laboratory approaches to programming variable-interval schedules vary so that no single feedback function can exactly model all VI schedules used. Most often, the variable-interval timer is stopped when a reinforcer has "set up" and remains stopped until the reinforcer is collected. Sometimes reinforcers can be accumulated; that is, when a reinforcer is read from the timer, it is stored and the VI timer continues to advance (Rachlin, Green, and Tormey, 1988; Vaughan and Miller, 1984). Usually, there is no time constraint on when the reinforcer, once available, can be obtained. However, occasionally, a "limited hold" is placed on the reinforcer so that if a response

does not occur during this time period, the reinforcer is lost and the VI timer begins to run again. In most cases, reinforcer intervals are arranged exponentially so that there is a constant probability of reinforcement with time (Catania and Reynolds, 1968; Fleshler and Hoffman, 1962). However, intervals have also been arranged arithmetically so that there is a linear increase in probability of reinforcement with time since the previous reinforcer (e.g., Lobb and Davison, 1975; see also Taylor and Davison, 1983).

7 With conc VI–VI schedules, both timers are sometimes stopped together when a reinforcer sets up (Stubbs and Pliskoff, 1969) and are sometimes completely independent (Herrnstein, 1961). Sometimes only one timer is used, and the reinforcers are assigned randomly or quasi-randomly to one or the other alternative (Shimp, 1969).

8 As a technical point, estimates using equation (3.12) are statistically biased since C_i and R_i are both dependent variables that respond to changes in schedule parameters. That is, the error term implicit in statistical estimation of the coefficient values is correlated with the dependent variable, so that the resulting estimates are statistically biased. Under our procedures (one response required per reward, an FR-1 schedule), this can be avoided by substituting $p_i x_i$ for responding (C_i) on the left-hand side of equation (3.11), and x_i, the quantity of good i consumed for R_i on the right-hand side, and rearranging so that x_i / x_j, the ratio of quantities consumed is the dependent variable, leaving p_i / p_j as the independent variable in the regression (recall that under our procedures, p_i is the inverse of the amount of reward per lever press). Least-squares estimates employing this specification, which are free from bias, yield uniformly smaller estimates (larger negative numbers) for the parameter y in equation (3.11) for all rats.

   With the notable exception of Davison and McCarthy (1981), psychologists have generally ignored questions of statistical bias in the reported estimates of y. Davison and McCarthy argue that the resulting bias will generally lower the estimated value for y, which suggests that this is one source of "undermatching" in typical conc VI–VI schedules. Our results suggest that the bias is in the opposite direction, that the true value for y is lower than the estimated value using equation (3.11). Note, however, that we are dealing with concurrent ratio schedules, while Davison and McCarthy were concerned with concurrent VI schedules, which may explain the differences.

9 Hursh (1980) makes this same point, namely that antimatching will occur in the presence of inelastic demand for commodities.

10 Arguably, Herrnstein had no idea how wildly off the mark the matching relation could be with gross complements such as food and water that produce statistically significant negative values for y, well below 0.0. See Green and Freed (1993) for a review and discussion of the scaling of reinforcers.

11 An even more general version of the model would permit the bliss-point values to vary with relative activity costs or other endogenous forces, such as the weight or age of the organism. Similar generalizations are possible within the context of the minimum-needs hypothesis (see Pollak and Wales, 1980, for alternative specifications along these lines), but are not pursued here.

12 When the γs are < 0, it makes no sense to describe the individual as purchasing a necessary (negative) amount of the commodity. Further, with negative γ, the system of demand equations corresponding to (3.15) implies negative demand for commodities even at income levels sufficiently low to render behavior identifiable by the system; additional decision rules would need to be specified in order to characterize behavior in this region of the choice space.

13 Equation (3.6) is obtained from (3.15) when $v = 0$ through the application of l'Hopital's rule (see for example Chiang, 1974, pp. 519–21).

14 Also, technical problems and financial expenses increase nonlinearly for studies involving more than two goods, as nonstandard apparatuses are required.
15 Details are reported in Kagel, Dwyer, and Battalio (1985).
16 We can reject the null hypothesis of equal slopes across rats at better than the .01 significance level.

4

Labor-supply behavior I: Initial tests of the theory with some public policy implications

In this chapter, we apply the commodity-choice model developed in Chapters 2 and 3 to issues of labor supply. As early as 1953, B. F. Skinner noted that ratio schedules of reinforcement in laboratory animals studied by psychologists correspond to piecework labor. Later, Logan (1964) noted a strong analogy between the "free-behavior situation" (behavior in a closed economy) and the way in which a "piece-rate worker controls his income." (This work also produced some of the first demand curves for income as a function of effort price, although Logan did not refer to them as such.) In this chapter and in Chapter 5 we exploit the correspondence between piecework wage rates and ratio schedules of reinforcement in order to (a) test simple economic models of labor-supply behavior, and (b) explore issues in labor-supply behavior that because of both ethical and practical considerations are difficult to study experimentally with humans.

Whereas in Chapters 2 and 3 we described studies in which income and consumption opportunities were determined exogenously by the experimenter, and choices were between different commodities, here we are concerned with total earnings and the "work effort" required to obtain those earnings (where work effort is defined as *both* the time cost and physical effort required to obtain income). Simple piecework wage rate schedules that tie earnings directly to the work performed provide the most direct extension of the commodity-choice framework to labor-supply behavior. Organisms are again viewed as choosing between two or more positive outcomes, only in this case the outcomes are income and leisure. And once income and leisure levels are determined, work time is determined as well. Section 4.1 of this chapter formally extends consumer-choice theory to labor-supply behavior. Section 4.2 briefly summarizes the rather extensive experimental results from psychological research on ratio schedules of reinforcement as they relate to the economist's labor-supply model. Sections 4.3 and 4.4 report a series of our own experiments on the substitutability of income for leisure. In these experiments, we use income-compensated wage changes similar to the income-compensated price changes used to study choices between edibles. Income-compensated wage *decreases* have much in common with a negative income tax and other income-transfer schemes. This relationship is explored in some detail in Section 4.5. Section 4.6 concludes with a brief look at supply-side economics as applied to pigeons and rats. We examine competing theoretical explanations of the data in Chapter 5.

4.1. Labor-supply theory: Extending consumer-choice theory

The theory of labor supply, like that of commodity choice, has to do with deciding over a choice set. In the case of labor supply, the commodity choice set consists of a leisure activity, x_l, a work activity, x_h, and the rewards from the work activity, referred to as income or earnings, x_m.[1] Under ratio schedules of reinforcement, performance of the job task becomes a prerequisite for obtaining access to preferred activities. Job tasks for pigeons may consist of pecking a key and pressing a treadle, and for rats they may consist of pressing a lever and running on a wheel. For animals deprived of food or water, preferred activities typically consist of eating or drinking, although other reinforcers have been used as well.

4.1a The budget constraint

Under a ratio schedule of reinforcement, the job task must be performed a prescribed number of times (δ), on average, to obtain a prescribed amount (α) of the preferred activity. This experimentally induced constraint on behavior can be written as

$$x_m = w x_h \tag{4.1}$$

where $w = \alpha/\delta$, x_h is the total number of times the job task is performed and x_m is total access to the preferred activity. Equation (4.1) characterizes job-related earnings under a piecework pay schedule in a barter economy where w is the real wage rate, x_h is the total number of pieces produced, and x_m is the total payment derived from working.

The job task is available for a limited period of time each day (T). This imposes a second constraint on behavior:

$$T = T_h + T_l \tag{4.2}$$

where T_h and T_l refer to time spent on work and leisure activities, respectively. Note, we are assuming that income is consumed outside the time constraint, say, by stopping the session control clock during reinforcement.

Since the amount of time taken to complete a given key peck or lever press can, for all practical purposes, be treated as a constant, μ,

$$T_h = \mu x_h \tag{4.3}$$

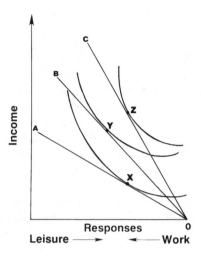

Figure 4.1 Indifference curves for income and leisure (not working) and the constraint on choices imposed by different ratio schedules of reinforcement. Wage rates are increasing (response requirements are decreasing) in going from OA to OB to OC. Equilibrium choice is where the constraint is tangent to the highest attainable indifference curve, e.g., point X for budget line OA.

Substituting (4.3) into (4.2) and rearranging,

$$T_1 = T - \mu x_h \qquad\qquad (4.4)$$

Equation (4.4) implies that responding directly competes for time with other activities ("leisure" in the economist's jargon), such as sleeping, preening, and the like, so that increases in responding, x_h, reduce the amount of time available for these other, unprogrammed, reinforcers, x_l.

Figure 4.1 shows graphically the constraints on choices associated with equations (4.1) and (4.2). The vertical axis measures income (e.g., number of food reinforcements). The horizontal axis measures the amount of time spent on leisure activities, as well as the time spent working. Both work and leisure can be represented on the horizontal axis since, as equation (4.4) shows, an increase in responding (work) directly reduces the time available for leisure (other) activities, and vice versa.

Simple ratio schedules of reinforcement are characterized by straight lines, such as OA in Figure 4.1. Any point on OA represents an income–work bundle attainable under this ratio schedule. At a zero response rate (all time devoted to leisure activities), total income is zero. Increases in the response rate result in proportionate increases in income. The other straight lines, OB and OC, are income-leisure bundles attainable under lower ratio requirements (the wage rate is higher).

4.1b Indifference curves and optimal choice

Workers' preferences between income–work bundles are represented by indifference curves, examples of which are also shown in Figure 4.1. The indifference curves are drawn as declining over most values, only becoming positively sloped as the level of leisure activities approaches its maximum value (when time spent working is close to zero). The positively sloped segment of the indifference curve indicates a willingness to work for free (or to pay for the right to "work"), as would likely be the case when wheel running is the job task for rats; that is, the work activity is valued as a "good" up to a certain point. Beyond some level of work, however, the individual is unwilling to spend additional time working unless she is compensated. Higher indifference curves represent more favorable income–work bundles because they have both more income and more leisure and would naturally be preferred.

Obviously, the positively sloped segments of the indifference curves need not exist; work may be regarded as a "bad," always requiring compensation. The slopes of the indifference curves are also affected by the nature of the leisure activities and the consumption goods available. For example, introducing a freely available running wheel into a rat's experimental chamber may increase the slope of the declining segment of the indifference curves, indicating that the rate of pay required to compensate for work rises as a result of an enhanced set of "leisure" activities.

As in the commodity-choice model, the individual is expected to choose the most preferred income–work bundle from those attainable. This is represented by the point at which the indifference curve is tangent to the budget line, point X for budget line OA in Figure 4.1. Specifying this equilibrium point for income and leisure is not very informative in its own right since there appears to be no independent way of determining whether this point has been achieved. However, the model does predict how changes in the budget constraint will affect the subject's willingness to work, and this is what the experiments focus on.

4.1c Income-compensated wage changes

Recall that in the commodity-choice framework, income-compensated price changes were those in which the relative prices of the commodities were changed *and* the budget constraint adjusted so that the individual could continue to consume the original combination chosen. To extend this concept to labor supply it is necessary to modify the wage rate while continuing to allow the same income–work bundle to be consumed. As in the case of commodity choice, the theory makes definite predictions regarding the effect of income-compensated wage changes: compensated wage decreases must result in reduced pay and increased leisure (less work), whereas compensated wage increases must result in increased pay and reduced leisure (more work).

Figure 4.2 illustrates an income-compensated wage decrease using the procedures from our first experiment. The job task was key pecking for pigeons working in an open economy (pigeons maintained at 80% of free-feeding body weight). Variable-ratio (VR) schedules of reinforcement were used, with the baseline schedule (line A in Figure 4.2) a VR 50 (that is, on average, every 50 key pecks resulted in the delivery of a food payment, which was a 3-second access to a grain hopper). Total time available for working was 40 minutes, and the session control clock stopped after each payoff so that eating did not count against total time available for work. Mean choices over the last five days of this schedule are shown by point X, along with data reported for two of the pigeons studied in this experiment (see Section 4.4a for a full explanation of the experimental results).

Under baseline (budget line A), bird 48 responded (pecked) an average of 6,908 times and earned an average of 137.3 trips to the food hopper; bird 49 responded an average of 5,290 times and earned an average of 106 payoffs. Income-compensation procedures involved delivering half of baseline earnings for free (delivered randomly throughout the session) while doubling the work requirement for earned income (halving the wage rate). For bird 48, this meant delivering 69 unearned (free) payoffs, while requiring 100 responses (VR 100) per earned payoff; for bird 49, this meant delivering 53 unearned (free) payoffs, while also requiring 100 responses for each earned payoff (budget lines B in Figure 4.2).

The income-compensated price changes ensure that if the birds worked as much following the wage change as they did before the change, their total income would be the same, only half of it would be unearned, with the other half earned at the lower wage rate. Responses to these compensated wage changes are shown by point Y in Figure 4.2. Bird 48 reduced its responding by around 38%, with total earnings reduced to 112.3 payoffs (69 free and 43.3 earned; a reduction of some 18%); bird 49 reduced responding by around 80%, with total earnings reduced to 63.5 payoffs (53 free and 10.5 earned; a reduction of 40%). As in the case of commodity choices, the compensated wage changes introduce relatively favorable trade-offs between the two goods: the percentage reductions in total earnings are half the percentage reductions in responding. As such, the birds are able to move to a new, higher indifference curve.

4.1d Income-constant wage changes

Under an income-constant wage change, the worker may or may not be able to achieve the income–work bundles originally chosen. The different budget lines in Figure 4.1 illustrate such changes. Going from budget line OC to OA involves a reduction in the real wage rate as a consequence of either a

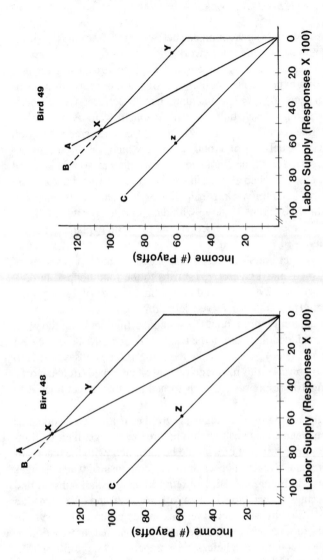

Figure 4.2 Effects of income-compensated wage changes with pigeons under open-economy conditions. Baseline budget line A is a variable-ratio (VR) 50 schedule. Compensated wage change line B halves the wage rate and delivers half of baseline earnings for free. Equilibrium choice points X (baseline) and Y (wage change) show reduced income and responding. Budget line C has the same wage rate as B but no unearned income. Choice point Z shows income and leisure to be a normal good in both cases. Data from Battalio, Green, and Kagel (1981).

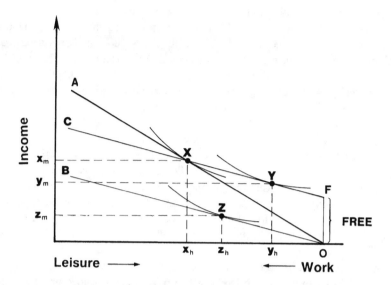

Figure 4.3 Income and substitution effects resulting from a wage decrease. Original budget line is OA. Budget line OB results from a wage decrease. Budget line OFXC represents an income-compensated wage decrease with the resulting reduction in labor supply, $x_h - y_h$, the substitution effect of the wage decrease. Budget line OB has the same response requirement for earned reinforcers as OFXC, but no unearned income, with the increase in labor supply, $y_h - z_h$, the income effect of the wage decrease.

higher work requirement per unit of reinforcement (δ), or a reduced level of consumption offered per unit of reinforcement (α).

The effect of the change in wage rates depicted in Figure 4.1 is an initial increase in labor supply from point X to point Y, as the budget line goes from OA to OB. This is followed by a decrease in labor supply, from point Y to point Z, when the budget line is changed to OC. These trends in work represent what is called a *backward-bending labor-supply* schedule, which a number of economists (or economic textbooks, at least) use to characterize behavior. We will have more to say about the shape of the labor-supply schedule later in this chapter. What is important to note right now is that an income-constant wage increase can lead to either an increase or a decrease in labor supply. Without further restrictions, either is acceptable from the point of view of the theory. However, income will normally increase as the wage rate is increased.

As with income-constant price changes, income-constant wage changes can be characterized in terms of an income and a substitution effect. Figure 4.3. illustrates this point, with an example of a wage rate reduction (change from budget line OA to OB). Budget line OFXC represents an income-compensated wage decrease in relation to the original budget line OA. The new budget line serves to define the substitution effect of the wage change (the reduction in labor supply from x_h to y_h). The shift from budget line OFXC down to OB is analogous to a decrease in income in the commodity-choice model and is the result of eliminating the unearned (free) income component (OF) of schedule OFXC while holding constant the relative wage rate. The resultant change in work level is referred to as the income effect of the wage rate change. Assuming that leisure and income are both normal goods (a natural assumption), the reduction in unearned income will result in reduced leisure (increased work) andreduced income, as represented by the movement from y_h to z_h and from y_m to z_m, respectively.

While labor supply may increase or decrease in response to an income-constant wage change, assuming that income is a normal good, the effect on income is clear-cut: The substitution effect of the wage decrease reduces income (the movement from x_m to y_m) and the income change reduces it as well (the movement from y_m to z_m). If the effort price of income is defined as the inverse of the wage rate $(1/w)$ (i.e., effort price increases as the wage rate decreases), then the "law of demand for income" (Robbins, 1930) holds that income will move inversely to its effort price: as effort price increases, income decreases. Finally, one can readily show that when the demand for income is elastic in terms of its effort price, labor supply will increase when wages increase; where the demand for income is inelastic, however, labor supply will decrease with increases in the wage rate.[2]

Figure 4.2 illustrates the effect of unearned income on choices. Budget line C has the same work requirement as budget line B (100 responses, on average, per payoff), but no unearned income. Average choices under C are shown by point Z. There is reduced income and increased responding (reduced leisure) in relation to the income–leisure bundle chosen under the compensated wage change (point Y). Both income and leisure are, therefore, normal goods, as we would anticipate.

4.2 Behavior in the laboratory: Results from prior studies

The foregoing has established an explicit connection between ratio schedules of reinforcement and labor-supply theory. Ratio schedules of reinforcement have been extensively studied by psychologists ever since Ferster and Skinner's influential book, *Schedules of Reinforcement* (1957). In this section, we briefly review these studies as they relate to the concepts developed in Section 4.1 in order to provide the necessary background to our own experiments.

4.2a Backward-bending labor-supply curves

Textbook diagrams of labor-supply functions usually show a forward-rising curve at very low wages, which becomes vertical and finally bends back at higher wage rates. Albert Rees (1974, p. 164) noted that "unfortunately, there is no empirical basis for the forward sloping portion of the curve." Although one can dispute Rees's assertion on the basis of a number of econometric studies showing female labor supply to be increasing as wage rates increase, this statement appears to be correct with regard to prime-age, male heads of households (Pencavel, 1986), and definitely captures the fact that virtually no econometric research reports a bitonic labor-supply curve for an *individual* worker, or even for a homogeneous collection of workers. However, results from ratio-schedule experiments show that for a number of different species, under a variety of experimental conditions, the bitonic shape of the textbook diagrams are fulfilled; for example, humans and rats pressing levers for access to alcohol (Bigelow and Liebson, 1972; Meisch and Thompson, 1972, 1973); rats pressing levers for food pellets (Barofsky and Hurwitz, 1968) and concentrated sucrose solutions (Collier and Jennings, 1969); mice pressing levers for a fortified milk diet (Greenwood et al., 1974); and pigeons pecking a response key for access to food (Battalio, Green, and Kagel, 1981; Green, Kagel, and Battalio, 1987). Figure 4.4 reproduces data from some of these studies. (Before looking at the figure caption, try to determine which of the three curves depicts data for humans and which depicts data for rats.) In cases where the labor-supply function is not bitonic, it is usually negatively sloped throughout.[3]

4.2b Demand for income as a function of effort price

Irrespective of the shape of the labor-supply function, demand for income is found to be inversely related to effort price ($1/w$). This pattern is displayed by rats, pigeons, monkeys, and humans working for such items as food, water, saccharin and sucrose solutions, alcoholic beverages, and intravenous injections of all sorts of drugs, addictive and otherwise (for reviews of these results, see Allison, 1979; Hogan and Roper, 1978; Lea, 1978). Figure 4.5 shows the relationship between income earnings and effort price for the labor-supply data of Figure 4.4. Note that income decreases as effort price increases, even though subjects had adequate time to maintain consumption levels at all but the lowest wage rates. Thus, hypotheses of target income-earning behavior, whereby workers are thought to work just hard enough to maintain a given level of income, do not do well when applied to the kinds of piecework job tasks and with the species employed in these studies. The nearly universal nature of this inverse relationship between income and effort price suggests that in those cases where the relationship breaks down, we should look for shifts in preference patterns, or undetected changes in experimental conditions, to explain the behavior.

4.2c Responses to nominal wage-rate changes holding real wages constant

Equation (4.1) implies that labor-supply behavior depends on the ratio of the amount of the preferred commodity received (α) in relation to the

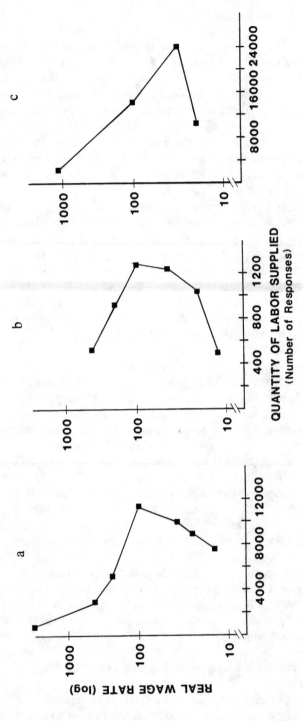

Figure 4.4 Backward-bending labor-supply functions. Panel a: Group data for mice lever-pressing for access to a fortified milk solution, their sole source of food intake (Greenwood et al., 1974). Panel b: Group data for rats lever-pressing for access to 64% sucrose solution (Collier and Jennings, 1969). Panel c: Data from an individual human lever-pressing for access to alcohol (Bigelow and Liebson, 1972).

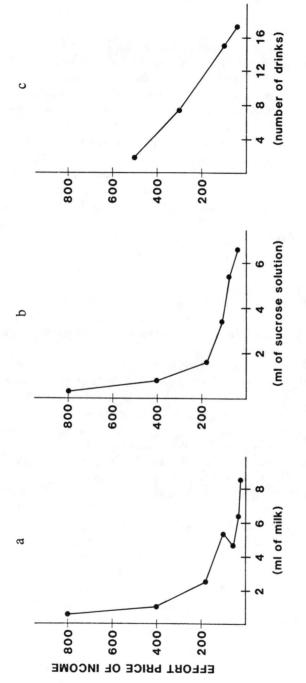

Figure 4.5 Demand for income as a function of effort price. Data in panels a, b, and c correspond to labor supply data of Figure 4.4

number of responses required to complete the job task (δ), and not on their absolute values (the ratio of these two values is called the *real wage* rate). Allison, Miller, and Wozny (1979) have tested this prediction with rats pressing levers (holding a lever down) in order to drink from a water spout. In their first experiment, the ratio of seconds of lever pressing to seconds of drinking varied from 5:5 sec, to 10:10 sec, to 20:20 sec with total session time held constant. The rats spent 17.0, 17.4 and 18.7% of the session lever pressing, differences that were not statistically significant. This result was replicated in a second experiment in which ratios of pressing to drinking varied from 20:20 sec, to 30:30 sec, and from 10:20 sec to 20:40 sec. Although labor supply varied systematically when the ratio values of pressing to seconds of drinking differed (i.e., from 1 to 1 versus 1 to 2), the amount of labor supply was constant between identical ratio values. These data, and those from other experiments, indicate that behavior is relatively insensitive, over a fairly wide range of values, to changes in the nominal work requirements as long as the real wage (α/δ) remains constant (for data on human workers, see Bickel et al., 1991).[4]

4.2d Choice between alternative jobs with differing wage rates

It is a well-established principle of labor-supply behavior that if workers have a choice between two (or more) jobs that yield no differences in nonpecuniary returns, they will exclusively work on the job with the higher wage rate (see, for example, Becker, 1971, pp. 166–70). In choosing between concurrently available ratio schedules of reinforcement (recall Section 2.5), animals essentially face this situation, and, as already noted, work almost exclusively on the job with the higher real wage rate.

4.2e Effects of unearned income on labor supply

Faced with the choice of working for food, or eating identical and continuously available free food, animals show a near-exclusive preference for the free food, provided stimulus signalling conditions (changing color, lights, sounds, etc.) associated with both alternatives are the same. However, in experiments where stimulus signals were associated only with the earned income, with no corresponding signals for the unearned income, subjects (including humans) continue to work, often obtaining 50 percent or more of their total income by working (for a review of this literature, see Osborne, 1977). Thus, neither pigeons, rats nor humans work for bread alone; the stimuli typically programmed to coincide with food deliveries have the status of "nonpecuniary" sources of income commonly thought to influence labor-supply behavior within market economies.[5]

4.3 Income-compensated wage-changes: Procedures

Laboratory studies of ratio-schedule performance disclose results that accord remarkably well with expectations based on neoclassical economic theory. It is this consistency that motivated the income-compensated wage-change tests we report below. Although labor-supply theory allows the labor-supply curve to be of any shape, and even permits, over portions of the choice space, increases in income with increases in effort price (so that income is a Giffen good), the predicted response to income-compensated wage changes remains unambiguous.

4.3a   Open versus closed economies

In the commodity-choice experiments, we distinguished between essential and nonessential commodities. The analogous distinction in the labor-supply experiments is between closed and open economies. Under a closed economy, all consumption is obtained as a consequence of within-session labor supply, with sessions lasting for extended periods of time (typically 20–24 hours). As a consequence, body weight varies with labor supply, and within-session earnings are essential to the organism's well being and survival.

In open-economy experiments, on the other hand, subjects work for a brief period (typically 40–60 minutes) each day strictly for food reinforcement, having ad-lib access to water outside the experimental sessions. In addition, subjects are maintained at a constant body weight (typically 80% ± a few grams) in order to keep weight changes from confounding the results. This is achieved through a regimen of postexperimental feeding that varies inversely with the level of within-session earnings. Although these supplemental feedings are sufficiently delayed and irregular enough so that the animal will still be induced to work within the experimental session, they are a source of consumption not available under closed-economy conditions. Under moderate deprivation levels, these extra feedings might be expected to promote greater substitutability of income for leisure than would be found in a closed economy (see Hursh, 1980, 1984).

In addition to the differences between open and closed economies, we have explored the effects of different methods of implementing compensated wage changes. Differences in method have sometimes been dictated by differences in other treatment variables, such as going from an open to a closed economy. At other times, a method has been changed in an effort to eliminate rival explanations of certain results.

4.3b   Income-compensated wage decreases with pigeon workers

All of our experiments with pigeons took place under an open economy using variable-ratio schedules and income-compensation procedures similar to those described in Section 4.1c. However, two different methods were used for reducing the wage rate for the earned reinforcers: (a) the number of responses required per earned reinforcer were increased (series I); and (b) the amount of food delivered per earned reinforcement was reduced (series II).[6] In terms of the static model of labor supply developed in Section 4.1, behavior should be the same under the two compensation procedures. This is explicit in equation (4.1) in which the controlling variable is the real wage rate. In terms of reinforcement theory, however, the two procedures may have quite different effects. Reinforcement theorists might criticize compensation procedures involving increased response requirements (series I) on the grounds that, given the impact of reinforcement delays on choice (see Chapter 7), increased delays to reinforcement, necessarily brought about by increases in the number of responses required, could completely account for any observed reductions in responding.[7] The series II procedure controls for this potential artifact.

4.3c Income-compensated wage decreases with rat workers

In labor-supply experiments with rats, we used mostly a closed economy. The task was to press a lever for the consumption goods food and liquid. Two levers were available for pressing at all times, one for each commodity. Work requirements were always the same for both commodities so that food and fluid may be viewed as a composite commodity, "income." Fixed-ratio schedules of reinforcement were used throughout.

Income-compensated wage changes were implemented using a two-part wage schedule: The "unearned" income was delivered in the first part of the schedule in which each response produced a payoff. Once the rat attained a predetermined level of unearned income, the second wage rate (response requirement) took effect. In the second stage, more work was required per unit of income than under the baseline wage rate. The amount of "unearned" income from the first stage and the wage rate in the second part of the schedule were set so that if the rat responded the same number of times as it had under baseline, it received the same total income.

For convenience, we delivered unearned income at the beginning of each session, rather than randomly throughout the session, because we were dealing with two commodities and a 24-hour time period. However, this method of delivering unearned income also addresses a methodological criticism of the pigeon experiments. A reinforcement theorist might attribute the reduced responding and consumption associated with random delivery of free goods to "superstitious" behavior (Skinner, 1948).[8] According to this explanation, unearned income adventitiously reinforces nonwork behavior, thereby increasing the relative frequency of nonwork, and decreasing total work and total income. Marginal wage rates have no role to play in this alternative explanation. Thus, the two-part wage schedule used to introduce compensated wage decreases in our rat studies preserves the mechanism, which, according to consumer-demand theory, underlies the substitutability of income for leisure. It also eliminates adventitious reinforcement that could give rise to superstitious behavior and thus contaminate our results.

As in our commodity-choice experiments, we maintained experimental conditions for a minimum time period (generally between 14 and 30 days) and did not change conditions until subjects satisfied a stability criteria. Unless noted otherwise, all data refer to averages computed over the last several days of an experimental condition, the period in which the stability criteria were satisfied.

4.4 Income-compensated wage changes: Results

4.4a Income-compensated wage decreases

Extending the fundamental law of demand to labor-supply requires that both work and earnings decrease following income-compensated wage decreases. Figure 4.2 (Section 4.1c) illustrated responses to these wage decreases.

Table 4.1 summarizes the results of all the income-compensated wage decrease tests we have conducted. In 57 out of 61 (93.4%) cases, both earnings and work decreased, as the theory requires. This is, of course, far more than one would expect by chance alone. There appear to be no significant differences between the three procedures in terms of their agreement with labor-supply theory.[9] The consistent reductions in labor supply under the differing procedures rules out the reinforcement-delay hypothesis and the superstition model as explanations of the animals' behavior. Also, note the consistent reduction in labor supply under both open- and closed-economy conditions.

The effects of income-compensated wage decreases were quite large in the open-economy studies: the elasticity of labor supply was greater than 1.0 in absolute value at all but the very highest wage rate.[10] For compensated wage changes initiated at the lowest wage rates, a number of birds stopped responding almost completely. Consequently, virtually all their consumption was unearned, being reduced to some 50% of baseline levels. Even at higher wage rates, reductions in labor were typically quite large under the income-compensated wage changes, with concomitantly sharp reductions (averaging about 30% of baseline) in the animals' within-session consumption. In addition, there was a consistent pattern of smaller substitution effects (smaller reductions in labor supply) at higher wages (lower ratio schedule requirements) as reflected in the elasticities of substitution reported in Table 4.1.

In the closed-economy studies, reductions in the labor supply of 20% or more were not uncommon. These translate into reductions in food and fluid consumption of some 13%. Even in the closed economy, animals substituted reduced income for reduced workloads following income-compensated wage reductions. The extent of these reductions in labor supply were, however, generally smaller than in an open economy, particularly at the lower wage rates, as indicated by the labor-supply elasticities reported in Table 4.1.

Of the four inconsistencies reported in Table 4.1, only two would prove statistically significant, given the day-to-day variability in the data. In contrast,

Table 4.1 *Income-compensated wage-decrease results*

Economy	Percentage consistent choices[a]	Median elasticity of labor supply (range)[b]		Compensation procedure	Subjects (no.)
		Highest wage rate	Lowest wage rate		
Open	86.4 (19/22)	−0.23 (0.04 to −0.68)	−1.81 (−0.88 to −2.94)	Series I: random delivery of free; increased response requirement per payoff	Pigeons (6)
Open	100.0 (16/16)	−1.48 (−1.30 to −1.81)	−2.33 (−0.82 to −2.86)	Series II: random delivery of free; reduced payoff per reinforcement	Pigeons[c] (4)
Closed	95.6 (22/23)	−0.69 (0.04 to −1.14)	−0.88 (−0.12 to −2.10)	Two-part wage schedule	Rats (6)

[a]Number of consistent choices divided by number of trials in parentheses.
[b]Elasticity of labor supply varies with the baseline wage rate underlying the compensated wage change.
[c]All four subjects had also participated in the Series I experiment.

virtually all the consistent responses would pass such significance tests (Battalio et al., 1981; Battalio and Kagel, 1985). These inconsistencies, moreover, all occurred at the highest wage rate (lowest response requirement). The extent of income-leisure substitution, particularly under an open economy, was inversely related to the baseline wage rate. That is, there were smaller reductions in responding and income at the higher wage rates (lower VR schedule values). Hence, given a constant degree of inherent variability in response patterns, one would expect to find more inconsistent choices with higher wages.

4.4b Income-compensated wage increases

Whereas income-compensated wage decreases reduce labor supply and earnings, compensated wage increases should achieve the opposite effect. To test this prediction, we set rats the task of lever pressing for food and liquid in a closed economy. Figure 4.6 illustrates our procedure. Starting from a baseline ratio schedule of reinforcement (line OA with equilibrium choice point X), a two-part wage schedule was implemented (OBC); only now, work requirements in the first part of the schedule were greater than during baseline (segment OB). The wage rate in the second stage was increased to 1 response per payoff after a fixed level of income had been earned in the first stage (with no limit as to how much earnings could be in any 24-hour period once the wage increase went into effect; segment BC). As with compensated wage decreases, if the rat responded the same number of times as it had under baseline, it would receive the same total earnings.

Within the framework of static consumer-demand theory, the increase in marginal wage rates in the neighborhood of point X promotes increased earnings and increased levels of work; this should lead to an equilibrium point such as Y in Figure 4.6. However, the strict convexity of the constraint also permits an equilibrium at a point such as Z, along the first segment of the compensated wage increase schedule. Such an equilibrium would represent a *local maximum* (a tangency point between an indifference curve and the budget line) in contrast to the *global maximum* at Y (another tangency point between the budget line and an indifference curve, but on a higher indifference curve). Boland (1981), in discussing the falsifiability of the maximization hypothesis within the neoclassical paradigm, argues forcefully that observing a local as opposed to a global maximum, when either of the two can be attained, delivers a devastating blow to the maximization hypothesis, a blow that would be difficult, if not impossible, to rebuff. Our procedures permit either equilibrium point to be achieved.

These are not the only alternatives open to the rats, however. They can "store" income internally by eating larger than normal amounts at one time and use this accumulated energy to tide them over extended periods of deprivation. This capacity to store food permits a dynamic solution to the constraints imposed, as the rats could operate on different segments of the two-part schedule on differ-

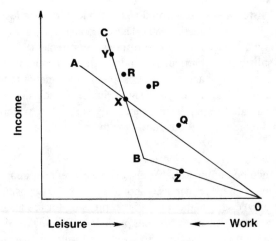

Figure 4.6 Income-compensated wage increase procedure. Baseline wage rate determined by a ratio schedule of reinforcement (budget line OA) with choice point X. Income-compensated wage increases employ a two-part wage schedule with an initial low wage rate (line segment OB), followed by a high wage rate (line segment BC). Text characterizes alternative choice points in relationship to the theory.

ent days. In other words, on one day a rat could operate strictly on the initial segment (OB), while the next day it could operate along the second segment (BC). If the animals alternate appropriately between these two values, their average choices can lie *above* the constraint OBC.

A number of possible choices consistent with the theory exist within this dynamic framework: (a) a point such as P can be obtained that *dominates* the original equilibrium point, more earnings *and* less work; (b) average choice might contain more earnings and more work compared with the original equilibrium, a point such as R; or (c) average choice might contain less income and less work, a point such as Q in Figure 4.6. Without considerably more information, such as the animal's storage capacity and the depreciation rate of stored energy, as well as a substantially more complicated model than we care to develop here, it is not possible to predict which of these alternatives would be most preferred. However, were the average choice point to lie within, or on, the triangle XBO, behavior would be inconsistent with a dynamic variant of the weak axiom of revealed preference: under the original constraint these points were rejected in favor of point X; for them to be preferred now, even though superior choice points on higher indifference curves are available, would contradict the theory.

Table 4.2 summarizes the rats' responses to this procedure in terms of the solution alternatives presented in Figure 4.6. For 6 rats, a total of 18 income-compensated wage increases were implemented (at least 2 conditions per rat).

Table 4.2. *Effects of compensated wage increases*

Baseline wage index[a]	Inconsistent choices	Consistent choices		Percentage consistent choice
		Static solution	Dynamic solution[b]	
300	2	2	1 (0)	60
(20)				
150	0	0	3 (2)	100
(40)				
100	2	0	1 (1)	33
(60)				
66.7	1	0	3 (0)	75
(90)				
44.4	1	0	2 (1)	67
(135)				
Total	6	2	10 (4)	67

[a]Wage index = 100(1/ratio requirement)60. Baseline ratio requirement in parentheses.
[b]Number satisfying dominant solution in parentheses. Dominant solution involves less work and more consumption, on average, following compensated wage increases.
Source: Battalio and Kagel (1985).

In 12 of the 18 cases (67%), behavior satisfied solution alternatives offered by consumer-demand theory. Only at the highest wage rate condition was the static solution satisfied – more income and more work. Otherwise, consistent choice always followed one of the dynamic alternatives. In about half of these cases (4 out of 10), subjects achieved a dominant solution – less work and more earnings, on average, than during the corresponding baseline condition (recall point P in Figure 4.6). In the other cases, subjects chose less work and less consumption than under the baseline, a dynamic outcome like point Q in Figure 4.6.

With low initial wage rates, the procedure produced quite dramatic day-to-day variability in consumption. It was not uncommon for total consumption to vary by a factor of two or more between days. Figure 4.7 presents representative data from two rats, showing the day-to-day variability in their consumption. For example, rat 803 went from about 600 payoffs on day 6 to 100 on day 7, back to about 600 payoffs on day 8. Such extreme daily variations in consumption seem quite remarkable.

Distinctly different processes appear to underlie the inconsistent choices at the different wage rates. At the lower rates (wage index 150 or less), three of the four inconsistencies involved a static local maximum like the one characterized by point Z in Figure 4.6. In these three cases, subjects either never attained the switch point (B in Figure 4.6) where the higher marginal wage rate went into ef-

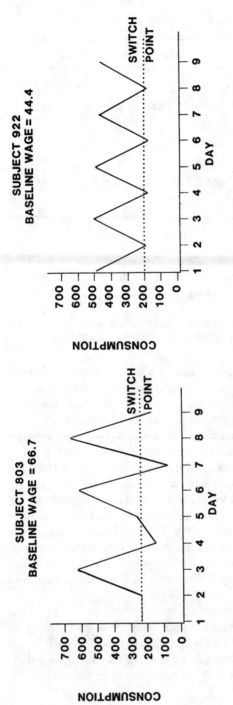

Figure 4.7 Daily variability in total consumption under income-compensated wage increase procedures. Data from Battalio and Kagel (1985).

fect, or they reached it only once or twice during the entire 14 plus days they were on the two-part schedule. This suggests that they might not have made contact with the wage change. To determine the role of "information" in these inconsistencies, we reduced the switch point (B) for two of these subjects to one that we knew they would reach. We maintained this condition for several (2–3) days, then gradually increased the switch point to its original value, where it was then maintained for 14 days. One subject now displayed consistent choices in the dynamic range, but the other rat continued to be inconsistent, although now operating within the triangle XBO. We suggest that any further exploration of behavior under these contingencies should employ signals providing advance information of schedule conditions, although these might be difficult to develop in practice.

For the two subjects that were inconsistent at highest real wages, labor supply fell somewhere along line segment BC each day of the period, but generally failed to exceed point X. In one case, the mean reduction in earnings and labor supply were not statistically significant given the day-to-day variability in the data. In the other case, replication of the rat's baseline condition showed a marked reduction in its earnings and labor supply in relation to its initial baseline levels, so that when we reimposed an income-compensated wage increase in relation to this new baseline, earnings and labor supply increased in accord with the static theory to a point such as Y in Figure 4.6. These two inconsistencies are similar in structure to those reported with income-compensated wage decreases: (a) they are not statistically significant (in relation to the day-to-day variability in the data) and/or are not replicable, and (b) they occur under the highest of wage rate conditions.

One of the most interesting aspects of these results is that the procedure evinced dynamic solution patterns. The two-part wage schedule clearly encouraged subjects to switch to a dynamic solution alternative when their baseline wages were low. Whereas the second segment of these schedules had the same work requirement, one press per payoff, the work requirement in the first segment was 50% greater than the baseline level. As a consequence, the total number of responses required to attain the switch point (B) increased dramatically as baseline wage rates decreased. For example, for rat 803 reported in Figure 4.7a, the response requirement in the first part of the wage rate schedule was 135 responses per payoff, and the second part of the wage schedule took effect after 240 payoffs, so that a fixed cost of 32,400 responses was required to obtain access to the one response per payoff segment of the schedule. In contrast, with the same switch point of 240 payoffs, but with a response requirement of 30 presses per payoff, a total fixed cost of only 7,200 responses would be needed to obtain access to the one response per payoff segment of the schedule. Thus, the fixed response cost of access to the same high marginal wage rate increased as wages decreased, thereby increasing the potential return for adopt-

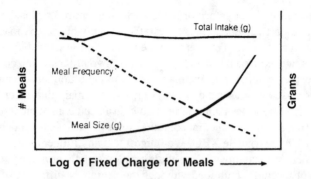

Figure 4.8 Effects of changes in fixed entry fee on meal frequency, meal size, and total food intake. Idealized data from a number of different experiments and species (Collier and Johnson, 1990).

ing a dynamic, as compared with a static, solution alternative. The latter would involve paying these fixed costs each day. The dynamic solution alternative, on the other hand, involves less frequent payment of the fixed costs and "stocking up" during the high marginal wage rate periods.

Collier and his associates have reported that a variety of animals adopt a feast-or-famine strategy in the presence of increased fixed costs of consumption, under procedures quite different from those employed here (Collier, 1982). In Collier's studies, subjects were housed in a cage with a tunnel attached to the front wall. Food was available at the end of the tunnel. Access to the food was contingent on the subjects' paying a fixed access fee, typically pressing a lever a predetermined number of times. Upon completion of the access fee, the subjects had continuous access to the food as long as they did not remain out of the tunnel eating area for more than ten consecutive minutes. That is, all subjects paid a fixed fee to enter the "cafeteria" and could remain and eat as long as desired. In examining subjects' responses to changes in the fixed entry fee, Collier found that they reduced meal frequencies and ate more per meal as the fixed cost increased, with little impact on total food intake (see Figure 4.8).

The similarity between Collier's results and ours is that both involve what might be characterized as solutions to dynamic optimization problems. In this context, the question that naturally arises concerns the extent to which the animals' behavior involves anticipation of future needs and contingencies, versus reactive responses to the deleterious effects of severe consumption deficits. Collier and his associates (Collier, 1986; Collier and Johnson, 1990) address this issue. They compare the standard homeostatic deficit/repletion model, in which feeding is presumed to begin and end in response to deficits and immediate food needs, with a more ecological/economic model in which decisions of what to eat and how much to eat are based not only on characteristics of currently available food resources, but also on anticipated food resources. Collier comes down squarely in favor of the ecological/economic model on two grounds: (a) the frequency of meals and their size are quite sensitive to the fixed costs of feeding, so that changes in meal patterns following increases in access price can be interpreted as a means of minimizing feeding costs; and (b) although average meal size increases with cost, the fine-grain control over eating implied by the homeostatic control mechanism is not present. For example, after controlling for changes in the fixed cost of meals, the correlation between meal size and the preceding intermeal interval varies around zero. Collier notes that behavior is anticipatory, in the sense of the animal being prepared, although the behavior is not necessarily anticipatory in terms of the animals' intentions, which, of course, are not observable.

To summarize the results from this section: Income-compensated wage increases produced results that were generally consistent with the predictions of the theory. The experimental procedures we employed encouraged a dynamic rather than a static solution, whereby the rats varied consumption by large amounts on a daily basis (see Figure 4.7).[11] We did not anticipate this pattern of dynamic solutions, but because the data yielded testable implications for the theory and the response patterns were so fascinating, we continued with the procedures. The daily variability in our rats' consumption, and the motivations for it, have much in common with Collier's investigation into the way in which changes in fixed costs of responding affect consumption patterns in rats.

4.5 Animal labor supply and the incentive effects of public welfare programs

4.5a Static considerations: Effects of a negative income tax

An income-compensated wage decrease employs similar contingencies to those involved in a negative income tax program. A negative income tax program (and most welfare plans, for that matter) delivers unearned income while effectively reducing the wage rate. The reduction in the wage rate comes about because any increase in earned income causes the recipient to lose unearned income, typically at very high marginal tax rates. Economists, and others, have voiced concern about the potential disincentive effects of such programs. These effects are illustrated in Figure 4.9. Budget line OA depicts net earnings after whatever income taxes are in effect, where there is no income-guarantee program in the system. (For the sake of simplicity, we assume a simple proportionate tax system.) Budget line OFBA shows the budget constraint under a guaranteed income program: OF is the maximum level of unearned income provided to the recipient when earned income is zero; b_m is the earned income level at which all benefits are lost, that is, when the recipient's earnings

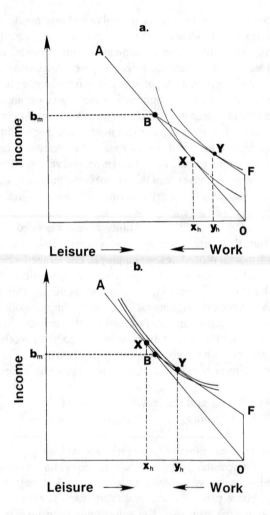

Figure 4.9 Effects of a guaranteed income program. Guaranteed income program generates budget constraint OFBA compared with budget line OA in the absence of the program. (a) Equilibrium income–work bundle (X) in the absence of the program is below break-even point (B). Point Y shows equilibrium under the program, assuming income and leisure are normal goods. (b) Equilibrium income–work bundle (X) in the absence of the program is above break-even point (B). Point Y shows possible equilibrium under this program.

equal the income limitations of the program (this is referred to as the break-even income level); and the slope of the line segment FB in relation to OB indicates the marginal tax rate, or the loss in benefits, as a consequence of earning income.

For workers whose earnings lie below the break-even income level, the income guarantee program is bound to cause a reduction in labor supply, in relation to preprogram levels, as long as leisure is a normal good. Figure 4.9a illustrates this case. Under these circumstances, movement from X to Y is the likely response to the program; the distance from x_h to y_h indicates the reduction in labor supply that would result. Under the circumstances, the recipient can reduce labor supply while at the same time maintaining or even increasing total income.

The existence of the income-guarantee program might also be expected to have a disincentive effect on the labor supply of those working poor whose income, prior to the program, is in the neighborhood of the break-even point. Figure 4.9b illustrates such a case. The guarantee program permits the working poor to move from X to Y and thus achieve a higher indifference curve with less income and more leisure. Of course, the size of the disincentive effect depends on the substitutability of income for leisure and the income elasticity of demand for leisure (that is, how much leisure increases in response to the unearned income).

Our experiments with pigeons and rats validate not only the economist's static labor-supply model, but also the potential disincentive effects of guaranteed income programs on labor supply. In drawing an analogy between our experimental procedures and welfare programs, we caution the reader to bear in mind that our results have little to say regarding the crucial question of the likely magnitude of any disincentive effects in humans. However, it is important to note that related research has shown that disincentive effects of guaranteed income are likely to be attenuated by the recipients' level of need: income-compensated wage decreases produced smaller income-leisure substitution for more deprived rats (Green and Green, 1982). In addition, our results validate the argument that the very high marginal tax rates present in a number of income transfer plans – rates at or above 100%, as in plans that would forfeit all benefits once income exceeds some threshold level – cause maximum work disincentive and should be replaced by more sensible marginal tax rates. We believe, in addition, that inasmuch as some disincentive effects are unavoidable, we must accept them as necessary costs of achieving desired improvements in individual and societal welfare. (See Schrader and Green, 1990, for a fuller presentation of the experimental procedures and results of animal experiments in relation to negative income tax programs, along with a discussion of the implications.)

4.5b Dynamic considerations:The welfare trap hypothesis

We have examined the disincentive effects of a guaranteed income program within a static theory of labor supply in which preferences are constant over time. Although few economists would dispute the short-term disincentive effects of a negative income tax (or similar welfare programs), the longer-term dynamic effects of such programs are still in question. The literature contains two distinctly different points of view on this question. On the one hand, Conlisk (1968) can imagine a world in which the delivery of unearned income, since it tends to increase total consumption, may, contrary to the static model, enhance labor supply in the long run. This could occur because the unearned income generates a taste for increased consumption ("getting hooked" on income). On the other hand, some argue that the income transfers inherent in welfare programs could cause tastes to change in the opposite direction (individuals could "get hooked" on leisure) and thereby create even greater dependency and contribute to poverty cycles. This is sometimes referred to as the "welfare trap" hypothesis (Plant, 1984; Sawhill, 1988).

In an experimental analysis of labor supply, the question of dynamic responses to unearned income reduces to determining the repeat reliability of the labor-supply data. That is, after periods of high levels of unearned income, are there systematic deviations in labor supply at lower levels of unearned income? What is the relative magnitude and direction of any deviations observed, and what forces are responsible for these deviations?

Our experiments have generated just these sorts of data as a natural by-product of the experimental design, which called for systematic replication of conditions. That is, we first measured baseline earnings without any unearned (free) income, introduced unearned income while holding wage rates constant, and then eliminated the unearned income. This procedure enables us to compare earnings and labor supply before and after the delivery of unearned income. The relevant results are provided in Table 4.3. The data in all cases are averages computed over those days on which performance satisfied our usual stability requirements. As such, the results are applicable to dynamic adjustment models (see, for example, Conlisk, 1968), where behavior converges to a steady-state level.

The data presented in Table 4.3 clearly favor the welfare trap hypothesis. When baseline earnings were compared before and after the introduction of unearned income, in 8 out of 11 cases less work was performed following the complete elimination of unearned income. Further, in 5 out of 6 cases, less work was performed following partial elimination of unearned income (with comparable levels of unearned income provided before and after the partial elimination). In total, in 13 out of 17 cases less work was performed following either partial or complete elimination of unearned income. Using a binomial sign test, we find there is less than a 2.5% chance of this happening if there were no systematic effect (under the null hypothesis that it is equally likely that replication values will show more or less labor supply than originally). The quantitative effect is small, however. For replication points with zero free income, reductions

Table 4.3. *Effects of unearned income on labor supply*

Amount of unearned income eliminated	Frequency with which labor supply increased or decreased following elimination of unearned income		Mean percentage change in labor supply[a]
	Increased	Decreased	
All	3	8	5.8 (2.69)
Partial	1	5	9.1 (6.50)
Total	4	13	7.0 (2.78)

[a]Standard error of mean in parentheses.
Source: Kagel (1987).

in labor supply averaged 5.8% of baseline levels. Such relatively small shifts in preferences between income and leisure are similar to Plant's (1984, pp. 679–80) finding from the U.S. economy that there exists "a small welfare trap leading to more persistence [on welfare] than would otherwise be predicted" (owing to shifts in income-earning opportunities).

It may be that our results tend to support a welfare trap hypothesis because the income elasticity of demand for leisure was higher than for income in these experiments. That is, unearned income usually increased leisure proportionately more than it increased total income in these experiments (the difference between points Y and Z for bird 49 in Figure 4.2 is more representative than the difference between these points for bird 48). Getting "hooked" on leisure or consumption as a consequence of past choices may well be a function of the relative impact of unearned income on these two competing outcomes. It would be of considerable interest, then, to look at preference shifts under altered conditions in which unearned income produces proportionately greater increases in consumption compared with leisure.

Although the direction of the changes in labor supply in our experiments are consistent with the welfare trap hypothesis, the magnitude of the changes are simply far too small to suggest major shifts in preferences. As a result, we would argue that our results point toward an absence of income-earning opportunities in relation to the welfare alternative, rather than to any nefarious shift in preferences, as in the welfare trap hypothesis, as the motivating force for that segment of the population who are long-term users of welfare.[12] In this case, our results agree with the limited econometric evidence available (Plant, 1984; Sawhill, 1988, and references cited therein).

4.6 Animal labor supply and supply-side economics

Taxes affect labor supply since they alter take-home wages. The higher the taxes, the lower the take-home wage. With a simple proportionate tax system

$$\bar{w} = w\,(1 - t)$$

where $\bar{w}$ is the take-home wage, w is the wage the employer pays, and t is the tax rate. Presumably, labor supply is responsive to after-tax wages, $\bar{w}$, rather than before-tax wages, w.

In recent years, the public has become aware of something called supply-side economics. One of its propositions that has found particular favor in some political circles is that reductions in tax rates might actually lead to greater government revenues. The argument is that the resultant increase in take-home wages would generate sufficiently large increases in labor supply, and therefore in earnings, to make up for the cut in tax rates. For this part of the supply-side argument to hold, individuals must be operating on the positively sloped portion of their labor-supply curves. And even then, an increase in tax revenues is far from assured, for not only must labor-supply increase, but it must increase enough so that more revenue is generated from a smaller tax rate. If, on the other hand, individuals are operating on the negatively sloped portion of their labor-supply curves, then the tax cut will lead to decreases in work and reductions in revenue.[13]

What is clear from the pigeon and rat experiments is that wage rates must be relatively low for the worker to be on the positively sloped portion of the labor-supply curve (recall Figure 4.4). And before a reduction in tax rates can push a worker very far along the positively sloped portion of the labor-supply curve, the existing tax rates must be exceptionally high. The supply-side argument is much more likely to be realized on a local or state level than on the national level, since workers are likely to vote with their feet in response to high local and state taxes. Although these insights into supply-side economics are hardly novel (see, for example, Browning and Browning, 1983), it is somewhat sobering to recognize that one reaches a similar conclusion using data from pigeons and rats, as well as one would from data drawn from national economic systems.

4.7 Summing up

This chapter has extended the commodity-choice model to labor-supply behavior. We showed that ratio schedules of reinforcement studied by psychologists may be viewed as simple piecework job tasks, and we explored labor-supply behavior on that basis. Our experiments have demonstrated that the fundamental law of demand extends to labor-supply behavior. That is, income-compensated wage decreases result in both reduced labor supply and reduced earnings. This occurs with a number of different compensation procedures and in both open- and closed-economy experiments.

Income-compensated wage decreases have a number of incentive properties in common with a negative income tax. Less well known, at least theoretically, are the longer-run effects of such programs. There is some concern that the income transfers inherent in welfare programs will cause tastes to change in favor of leisure, and thereby foster even greater dependency on welfare and create poverty cycles (the "welfare trap" hypothesis). We look at this issue by comparing labor supply under a given wage rate both before and after individuals received unearned income. Our data show more leisure following the delivery of unearned income, which is consistent with the welfare trap hypothesis; however, the quantitative effects of the changes are quite small. These results parallel those reported from the United States economy. The suggestion is that, to the extent poverty cycles exist in market economies, one must look to factors other than "taste changes" resulting from welfare payments to explain the behavior.

Income-compensated wage increases were implemented using a two-part wage schedule that promoted a dynamic, rather than the predicted static, solution, with the rats' earnings (and consumption) varying by large amounts on a day-to-day basis. This feast-or-famine strategy was a response to the high fixed cost of reaching the high wage rate segment. The daily variability in our rats' consumption, and the motivation for it, have much in common with Collier's studies of the effects of the fixed costs of consumption on meal size and meal frequency.

Notes

1 Each activity may be broken down into a further set of activities, provided relative prices within the activity set remain constant, or that these activities are performed in fixed proportions.

2 Let p_m be the effort price of consumption, defined as $1/w$. It can be shown that the elasticity of demand for consumption with respect to effort price $\xi_m = (\partial x_m/\partial p_m)(p_m/x_m) = [1 + \xi_h]$, where $\xi_h = (\partial x_h/\partial w)(w/x_h)$ (the elasticity of labor supply with respect to wage rate changes). When $\xi_h > 0$ (the labor-supply curve is positively sloped), demand for consumption is elastic ($\xi_m < -1$). When $\xi_h = 0$ (vertical labor-supply curve), demand for consumption is unitary elastic ($\xi_c = -1$). When $-1 \leq \xi_h < 0$, the labor-supply curve is negatively sloped (backward-bending) and elasticity of demand for consumption with respect to effort price is negative and inelastic ($\xi_m > -1$).

3 In an informal review of some 40 different experiments, Staddon (1979a) notes that about half of the studies obtained bitonic labor-supply functions.

4 Changing income-to-labor proportions in the animal experiments also involves changing time to reinforcement, which will, at some point, introduce sufficient changes in the absolute sizes of α and δ to affect this prediction (see Chapter 7).

5 In our laboratories, we have found that if a dish of food pellets is left on the cage floor, or if a water tube is hung on the door of the experimental chamber, the amount of lever

pressing that pays off in that same currency is greatly diminished, although responding does not drop to zero (except when lever pressing fails to result in any income being earned whatsoever, or when the ratio value is extremely high). This responding occurs even though there is no evidence to suggest that in the presence of ad-lib access to free food and/or liquid, rats would ever *learn* the lever-pressing task. This phenomenon suggests two possibilities. First, the "nonpecuniary" returns associated with the lever pressing are learned; that is, the lights and sounds paired with the delivery of earned reinforcers become conditioned reinforcers. In contrast, standard economic theory takes such tastes as given. Second, we know these "nonpecuniary" returns are not sustainable in the complete absence of primary reinforcement, so it is fair to assume that the stereotypical individual who works for "the love of the job" would behave otherwise in the absence of any monetary rewards.

6 In series II procedures, a photoelectric cell was introduced into the food hopper to ensure precise control of eating time (for details, see Green et al., 1987).

7 Bauman (1991) attempts to isolate the effect on labor supply of delays to reinforcement inherent in ratio schedules, as distinct from the effort and time cost (opportunity cost relative to other activities) of responding.

8 Joel Cohen first suggested this alternative explanation of the data.

9 $\chi^2 = 3.1$, d.f. $= 2, p = .21$.

10 Typically, a single compensated wage change was implemented to compare with a given baseline wage rate. Since labor supply varied systematically with the baseline wage rate, the elasticity of labor supply is measured using an arc elasticity measure at each wage rate (defined as the $[(x_1 - x_2)/(x_1 + x_2)]/[(w_1 - w_2)/(w_1 + w_2)]$, where x_1 and x_2 are the number of responses under the baseline and compensated wage change conditions and the w's are the corresponding wage rates).

11 Limited results, under different procedures that did not permit a consistent dynamic solution to income-compensated wage increases, are reported in Battalio and Kagel (1985). Under these procedures, both labor supply and earnings increased following compensated wage increases, as the theory predicts.

12 An alternative version of the welfare trap hypothesis attributes the trap to the deterioration in recipients' "human capital" as a consequence of unemployment, rather than to any shift in preferences. These two effects are difficult to disentangle, observationally. Moreover, to the extent that a welfare trap can be shown to result from deterioration in human capital stock as opposed to a shift in preferences, public policy responses would be quite different. The only interpretation open to us given our data is that of a shift in preferences, since the "pigeon capital" involved in learning how to key-peck is minimal or nonexistent.

13 Under a progressive income tax system, which is the more usual case, the analysis becomes considerably more complicated. Nevertheless, the essential features are unaffected.

5

Labor-supply behavior II: Tests of competing motivational processes and earnings distributions for animal workers

In this chapter we discuss further the competing motivational models developed in Chapter 3 and apply them to an animal's labor supply (Sections 5.1–5.3). Section 5.4 examines the effect of varying economic conditions (different wage rates, open versus closed economy) on an individual animal's labor supply. Because the distribution of earnings and inequality of incomes among individuals is a topic of continuing interest to social scientists, we construct earnings distributions and compare them with theoretical and empirical properties of earnings distributions reported in the literature.

5.1 Random behavior models

The random behavior models developed in Section 3.1 extend directly to labor supply. Recall that there are two polar random decision models for the individual consumer: he may be a pure random goods decider (equations (3.3) and (3.4)) or a pure random money decider (equations (3.1) and (3.2)). Random goods deciders select a collection of goods at random, in this case income and leisure. The model predicts, just as in the commodity-choice case, that this collection of goods is unaffected by income-compensation wage changes. In contrast to this prediction, the experimental data clearly indicate that the earnings-to-leisure ratio decreases in response to income-compensated wage decreases (recall Table 4.1).

The pure random money decider, on the other hand, spends a constant proportion of his income on goods in the choice set. A natural translation of this decision rule would be that subjects spend a constant proportion of their time engaged in leisure activities; or, what amounts to the same thing, a constant proportion of their time is spent working,

$$\frac{T_h}{T} = \beta \tag{5.1}$$

where, following our earlier notation, T_h is time spent working, T is total time, and β is a constant (between 0 and 1). Assuming that the time needed to complete a response, μ, is a constant, $T_h = \mu\, x_h$, where x_h is the number of responses. Substituting into (5.1) and rearranging yields

$$x_h = \left(\frac{\beta}{\mu}\right)T \tag{5.2}$$

Equation (5.2) implies a constant amount of labor supply, irrespective of wage rates (response requirements), and clearly fails to characterize the data (recall Figure 4.4 and see Figure 5.7).[1]

A weighted average of the two pure random behavior models once again results in a restricted form of the linear expenditure model. The labor-supply function for this model, in the absence of any unearned income, is

$$x_h = \frac{\gamma_m}{w} + \beta\left[\frac{T}{\mu} - \frac{\gamma_m}{w} - \frac{\gamma_l}{\mu}\right] \tag{5.3}$$

where γ_m, $\gamma_l > 0$ represent random income and random leisure purchases, respectively, and the bracketed term represents the number of free responses left over after these purchases. Differentiating (5.3) with respect to w shows that the labor-supply curve must be negatively sloped throughout, since $0 < \beta < 1$. Although much of the experimental data show an inverse relationship between wage rates and labor supply, this model fails to account for the positively sloped portion of the labor-supply curve, which is consistently observed at the lowest wage rates in an open economy.[2]

5.2 The matching law

The matching law and the labor-supply model developed in Chapter 4 conflict on a number of predictions, one of which is the shape of the labor supply curve, discussed in Section 5.2a. Section 5.2b shows that well-known differences in response rates on variable-interval (VI) and variable-ratio (VR) schedules of reinforcement can be accounted for in terms of income-leisure trade-offs and compares this account with the matching law's explanation. Section 5.2c looks at concurrent VI–VR schedules, a procedure developed by matching proponents to distinguish between matching and maximizing accounts of labor-supply behavior. Finally, Section 5.2d looks at progressive ratio schedules, which help to distinguish sensitivity to marginal versus average rates of reinforcement. As noted in Section 3.2a, matching implies sensitivity to average rates of reinforcement while maximizing implies sensitivity to marginal rates of reinforcement.

5.2a Matching and the shape of the labor-supply curve

As noted in Section 3.2, the matching law is an effort to quantify the "law of effect" – which states that greater reinforcement produces greater response strength (Hull, 1942; Skinner, 1938; Thorndike, 1911). The matching law (Herrnstein 1961, 1970) uses relative frequency of responding as the measure of response strength in choosing between concurrently available reinforcers. The model extends quite naturally to absolute rates of responding. Herrnstein (1970) develops this extension as follows: Let P represent the response rate (e.g., rate of key pecking for a pigeon, rate of lever pressing for a rat), R represent the obtained rate of reinforcement from responding, and R_o represent "other" reinforcers present in the environment that compete with the programmed reinforcers. (Note that these other reinforcers correspond directly to the economists' notion of "leisure" activities, although this term is not used.) The extension of the matching law to absolute response rate is

$$P = \frac{kR}{R + R_o} \tag{5.4}$$

where k is a positive constant that might be expected to change between different job tasks and with changes in the other (leisure) activities in the environment. Note that equation (5.4) captures directly the notion that the absolute rate of responding increases with the rate of reinforcement (R) and yields matching for concurrent schedules of reinforcement.[3]

Equation (5.4) did a fine job of characterizing response rates on variable-interval schedules of reinforcement at the time it was formulated (recall that on a VI schedule, subjects, on average, receive reinforcement for the first response made after a prescribed period of time has elapsed). However, it was clear from the start that response rates on ratio schedules were inconsistent with the model (Pear, 1975; Timberlake, 1977) (recall that on a ratio schedule a fixed number of responses must be made for each payoff). The problem with assuming that k and R_o are constant for a given job task, as the matching law does, is that response rates will then always *decrease* with *increases* in the ratio requirement, since R (the reinforcement rate) moves inversely to the ratio requirement. Consequently, as the ratio requirement increases, reinforcement rate (R) decreases, and responding (P) therefore decreases. In other words, the matching law predicts a *positively* sloped labor-supply curve throughout, so that responding increases as the ratio value decreases (the wage rate increases). At the time this implication of the matching law was clearly understood, a considerable body of data already existed showing that labor-supply curves were negatively sloped over a fairly wide range of ratio schedule values (recall Figure 4.4) (Timberlake, 1977).

One fallback position offered for the matching law in the face of these data was that the overall response rate is not an appropriate measure of responding since it includes time in which the animal is engaged in other behaviors. That is, response rates should be calculated on a time base obtained by subtracting reward time and postreinforcement pause time (pauses in responding following reinforcement) from total session time (for a statement of this position and citations to the relevant literature, see Prelec, 1982; and Timberlake, 1977). This effectively nullified much of the data reported up to this point since the experiments conducted (a) typically counted reinforcement time against total session time, and (b) used fixed-ratio (FR) schedules in which pauses typically follow reinforcement, in contrast to the more steady responding observed under variable-ratio schedules.[4] However, our open economy labor-supply procedures excluded reward time from total session time – the session control clock stopped whenever reinforcement occurred – and our use of VR schedules largely eliminated postreinforcement pauses associated with FR schedules. Nevertheless, we continued to observe a negatively sloped labor-supply curve over a relatively wide range of wage rates, in contrast to the matching law's prediction. Further, more recent research (Dougan, 1992; Timberlake and Peden, 1987) reports negatively sloped portions of labor-supply curves even under variable-interval schedules that typically produce slow, steady response rates. VI schedules also lack the postreinforcement pauses on which matching proponents base this defense.

Of course, as with commodity-choice behavior, it is possible to explain these violations of the matching law by arguing that with high wage rates (low response requirements), earned reinforcers are valued less than at low wages. But this invokes, in an ad hoc fashion, the kind of income effects that are built into the economic model of labor supply. Further, under the matching law, these "income effects" come into play through changes in within-session deprivation levels that change the value of the reinforcers (recall Section 3.2c). Dougan (1992) addresses the issue of satiation effects by looking at within-session response rates on VI schedules. He finds that response rates are *lower* in the first minute of high wage sessions, before satiation could have possibly occurred. He therefore concludes that his data are inconsistent with the matching law.

From a different perspective, the matching law's prediction of a positive slope throughout the labor-supply curve follows directly from its failure to account for the relatively inelastic demand for income at higher wage rates. Labor-supply curves are positively sloped whenever demand for income is elastic with respect to effort price, but they are negatively sloped with inelastic demand for income (see Chapter 4, note 2). Thus, the possibility of inelastic demand for goods, which the matching law failed to account for in commodity choice and which produced antimatching in that context, is responsible for negatively sloped labor-supply curves that the theory has similar difficulty accounting for.

5.2b Differential response rates on interval and ratio schedules of reinforcement

A variable-interval schedule of reinforcement provides reinforcement for the first response after a variable period of time has elapsed. In contrast, a

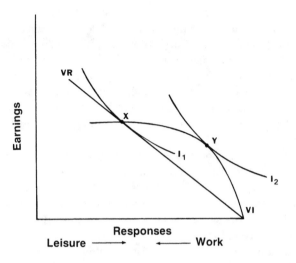

Figure 5.1 Contrasting VI and VR constraints: The straight line represents a VR schedule and the bowed curve represents a VI schedule. Average reinforcement rates are the same at the point of intersection (point X). I_1 and I_2 are hypothetical indifference curves for income and leisure.

variable-ratio schedule of reinforcement provides reinforcement strictly on the basis of the animal's response rate. It is commonly acknowledged that over most ranges of reinforcement, responding under VR schedules is considerably greater than under VI schedules with comparable rates of reinforcement. The response rate differential is commonly in the neighborhood of 2 to 1 in favor of the VR schedule (see, for example, Catania et al., 1977).

The uncertainty concerning the timing of rewards under a VI schedule, in conjunction with the requirement that a response must be produced after the interval has elapsed in order to collect the reward, establishes a production technology (a reinforcement feedback function, as the psychologists call it) in which the expected rate of return for responding is positive throughout, but subject to rapidly diminishing *marginal* returns (as indicated by the bowed curve in Figure 5.1). In contrast, VR schedules maintain a constant marginal and average reinforcement rate throughout (the linear function in Figure 5.1). The net effect, in cases where both schedules produce the same rate of reinforcement given the same rate of responding, is comparable to the situation shown in Figure 5.1 at point X. The marginal reinforcement rate under the VI schedule (the slope of the bowed curve at this point) is approximately zero, whereas that of the VR schedule is a positive constant. The situation is thus completely analogous to an income-compensated wage decrease: Compare Figure 5.1 with Figure 4.2 or 4.3. The difference is that the compensated wage change lines in

Figures 4.2 and 4.3 employ discrete changes in the slope of the budget line (the marginal reinforcement rate), in contrast to the VI schedule in Figure 5.1 which involves a continuous change in the slope of what is, in effect, a compensated wage-change line. As with the income-compensated wage decreases reported in Sections 4.1c and 4.4a, the labor-supply model predicts substitution of income for leisure (in this case, very small reductions in income since the VI schedule is practically flat in the neighborhood of X). The net result is a choice point such as Y under the VI schedule as the animal moves to a higher indifference curve (I_2 versus I_1).[5]

To explain the observed response rate differential between VI and VR schedules, matching proponents have argued that it takes longer to produce a VI than a VR response, even to the point of arguing that it takes twice as long to produce a VI response (for arguments to this effect, see Prelec, 1982). That is, the value of the variable k varies systematically between VI and VR schedules, because it takes up to twice as long to respond on VI as it does on VR schedules. Note, however, that their argument is circular and offers no explanation as to *why* it should take so much longer to respond on the VI schedule, other than the fact that responding occurs at a lower rate.

5.2c Concurrent VI–VR schedules

In a concurrent VI–VR schedule, a pigeon has a choice of responding on either a VI or a VR schedule. Responding on the VR schedule produces a joint output: payoffs from the VR schedule, as well as reward setups from the VI schedule (which can only be collected by switching to the VI schedule). The VI schedule is independent; time spent on it only affects payoffs from that schedule. These contingencies are generally established as follows: The VR schedule advances only when the animal is responding on it. The VI schedule, however, advances whether the animal is responding on the VR or the VI schedule. If the VI interval lapses while the subject is responding on the VR schedule, the reward is held until the animal returns to the VI schedule and makes the response required to collect it. In addition, the VI timer stops between the time reinforcement is set up and collected, so the animal must switch to keep the rewards coming from the VI schedule. And a fixed cost is imposed in terms of a changeover delay (COD) so that both schedules are inoperative for a period of time, when the animal switches between them.

With perfect information regarding the availability of reinforcement on the VI schedule and no fixed costs for switching between schedules, the most efficient strategy, in a world where food is valuable and responding is costly, is to respond exclusively on the VR component until a reward is set up on the VI component, switch to the VI component, collect the reward, and return to the VR component. The introduction of uncertainty and the fixed cost of switching between schedules makes the situation substantially more complicated.

The concurrent VI–VR experiment (Herrnstein and Heyman, 1979) has been cited as an important means of discriminating between maximizing and matching accounts of behavior. The characteristic outcomes of this experiment are that (a) local response rates on the VR alternative are approximately twice that of the VI schedule, (b) there is a time bias in favor of the VI schedule that reduces the maximum possible rate of food intake by approximately 30%, and (c) unbiased response matching (equation (3.11) with h and $y \approx 1.0$ provides a reasonably good fit to the data). Herrnstein and Heyman (1979, p. 209) concluded that the results are "incompatible with maximization of total [food] reinforcement, given observed local rates of responding and rates of alternation between schedules" and, instead, are in favor of matching-based explanations.[6]

Prelec (1982) expanded Herrnstein and Heyman's argument, noting that if the time cost of responding is a simple proportional function of the level of responding (as in equation (4.3)), and subjects are indifferent between responding on the VI or VR components, then efficiency dictates that the marginal reinforcement rate (MRR) for responding be the same on the VI and VR components. In fact, however, the MRR realized on the VI component is well below the MRR on the VR component in Herrnstein and Heyman's experiment. From this, Prelec argues that the subjects could have increased their rate of food intake without increasing their work, by reallocating responses from the VI to the VR component.

In analyzing behavior under concurrent VI–VR schedules, two issues are of particular interest. First, why, given the observed response rates on the two schedules, does the animal fail to maximize total food intake? Second, why do we observe different MRR's for the two schedules, and do these reflect serious efficiency losses and loss of value to subjects?

The higher response rate on VR compared with VI schedules suggests that important income-leisure trade-offs are occurring that help explain why animals fail to maximize total food intake. Figure 5.2 illustrates this point. The functional relationship between time spent on the VI schedule (T_i) and income under a concurrent VI–VR schedule is shown by the humpback curve, with maximum earnings at point M*. Increases in time spent on the VI schedule beyond the maximum earnings point will *reduce* the overall rate of food intake but *increase* the amount of leisure time (since response rates are lower on the VI than on the VR schedule). If we postulate standard, negatively sloped indifference curves between income and leisure, such as I_1 and I_2 in Figure 5.2, equilibrium *must* lie to the *right* of the maximum earnings point, M*. In other words, maximizing utility where *both* income and leisure are arguments of the utility function *must* produce an equilibrium to the right of the point of maximum food intake under concurrent VI–VR procedures. Furthermore, simulations based on a CES utility function with parameter estimates obtained from the income-compensated wage change studies reported in Chapter 4 show that

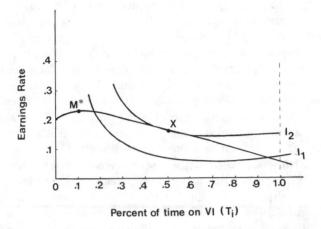

Figure 5.2 Feedback function for concurrent VI–VR schedule and hypothetical indifference curves (I_1, I_2) for income and leisure. Leisure (not working) increases as time spent on the interval schedule (T_1) increases since responding is twice as high on the ratio schedule. Point of maximum food intake is M*, whereas the equilibrium choice point X, *must* lie to the right of this if there are labor–leisure trade-offs. From Green, Kagel, and Battalio (1982).

it is plausible for a utility maximizer to willingly reduce income by 30% (or more) from the maximum attainable, given the response rate differentials between the two schedules (Green, Kagel, and Battalio, 1982).

This explanation leaves open the question of why we observe a lower MRR on the VI than on the VR schedule. In computing MRR's on the VI and VR schedules, matching proponents take no account of the fixed cost of switching between schedules (the COD). The fixed cost acts as a barrier to equating MRR's; that is, once the animal has switched to the VI schedule, an efficient decision maker must weigh the marginal return for an additional peck on the VI schedule against the marginal return from pecking on the VR schedule *and* the COD cost of switching. Further, once we abandon the assumption of constant response costs, as the matching law must do to explain the differential response rates on VI and VR schedules, there is another way to explain any observed MRR differentials. Suppose we argue that the cost of pecking varies with the pecking rate so that it is more costly (it involves more effort or disutility) to respond at a faster rate. Then it is no longer relevant to compare MRR's across VI and VR schedules strictly in terms of their productive consequences, as the (dis)utility of responding is different between the two schedules.

The advantage of an experimental analysis of behavior is that the opportunity is always available to test between competing models, providing the experimenter is clever enough to devise a technique for distinguishing between them. Concurrent VI–VR schedules have attracted a great deal of such attention. We briefly review several of these studies.

Green, Rachlin, and Hanson (1983) devised an experiment aimed at eliminating the income–leisure differences between the VI and VR schedules while still maintaining the basic contingencies of the procedure. To do this, they conducted an experiment with two VR schedules: Pecks on one schedule – which we refer to as the "VI" schedule – counted toward satisfying the work requirements of that schedule alone. Pecks on the other schedule – which we refer to as the VR schedule – counted toward satisfying the VR requirement on that schedule, as well as the work requirements of the "VI" schedule. Thus, the between-schedule contingencies are the same as in the standard conc VI–VR procedure, but if two VR schedules are used, the local rate of responding (hence, income-leisure trade-offs) are similar. Further, Green et al. (1983) eliminated the COD cost of switching between the two schedules.

The premise that income–leisure trade-offs and switching costs affected Herrnstein and Heyman's results, leads to the weak prediction under Green et al.'s procedure that there will be a bias in favor of the VR schedule. This was, in fact, the case, since all but one observation (out of a total of 32) deviated from the predictions of unbiased matching in favor of the VR schedule. For example, with equal rates of reinforcement from the two schedules, the pigeons pecked 2.7 times more on the VR schedule, although with equal average rates of reinforcement Herrnstein and Heyman's pigeons pecked at the same rate on both the VR and VI keys.

The strong prediction for Green et al's procedures is that their pigeons would show no systematic deviations from the maximum rate of food intake. This was not the case, however. Rather, the response allocations fell squarely between the predictions of matching and maximizing. Figure 5.3 shows the actual results for individual subjects (crosses) along with computer-simulated curves for matching and maximizing.[7]

Consider the VR-15, "VI"-30 condition. The experimental contingencies imply that, on average, every 30 responses on the VR schedule result in two reinforcements from that schedule as well as one payoff from the "VI"-30 schedule, provided an additional response was made on the "VI" schedule once reinforcement was set up. Unbiased matching dictates that the animal will spread its responses equally across the two response keys, since each response on the VR key counts toward fulfilling its response requirement as well as half the response requirement on the "VI" key. In other words, the pigeons will not perceive, or not respond to, the interdependencies between the two schedules, presumably because they are only biologically equipped to follow the simple strategy of equating average reinforcement rates, rather than the more complicated maximization strategy (see Herrnstein and Prelec, 1991; Herrnstein and

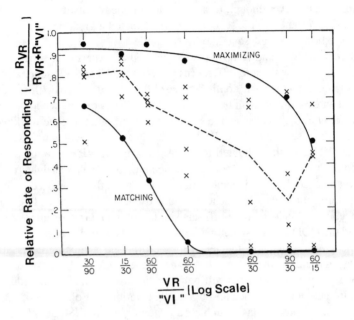

Figure 5.3 Relative rate of responding resulting in maximizing or matching as a function of the relative rate of reinforcement (ratio of VR to "VI" response requirements). The solid points are from the simulation. The crosses are relative rates of response of actual individual pigeons. The dashed line is the median of the individual subjects. From Green, Rachlin, and Hanson (1983).

Vaughan, 1980; Vaughan and Herrnstein, 1987).[8] In the pure maximization model, on the other hand, the subject must completely integrate the interdependencies between schedules and thereby allocate close to 90% of its responses to the VR schedule. As Figure 5.3 shows, the actual data fall somewhere in between.

Shurtleff and Silberberg (1990) have taken a different approach to the question of maximizing versus matching on conc VI–VR schedules. To determine the effect, if any, of income maximization on behavior, they conducted conc VI–VR experiments in a closed economy (so that all food was earned from within the experimental session) and with time-constrained sessions of varying length. This contrasts with Herrnstein and Heyman's procedures, which dealt with an open economy in which sessions terminated after a fixed number of payoffs had been earned, so that the animals' choices had no effect on their income or body weight. Further, to control for income–leisure trade-offs, Shurtleff and Silberberg employed two VI schedules while preserving the schedule interdependencies underlying the conc VI–VR procedure (that is, time on one of the VI schedules counted toward completion of the requirements of both

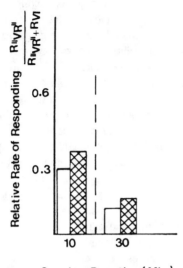

Figure 5.4 Mean relative rate of responding on "VR" schedule in concurrent VI–VR procedure as session duration (10 min and 30 min) varies in a closed economy. First and second determinations for each condition are represented by open and crossed hatched bars, respectively. From Shurtleff and Silberberg (1990).

schedules; time on the other schedule counted toward completion of only that schedule's requirements). They found that with reduced income (shorter session), choice of the "VR" schedule (the joint output schedule) was greater than under longer sessions when income was greater (see Figure 5.4). The suggestion is that when sessions are reduced, income-earning considerations become more prominent, in relation to whatever other forces are at work in this complicated environment, and the result is greater choice on the "VR"-like schedule. Shurtleff and Silberberg (1990, p. 283) conclude that "although the operation of an income-maximizing process is apparent in the results of this study, it offers an incomplete account of choice on concurrent VR–VI schedules because the inverse relation between income level and VR preference was typically too small to maximize income or defend body weight completely. Hence, some other processes must also contribute to the determination of choice on this procedure."

Silberberg, Thomas, and Berendzen (1991) studied human choice on conc VI–VR schedules. To keep procedures as similar as possible to the pigeon experiments, they used as reinforcers the brief delivery of heat to cold subjects (volunteers were paid a fixed fee to participate, and a physician was in attendance throughout the experiment). Further, as with pigeons, instructions were kept to a minimum so that the schedule contingencies had to be learned strictly by experiencing them. Silberberg et al. compared maximizing against matching ordinally: if maximizing is present, the relative rate of VR responding and VR time allocation should *exceed* the relative frequency of VR reinforcement. In terms of relative response rates, only 3 of 11 choice conditions were consistent with matching, whereas all the others deviated in the direction of maximizing the reinforcement rate. Moreover, a control condition showed that it was only when subjects did *not* respond at a substantially higher rate on ratio than on interval schedules (the result obtained when these schedules are studied with pigeons) that matching was satisfied. That is, only when the humans failed to show the absolute VR–VI response rate differences always found in pigeons (which implies that they were out of touch with the schedule contingencies) did they satisfy unbiased matching on the conc VI–VR schedule.

In view of the standoff between matching and maximizing accounts found in these experiments, it would be interesting to investigate whether enhanced information regarding the interdependencies between schedules would improve subjects' efficiency in allocating responses. The role of information and information-processing capacities has received only limited attention in the debates over matching and maximizing (Silberberg and Ziriax, 1985). Nevertheless, it is increasingly clear that significant deviations from optimal performance reported in psychology experiments occur in situations where the relationship between actions and payoffs is ambiguous or obscure (Staddon and Reid, 1987), as tends to be the case under conc VI–VR schedules. We return to conc VI–VR schedules in Section 7.5, where we review an experiment by Silberberg, Warren-Boulton, and Asano (1988) that accounts for the effects of time discounting and uncertainty on behavior under this procedure.

5.2d Progressive ratio schedules

Progressive ratio schedules can be used to determine if animals maximize average or total rate of reinforcement. Consider the following experimental procedure. An animal has two response mechanisms available. One is programmed according to a standard fixed-ratio (FR) schedule: following every X number of responses, a payoff is delivered. The other mechanism is programmed according to a progressive ratio schedule (PR): starting from some initial fixed-ratio value (say, FR 10), completion of each ratio requirement increases the response requirement for the next payoff by some fixed amount, say 20 responses. Thus, under the PR schedule, there is a sequence of fixed ratio requirements; in this example, FR 10, FR 30, FR 50, FR 70, FR 90. . . . Now, the really interesting part of this procedure is when a reset condition is employed. Under the reset condition, once the animal starts on the PR schedule, it can reset the PR to the starting value of the sequence (e.g., FR 10) *anytime* it switches and completes the response requirement on the stationary FR schedule.[9]

Under these procedures, matching and maximizing yield widely different predictions. Consider the case where the stationary FR requirement is 120 and the PR uses increments of 20 starting from an FR 10. An animal that obeys the matching law, which requires equating the average rate of reinforcement between the two schedules, must continue on the PR schedule for 12 reinforcements (up to the FR 230 requirement; this totals 1,400 responses for 12 payoffs, thus equaling the FR 120 schedule) before switching to the stationary FR 120. An animal that satisfies melioration theory does not have to be quite so pathological. According to melioration theory, it is the local rate of reinforcement that guides behavior, so in each case the animal compares alternatives ignoring the reset condition – FR 10 versus FR 120, FR 30 versus FR 120, FR 50 versus FR 120, and so on – and chooses the alternative with the higher rate of return. Under this rule, the animal switches from the PR to the FR schedule when the marginal work requirements are equal (120:120). A maximizer, on the other hand, switches well before the PR 120 – after PR 50 in this example.

Several experiments have been conducted along these lines using different species. In all of these experiments the animal learns the contingencies through experience and exploration, so that the contingencies are maintained for an extended period of time until some sort of stable response pattern is observed. Although there are differences across species in terms of the exact degree of conformity to maximizing outcomes, in all cases the animal switches in advance of, or at, the equality point, and long before the point predicted by matching. Figure 5.5 shows results for juvenile rhesus monkeys under this procedure. They are almost perfect maximizers (Hineline and Sodetz, 1987). Pigeons, on the other hand, tend to switch later than they should if they are to minimize response requirements (Wanchisen, Tatham, and Hineline, 1988). Experiments with human subjects fall somewhere between these two extremes (Wanchisen, Tatham, and Hineline, 1992). As we show in Chapter 7, switching that occurs later than maximization theory would predict with pigeons is due in part to the pigeons' heavy discounting of future as compared with immediate rewards. In the experiment with humans, procedures could have been a bit tighter since, as the authors point out, total earnings were determined by both the rapidity of responding and the point within the PR sequence at which the subject switched. Thus, by responding more rapidly, but a little less efficiently, one could, and sometimes did, produce higher total earnings.

5.3 Bliss points versus minimum needs

Under the assumption of a constant time cost per response, the generalized minimum-distance (MD) and the generalized minimum-needs (MN) models yield labor-supply functions of the form

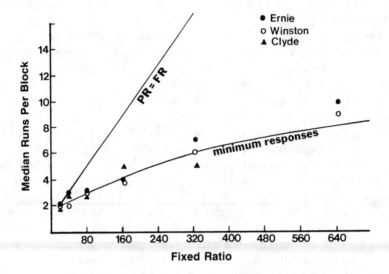

Figure 5.5 Data for three monkeys on concurrent PR-FR procedure with re-set. A "block" is a sequence of choices of the PR terminated by selection of the FR. "Runs per block" is the number of ratio completions (both PR and FR) in a block. The upper, straight line shows block lengths that would result if the monkeys switched to the FR only when the PR = FR. The lower solid line shows the optimal choices, that is, the runs per block that minimize the number of responses per payoff at each size of the FR. From Hineline and Sodetz (1987).

$$x_h = \frac{p_m(\gamma_m - F)}{\mu} + \frac{\beta_m p_m^{1-\sigma}}{\mu \sum_k \beta_k p_k^{1-\sigma}} \left[T + p_m F - \sum_k \gamma_k p_k \right], \ k = l, m \quad (5.5)$$

where x_h is the number of responses; T is total session time; μ is response time; p_m and p_l are the time cost of obtaining, respectively, income and leisure; γ_m, γ_l represent the respective set points of the models; and F is the level of un-earned income.[10] As in the commodity-choice case, what differentiates the two models is the contrasting parameter restrictions (recall Table 3.1), which yield contrasting predictions regarding the substitutability of income for leisure as income varies (recall Figure 3.3 and its discussion): In the MN model, as the worker becomes wealthier, income and leisure become more substitutable; expansion paths fan up and out from the MN point. In the MD model, however, expansion paths fan down and out from the bliss point so that income and leisure become less substitutable as workers become wealthier.

Table 5.1. *Parameter estimates of best-fitting model*

Subject	σ	γ_m	γ_l	β_m	R^2	N
47	0.979	−22.3	1,575.8	0.531	.783	28
	(.201)	(13.0)	(176.6)	(0.127)		
48	0.427	−136.2	1,117.1	0.422	.788	25
	(.557)	(305.3)	(1,071.7)	(0.284)		
49	0.852	−16.5	−1,342.2	0.137	.823	24
	(.101)	(8.0)	(1,255.8)	(0.049)		
50	0.685	−43.0	1,699.8	0.662	.786	31
	(.127)	(25.0)	(73.9)	(0.068)		
All subjects	0.652	−58.8	1,496.2	0.515	.434	108
together[a]	(.173)	(35.1)	(171.7)	(0.102)		

Note: $\beta_l = 1 - \beta_m$; R^2 = square of multiple correlation coefficient; and N = number of observations. Standard errors of estimates in parentheses.
[a]Likelihood ratio test statistic for pooling observations across subjects is $X^2 = 77.5$ with 12 degrees of freedom. This leads to rejection of the null hypothesis at better than the .001 level.
Source: Battalio, Dwyer, and Kagel (1987).

5.3a Some initial test results

Tests of the two models were conducted using pigeon workers in an open economy, and varying wage rates by changing the number of responses required per unit of reinforcement. The expansion paths were explored by delivering different amounts of unearned income. Table 5.1 shows the unrestricted estimates of equation (5.5) for the four pigeons studied. Estimates are reported for each pigeon separately and with the data pooled. The point estimates once again satisfy the parameter restrictions of the MN model.[11] In particular, the point estimates for σ are all positive as the MN model predicts, whereas σ must be negative to satisfy the MD formulation.

The constant terms associated with minimum-income requirements (γ_m) are negative in all cases.[12] As noted previously (Section 3.3), we interpret negative γs in the MN model to mean that subjects could get along without any of the items in question. Under an open economy this is indeed the case since subjects are maintained at 80% of free-feeding body weight throughout the experiment. This effectively eliminates any minimum-income requirements.

To determine whether members of the class of MD models could organize the data, we varied σ in equation (5.5) from -1.3 to 1.3 by increments of .1 and obtained the best-fitting model by the method of least squares. We define acceptable σ values in equation (5.5) as those for which, using a likelihood ratio test statistic and a 5% significance level, we cannot reject the null hypothesis that the estimated model fits the data as well as the best-fitting model reported in Table 5.1. Under this criterion, acceptable values of σ are all positive, with the exception of that for bird 48. Thus, for at least 3 of the 4 birds, the MD model does not provide a general characterization of labor-supply behavior, no matter what the metric involved in minimizing the distance to the bliss point (and in no case does it provide the best fit to the data).

5.3b Evidence for the possibility that both hypotheses work well

Detailed examination of the pigeons' expansion paths from this experiment does, however, suggest some basis for a reconciliation of the two models. Figure 5.6 shows the expansion paths for pigeons 48 and 50 under each of two wage rates (VR 25 and 100); the vertical axis represents total income (number of earned plus free food reinforcers), and the horizontal axis represents the number of responses as the amount of unearned income varies. The solid lines represent free-hand connection, and extrapolation, of the data points. Note that in both cases the expansion paths under the lower real wage rate condition (VR 100) have a pronounced nonlinear twist at higher levels of unearned income (when unearned income was between 130 and 260% of baseline earnings for bird 48 and between 230 and 300% of baseline earnings for bird 50). If these trends were to continue, the expansion paths would converge at a point in the upper right-hand corner of the choice space, involving modest levels of labor supply and substantial amounts of income. This is in fact what the MD model predicts. However, the MD model fails to do better on the statistical tests reported because most of the data were generated under lower levels of unearned income, where the MN model performs best.

It is, of course, perfectly possible, and intuitively quite plausible, that the MN model describes behavior well over a relatively wide range of the choice space, but breaks down once the constraint moves far enough away from the minimum-needs point, while the MD model holds in the relatively smaller neighborhood of the bliss point. The latter would be in accord with the intuitive notion that with a fixed set of consumption and leisure activities there must be a bliss point in the choice space representing satiation levels for these activities. However, the results reported in Figure 5.6 were far from universally observed under open-economy conditions (in these other cases, expansion paths were linear throughout and fan out from the origin, as the MN model predicts). Further, we have done virtually no exploration of expansion paths for labor supply under closed-economy conditions. Nevertheless, the data are suggestive and call for further exploration of expansion paths over extremely high levels of unearned income.

5.3c Further observations on the MN hypothesis

Within the context of the constant-elasticity-of-substitution functional form, the shape of the labor-supply function depends on the sign of γ_m and the

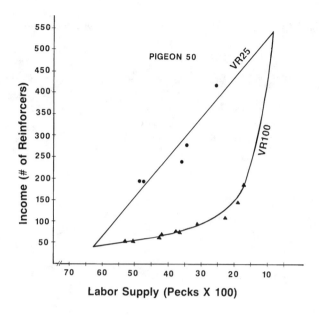

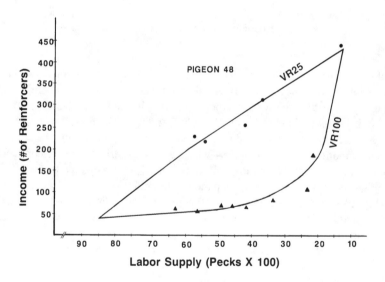

Figure 5.6 Income–leisure choices as free income varies for pigeons 48 and 50 under different wage-rate conditions (VR 25 and 100). Solid lines were fit by freehand to the data, converging at set points near the origin and near a "bliss point." Circles represent results under the VR 25 condition; triangles represent results under the VR 100 condition.

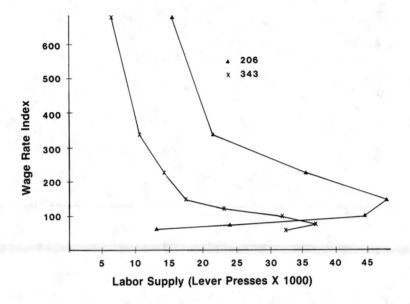

Figure 5.7 Labor-supply curves (number of lever presses) for two rats working in a closed economy. Wage-rate index is normalized to 100 for VR 135. The lower the VR requirement, the higher the wage index.

value of σ (within the MN model, σ is the elasticity of substitution between income and leisure for income above minimum needs).[13] In cases where $\gamma_m < 0$ and $\sigma < 1$, as they are for all subjects reported in Table 5.2, the labor-supply curve is positively sloped over low wages, bending back on itself beyond some wage rate. This is indeed the characteristic pattern of labor-supply behavior in open economies (recall Figure 4.4 where all the experiments were conducted under open economy conditions). If, however, $\gamma_m > 0$, as would be the case in a closed-economy experiment, and there is no source of nonwage income, then as long as maximum earnings are sufficient to cover minimum consumption requirements, the labor-supply curve is monotonic throughout, with the slope depending on the value of σ.

Figure 5.7 reports labor-supply data (number of lever presses as the wage rate varied) for two rats in a closed economy. Labor supply for one of the rats (rat 206) provides dramatic evidence for the existence of a bitonic labor-supply curve. Within the context of the MN model, this bitonicity could only be explained by the fact that, although this rat had no experimenter-supplied source of unearned income, rats in general have stored energy resources in the form of excess body weight. This provides an endogenous source of nonwage income (assets under the belt rather than in the bank, so to speak). Under this interpretation, the greater resistance of rat 343 to reducing its labor supply in the presence of falling wages is directly attributable to its lower body weight; rat 343 weighed only about 240 grams at its maximum response point, in comparison with rat 206, which weighed over 500 grams at its maximum response point.[14]

The impact of body weight on labor supply is further revealed in data provided by Timberlake and Peden (1987). They studied the labor-supply behavior of pigeons under a closed economy over a wide range of real wage rates. In their experiment, the pigeons were returned to their baseline body weights between each wage rate condition so that labor-supply behavior would not interact with cumulative body weight changes. Their data, generated under FR schedules, show a small positively sloped portion to the labor-supply curve under the lowest real wage rate condition (see especially experiment 2, pigeon 474), with a negatively sloped labor-supply curve prevailing over higher wage rates.[15]

This bitonic labor-supply curve contradicts the MN hypothesis unless (a) the pigeons had sufficient assets under the belt to cover their minimum needs, or (b) real wages were sufficiently low that minimum income requirements could not be met at maximal response levels, in which case the theory is silent regarding behavior. Since it is clear that Timberlake and Peden's pigeons were not terribly fat under baseline body weights (so that assets under the belt were minimal), we calculated maximum attainable consumption levels at these low real wage rates, assuming that the pigeons pecked continuously throughout the session, to determine whether consumption levels were sufficient for long-run survival.[16] The data suggest that they were not, since at best the pigeons could have achieved 20 to 50% of baseline earnings and, accordingly, their weights would decrease substantially. In other words, in this case the budget constraint appears to lie below the minimum-needs point, so that the MN hypothesis does not specify the shape of the indifference curves or the pattern of labor supply (recall the discussion in Section 3.3b).[17]

5.3d Postscript on the representative consumer hypothesis

For the pigeon data reported in Table 5.1, the weak form of the representative consumer hypothesis is satisfied, since the generalized MN hypothesis best fits each subject's data, as well as the pooled data. However, the strong form of the representative consumer hypothesis is rejected at the 1% significance level, since individual subjects' expansion paths fail to have the same slope. Further, the labor-supply responses to income-compensated wage changes differ by a factor of more than two to one across individuals (Battalio et al., 1981, pp. 627–8). The economic implications of rejecting the strong form of the representative consumer hypothesis were discussed in Section 3.4.

5.4 **Earnings distributions for animal workers**

A topic of continuing professional and nonprofessional interest concerns the distribution of earnings and inequality of incomes among individuals in an economy. A key question continues to be: What is the basis for these observed differences in earnings? Economists have not had to look far to find a host of factors that might be responsible for differences in income among individuals within national economic systems, although they have had great difficulty testing any hypotheses to this effect, given the available data.

Stigler (1987) provides a comprehensive discussion of the factors that may generate differences in earned incomes within national economic systems. There are fourteen such factors: (1) luck (which has to do with personal factors such as health and accidents; employer factors such as weather, fire, flood, and bankruptcy; and market factors such as general business conditions and finding the best job and best pay within a job); (2) direct occupation expenses (those occupations with higher expenses must offer higher wages to compensate for the increased expenses); (3) costs of occupational training and education (since occupational training and education are capital investments, more education and training should result in higher incomes as the higher earnings represent returns on capital investment); (4) lifetime concavity of earnings with respect to experience (earnings vary across generations, and those in their middle years tend to be at the peak of their lifetime earnings; those in their younger years and those nearing retirement tend to be at the low points of their lifetime-earnings profile); (5) variability or instability of earnings (those with more highly variable earnings should receive higher average earnings to compensate for the risk involved); (6) differences in cost of living; (7) occupational prestige and social esteem; (8) fringe benefits, life insurance, and the like; (9) monopoly power and restrictions; (10) inability to borrow investment funds for training; (11) imperfect foresight; (12) discrimination and nepotism; (13) relative desire for market income versus leisure; and (14) ability or productive capacity.

The first factor (luck) is stochastic in that it provides irreducible sources of variation in earnings; factors 2–8 are the compensatory or equalizing principles of Adam Smith that would exist in full competitive markets and cause wage incomes to differ even among workers of similar ability and taste for income. Factors 9–12 describe deviations from a perfectly competitive economy that can create additional income differences. Because of the very nature of our animal labor-supply experiments, factors 1–12 and 14 play a negligible role in accounting for observed inequality of earnings among individuals. Further, within a given strain of rats or pigeons, any genetic sources of earnings differences among individuals are limited as well, whereas cultural or socialization differences clearly have no role to play, as they would within national economies. With the data on animal labor supply we can investigate whether persistent and reliable differences exist in earnings among individuals in an economy in which the relative desire for income versus leisure is the primary force at work. If there are differences, how do these differences in earnings distributions compare with those reported from national economic systems? What, if any, economic conditions reliably result in wider or narrower earnings distributions?

The data in Table 5.2 provide descriptive measures of the distribution of earnings under different wage-rate conditions. In cases where we replicated the same experimental conditions, we averaged the earnings from those replications. Finally, in all cases, subjects worked in similar, and in some cases the same, experimental chambers.

Two measures of the distribution of earnings are reported in Table 5.2. The Gini coefficient is a traditional measure of earnings inequality. It ranges from 0, when all incomes are equal, to 1, when the highest income earner has all the income (for calculation details, see Kendall and Stuart, 1969, pp. 46–51). The lower the value of the coefficient, the less the disparity in incomes among individuals. Atkinson (1975, p. 45) offers the following characterization of the Gini coefficient: Suppose we choose two people at random from the income distribution and express the difference between their incomes as a proportion of the average income. Then this value turns out to be, on average, twice the Gini coefficient. For example, a coefficient of 0.4 means that the expected difference in incomes between two people chosen at random is 80 percent of the average income.

The coefficient of variation of earnings (C.V.) provides a second measure of the dispersion of earnings. It is the standard error of the variation in earnings divided by mean earnings. The coefficient of variation is 0 if earnings are the same for individuals and increases monotonically as the variance in earnings increases. For both the Gini coefficient and the coefficient of variation, the greater their value, the more disparity in the distribution of earnings among individuals. Also reported in Table 5.2 is the wage-rate index (and the ratio schedule) under which the earnings distribution was computed, along with mean labor supply (mean number of responses at each wage level).

The earnings distributions over most of the wage rates reported are quite compact, as the Gini coefficient rarely goes above .20 and commonly has values in the range of .05 –.15. In contrast, the Gini coefficient for the United States and other national economies often exceeds .40 when distributions include all sources of money income (before personal taxes) for all types of households. However, the general tendency within market data is for earnings to be more evenly distributed the more homogeneous the sample and the narrower the occupational classifications for which a coefficient is calculated. For example, Henle (1972) reports Gini coefficients of .28 and .26 for pretax wages and salaries of U.S. full-time male workers in all industry and manufacturing, respectively, and Hill (1959) reports a Gini coefficient of .21 for pretax wages

Table 5.2. *Distribution of earnings under varying wage rates*

Wage rate index[a]	Gini coefficient	Coefficient of variation	Mean labor supply (no. responses)	Number of subjects	Experimental conditions
25 (200)	.19	.37	4,170	4	Pigeons, open
50 (100)	.06	.10	5,240	4	economy conditions
100 (50)	.11	.18	5,470	4	Series I procedures
200 (25)	.14	.23	4,883	6	
400 (12.5)	.15	.26	3,608	6	
20 (400)	.46	.73	2,720	4	Pigeons, open
40 (200)	.25	.40	4,260	4	economy conditions
80 (100)	.14	.23	5,365	4	Series II procedures
60 (50)	.21	.33	5,153	4	
66.7 (90)	.22	.39	30.672	4	Rats, closed
100 (60)	.10	.18	20,693	4	economy conditions
150 (40)	.11	.18	16,133	4	

[a]Increases in the ratio requirement reduce the wage rate index. Ratio requirement in parentheses.

and salaries of full-time male employees in the United Kingdom. Given that our labor-supply experiments involve a considerably more homogeneous group of individuals and substantially narrower "occupational classifications" than these other data, the narrower distribution of earnings found here is not surprising. Indeed, depending upon one's beliefs concerning Stigler's (1987) contributory factors, one might even be surprised that our animal workers' earnings are not more similar.

In light of the compact earnings distributions reported in Table 5.2, the question arises whether the variation in earnings represents simply random variability unrelated to individuals, or differences in earnings that are reliably associated with certain individuals, in which case we would attribute them to differences in "taste" for income versus leisure. To determine this, we first looked at repeat measures of labor supply that we happened to have for wage rate indices 400 and 160 under series I and II procedures, respectively. In both cases, we compared individuals' ranks in the earnings distribution under the initial measure of labor supply with their ranks under the repeat measure. The rank-order distribution of individual subjects remained the same in each condition, so that at both wage rates we can reject the hypothesis (at the 5% significance level) that the rank-order distribution of individuals is random across repeated applications of the same experimental condition.[18] In addition, we compared the rank-order distribution of individuals under all the different wage-rate conditions for agreement in their rankings in the earnings distribution.[19] Under all three sets of experimental conditions, we reject the null hypothesis (at the 10% significance level or better) of random rankings of individual earnings across the different wage rates. Both tests, therefore, suggest that the variation in earnings among individuals results from inherent differences in their "desire" for consumption versus leisure.

The data in Table 5.2 also suggest that the dispersion of earnings in an economic system will vary systematically with certain institutional characteristics of the system. All three sets of data show a tendency for the distribution of earnings to become more uneven (higher Gini coefficients and larger coefficients of variation) as real wage rates decrease. These lower wage rates were in all cases linked to lower income levels. On the basis of his analysis of economic growth, Simon Kuznets (1955) hypothesized that a society's distribution of earnings would become more even in the course of its economic development. Kuznets and others working on this question have suggested that the gradual elimination of the "dual economy" (a modern industrialized sector versus a rural agrarian sector) may be the primary force behind a more even distribution of earnings in the course of economic development. But to the extent that economic development involves higher mean earnings for the population as a whole and a lower effort price for consumption, our data suggest that this outcome is promoted by additional forces as well.

Note, however, that the more even earnings distributions found in our results at higher wage rates occur within the context of a constant set of consumption goods and leisure time activities. A developing economy, on the other hand, has an expanding set of consumption goods and leisure time activities. Work by Motheral (1982, experiment 3) demonstrates that variation in earnings depends on the goods in the choice set. She found that when a running wheel (a favored leisure-time activity for rats) was introduced into the work chamber under open-economy conditions, the coefficient of variation increased substantially under each of several different wage rates she studied. Such results suggest that the expanding set of consumption goods and leisure activities available in the course of economic development will militate against greater income equality.

Notes

1 This behavior pattern is indistinguishable from subjects having a Cobb–Douglas utility function (recall equation (3.2)) so that this analysis also rules out the simple Cobb–Douglas utility function as an explanation for the observed behavior.

2 James Allison has developed a model with similar implications, but a different process is behind the behavior (Allison, Miller, and Wozny, 1979; Allison, 1981). See also Staddon's (1979b) commentary on Allison's model.

3 For example, in conc VI VI schedules, the absolute rate of responding on one key is given by $P_i = kR_i/(R_j + R_i + R_o)$ so that $P_i/(P_i + P_j) = R_i/(R_i + R_j)$. With constant time costs of responding, the matching relationship extends to time-based measures of labor supply as well.

4 While there is a theoretical basis within labor-supply theory to exclude reinforcement periods from total session time, particularly with short experimental sessions, there is no basis for excluding FR schedules on account of postreinforcement pauses. Until demonstrated otherwise, we assume that these pauses represent the subject's decision to allocate time to leisure, the timing of which is strictly a secondary phenomenon that neither matching nor the static labor-supply formulation addresses.

5 We assume throughout this discussion that the average rate of reinforcement on the ratio schedule is sufficient to maintain responding. That is, total response costs do not exceed total benefits from responding. Prelec (1982, 1983) ignores this point in arguing that behavior under VI in comparison with VR schedules favors a matching-based explanation. The interested reader should consult Prelec for a full elaboration of these arguments, and Kagel, Battalio, and Green (1983) and Rachlin (1983) for rebuttals.

6 Shurtleff and Silberberg (1990) note that matching often occurs over a wide range of choice ratios for the same VI–VR schedule. For example, in the last phase of their first experiment, they find approximate matching for birds 0 and 1, yet their respective response allocations to the VR schedule were 70% and 30%, respectively. That is, under exactly the same treatment condition, approximate matching occurs despite widely different choices between the two schedules. This gives matching extra degrees of freedom for fitting the data compared with the maximizing alternative.

7 Houston and Sumida (1987) offer an alternative solution for optimizing under Green et al.'s procedures. Comparing their Table 2 with Figure 5.3, there are some relatively small differences between predictions under the two specifications.

8 Once the VR response requirement exceeds that of the "VI" schedule, it is no longer technically possible to equate average reinforcement rates across the two schedules. In this case, unbiased matching requires the animal to respond exclusively on the "VI" schedule.

9 Needless to say, identical payoffs are received from both mechanisms.

10 $p_m = (\mu/w)$ and p_l is normalized to 1.0.

11 We need to specify a value for μ, the time to make a response, in order to identify γ_l, the constant associated with leisure. We assume a maximum response rate of 10 pecks per second in the estimates reported. The time value employed has no bearing on the distinction between MN and MD formulations.

12 The negative values for γ_m ensure that the regularity condition $(T - \gamma_l) + p_m(F - \gamma_m) \geq 0$ is satisfied at all points in the choice space. Since $T - \gamma_l$ is nonnegative and F

was restricted to nonnegative values, this regularity condition must be satisfied for $\gamma_m \leq 0$. Further, negative predicted values for amount of labor supplied occur at only two data points, once for subject 47 and once for subject 49, so the demand functions appropriately characterize choices at virtually all points of observed behavior.

13 $\partial x_h / \partial w \gtreqless 0$ as $A(T - \gamma_l)(1 - \sigma)w^\sigma \gtreqless (F - \gamma_m)(B\sigma w^{\sigma-1} + 1)$ where A and B are positive constants. With $(T - \gamma_l) > 0$, $(F - \gamma_m) > 0$ and $\sigma < 1$, the model implies a bitonic response pattern of the sort typically reported.

14 James Allison (1981) has suggested a similar basis for the positively sloped portion of the labor-supply curve commonly found with ratio schedules.

15 Timberlake and Peden (1987) report labor-supply data for VI schedules as well. Our analysis of labor-supply behavior under the minimum-needs hypothesis has not been extended to VI schedules, as we do not feel comfortable in accurately modeling the precise nature of the budget constraint under changing VI parameters (in comparison with knowing what the constraint looks like, *given* observed levels of responding).

16 Timberlake and Peden (1987) estimate that each key peck required 0.5 sec, which implies a maximum pecking rate of 120 pecks per minute, or 21,600 pecks in the three-hour experimental session (this is undoubtedly an overestimate of the upper bound as it ignores any minimal rest requirements). To determine maximum attainable consumption, we divided the maximum possible number of pecks by the ratio requirement in force when labor supply decreased, and multiplied this figure by the payoff value in effect.

17 Bauman (1991) reports reductions in labor supply under the highest FR requirements employed (the lowest wage rates) in a closed economy. However, he maintained wages for only a single day so that it is not clear if responding had stabilized, and it is difficult to determine whether his rats could meet minimum survival requirements.

18 Using Kendall's t statistic (Conover, 1971, pp. 249–53).

19 Using Kendall's coefficient of concordance (Conover, 1971, pp. 270–1).

6

Choices over uncertain outcomes

Chapters 2 through 5 considered animals' choices between certain payoffs, which constitute the framework in which consumer-demand and labor-supply theories were originally developed. In those few cases where the experimental procedures subjected animals to uncertain outcomes – for example, where their labor supply was studied under variable-ratio schedules of reinforcement (Section 4.3a) – we ignored the effects of uncertainty on choice and confined the analysis to the average rate of reinforcement. This chapter explicitly considers the effects of uncertainty on animals' choices.

Choice under uncertainty has been a subject of enduring interest to economists, psychologists, and behavioral biologists. Expected utility theory is common to much of the social sciences and has an extensive and long history of experimental studies in economics and psychology using primarily hypothetical choice protocols with humans. The study of nonhuman animals' choices over uncertain outcomes has a more uneven history. In the 1960s, psychologists focused on the study of alternatives with identical payoffs but with different probabilities of reward – psychologists called these "probability learning experiments." Economists know them as "tests of first-degree stochastic dominance." Section 6.1 develops the concept of first-degree stochastic dominance and reviews these early probability learning experiments, along with the discrete-trial choice procedures that underlie our experimental work.

In the early 1980s, biologists (most notably Caraco, 1981, 1982; Caraco, Martindale, and Whittam, 1980) extended the study of choice under uncertainty beyond questions of first-degree stochastic dominance to test for risk aversion over uncertain food payoffs. In these experiments, animals made choices between a certain food reward and an uncertain one with equal expected value. We review these results in Section 6.2, and also present the results of our own experiments in which we studied risk aversion and transitivity for alternatives with positive payoffs. Section 6.3 examines risk preferences un-

134

der varying levels of resource availability, a question of considerable interest to both economists and biologists. The choices that rats make when average payoffs are insufficient for long-run survival (i.e., deficit-resource conditions) are compared with similar studies using small birds and rodents. Risk preferences where average payoffs exceed survival requirements (i.e., surplus resource conditions) are also investigated, and these results are compared with predictions of the generalized minimum-needs and the generalized minimum-distance hypotheses.

In Section 6.4 we describe the procedures we developed for rats in an effort to mimic conditions that have reliably produced violations of expected utility theory in verbal protocols with humans. Reported violations of expected utility theory with humans have been criticized on the ground that the experiments involved hypothetical or low-stakes outcomes so that the choices lacked "saliency" (Machina, 1983).[1] Our animal experiments yield similar violations and are exempt from this criticism. Having established reliable violations of expected utility theory similar to those found with humans, we then go on to test between competing nonexpected utility models that were designed to explain these violations.

Section 6.5 briefly reviews the extensive psychological literature that demonstrates risk loving for variable delays to reinforcement. As we see it, this literature bears on the issue of risk loving for losses versus risk aversion over gains, a key concept in prospect theory (Kahneman and Tversky, 1979), which stands in marked contrast to the economist's traditional assumption of risk aversion for both gains and losses. We conclude this section with an experiment testing for the generality of risk loving for losses. Section 6.6 deals briefly with questions of search and information acquisition.

6.1 **Decisions under uncertainty: Some basic concepts**

For choices made in situations of uncertainty, the outcome of a decision will depend on events over which the individual has no control. These events are usually referred to as states of nature, or simply states. Obvious examples of states include the weather tomorrow and the result of a random toss of a fair coin. The effective state of nature is unknown at the time decisions are made, although the individual is assumed to have well-formed expectations regarding the distribution of possible states.

In most common applications of choice theory, including the one employed here, the individual chooses between acts that have *unidimensional* outcomes, so that utility is defined in terms of a single commodity and there is a probability function expressing the individual's beliefs as to the possible states of nature. We refer to the alternatives among which the individual chooses as prospects, where for a given prospect $X = [x_1, x_2, \ldots, x_x; \alpha_1, \alpha_2, \ldots, \alpha_s]$, x_i is the outcome in state i, and α_i is the subjective probability of state i. Common applications of the theory in economics deal with choices among final asset positions or income levels. However, the theory can be applied to any unidimensional outcome, such as the number of food pellets or amount of water received as a consequence of lever pressing. The theory also applies to losses, or aversive outcomes, where less is better, such as a higher effort level required per payoff, or numbers of shocks received as a consequence of lever pressing.

6.1a First-degree stochastic dominance

A central concept of consumer-demand theory is that more of a good thing is better then less. In choices between uncertain prospects, this implies that for any two prospects, X and Y, X *stochastically dominates* Y in the *first-degree* if (a) the probabilities of the different states are the same, but some or all of the payoffs in X are more favorable and none is less favorable than in Y, or (b) the payoffs under the different states are the same, but prospect X has higher probabilities associated with favorable states. Part (a) of this definition is a direct application of the notion that more (less) of a good (bad) thing is better, since the probabilities of the different states are identical between the different prospects. Part (b) extends the definition to differences in probabilities and implies, for example, that in choosing between two gambles, both of which pay $10 in the case of winning and nothing in the event of losing, the gamble with the higher probability of winning is preferred. Virtually all theories of choice, whether they involve optimizing behavior or not, predict preference for the dominant alternative, provided the dominance relationship is readily apparent.[2]

6.1b Probability learning experiments: Tests of stochastic dominance

Studies of first-degree stochastic dominance with animals have focused on choices between prospects with different probabilities of reinforcement. Most of the early research on this question employed a discrete-trials choice procedure using a T-maze, where rats ran down a straight alley, at the end of which they could turn left or right, with, for example, the left paying off with probability .75 and the right paying off with probability .25. These procedures typically did not involve any forced-choice trials, but instead employed correction procedures. Under a correction procedure, if the animal's initial choice on a trial is not rewarded, the animal is permitted to spontaneously correct itself, going to the other goal area to obtain the reinforcement. Psychologists refer to studies of this sort as probability learning experiments.

Results from these different procedures may be summarized as follows (Sutherland and Mackintosh, 1971, chap. 11): When trained without correction procedures, rats "maximize." That is, after a period of learning, the length of which varies inversely with the probability differences between prospects (see Section 6.6), the rats select one alternative on approximately 100% of all trials, and virtually all animals choose the alternative with the higher probability of reinforcement. These results are quite similar to those found under concurrent VR–VR procedures (Section 2.5c).

In the presence of correction procedures, however, virtually all studies show subjects failing to achieve exclusive (or nearly exclusive) choice, so that a consistent minority of free choices is allocated to the alternative with the lower probability of reinforcement. Sutherland and Mackintosh (1971) note that the frequency with which the higher probability alternative is chosen usually exceeds the probability of reinforcement on that alternative. Thus, under both procedures there is little evidence of "probability matching" (choice frequencies equaling the probability of reinforcement) (Estes, 1959, 1962; recall Section 3.2b).

6.1c   Tests of stochastic dominance using our discrete-trials choice procedures

We have conducted our own limited investigations of stochastic dominance. The primary goals of these studies were (a) to verify sensitivity to low-probability outcomes, and (b) to provide a benchmark against which to evaluate choices observed under other treatment conditions using our procedures.

Under our procedures rats choose between a single pair of prospects throughout an experimental session. A single press on one of two choice levers delivers the payoffs (food or water in the case of positive outcomes). Each experimental session begins with a fixed number of forced-choice trials, followed by a fixed number of free-choice trials, with trials separated by a constant time interval of 20 sec or more, irrespective of the choice made or the outcome obtained. The forced-choice trials serve to familiarize subjects with the alternatives. On these trials, only one of the choice levers is available. During free-choice trials, subjects could choose which lever to respond on. These trials serve to measure preference. Closed-economy procedures were used throughout so that with food payoffs, for example, all the rat's food would be obtained within the experimental session.

Preference is measured in terms of the relative frequency of choosing one prospect over the other during the free-choice trials. Our subjects' choices were rarely, if ever, exclusively confined to one of the prospects. Therefore, our results are consistent with the majority of data from comparable experiments involving human (Luce and Suppes, 1965) and nonhuman subjects (Caraco et al., 1980; Real, 1981).[3]

Experimental sessions were conducted daily with the same prospects associated with the same levers for a minimum number of days (usually 18) and/or until choices stabilized, based on a visual criterion. To control for lever bias, which can at times be severe in rats, we commonly reverse the payoffs associated with each lever. The choice frequencies we report represent the average

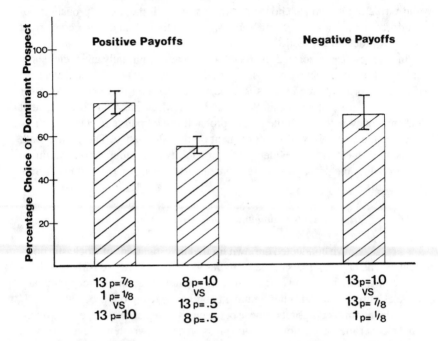

Figure 6.1 Frequency of choosing the dominant alternative. Bars indicate ± 1 standard error of the mean.

data from the last five days on each condition, which were averaged across side switches. By measuring preference in this way, we are assuming that lever bias, to the extent it exists, has an additive effect on choice, so that averaging across side switches effectively cancels out the bias.

Figure 6.1 reports the data from these studies. The first experimental condition involved positive payoffs, namely, different numbers of water-cup deliveries. The rats had a choice between two levers: responses on one of these levers led to a certain 13-cup payoff, while responses on the other lever led to a 13-cup payoff with probability 7/8 or a 1-cup payoff with probability 1/8. All the rats were quite sensitive to the 1/8 probability (1 cup) payoff: the average choice frequency (for four subjects) of the certain payoff was 75% (with a minimum choice frequency of 70%). Similar sensitivity to low-probability outcomes was evident with rats choosing between negative payoffs (i.e., delays to reinforcement). When faced with a certain 13-sec delay to reinforcement for responding on one lever, and a 13-sec delay with probability 7/8 or a 1-sec delay with probability 1/8, for responding on the other lever, subjects chose the dominant alternative (with its 1/8 probability of a 1-sec delay) approximately 70%

of the time (with the lowest choice frequency of any the seven subjects being 59%). The sensitivity to low-probability outcomes in these two cases would appear to be a direct function of the large difference between the worst payoff on the inferior alternative and the best payoff on the dominant alternative. When we compared choices between a 50-50 chance of a 13- or an 8-cup payoff and a certain 8-cup payoff, the dominant alternative was chosen 54% of the time (using the same four subjects as in the first positive payoff test). In this case, no subject's choice of the dominant alternative exceeded 57%, although none was less than 50%.

Unlike the probability learning experiments with T-mazes, our data do not show anything approaching exclusive choice of the dominant alternative. Part of the difference may result from the large number of forced-choice trials we employed at the beginning of each day's session. These forced choice trials likely reinforce sampling of both alternatives. Other factors promoting non-exclusive choice are lever bias, which can be strong in rats, and the fact that in an environment fraught with uncertainty, it is in the animal's long-term interest to sacrifice some immediate returns in favor of continued sampling of both alternatives.

Whatever the basis for less-than-exclusive choice of the dominant alternative, the choice frequencies in Figure 6.1 serve as our sought-after reference point against which to evaluate changes in choice frequencies when there is no dominant alternative. That is, in the context of testing for risk aversion, or for violations of expected utility theory, we would not expect to see differences in choices greater than the maximum reported in Figure 6.1, when differences between alternatives are clear, unambiguous, and are of first-order importance.

6.2 Risk preferences over positive payoffs: Response to reward variability

The expected value of a prospect is defined as

$$E[X] = p_1 x_1 + p_2 x_2 + \ldots + p_s x_s \tag{6.1}$$

where p_i is the (objective) probability of state i. For prospects with equal expected value, the riskier prospect is the one for which the probability of extreme outcomes (both favorable and unfavorable) is greater. For example, consider the following three binary prospects: X offers a certain payoff of 10, Y offers a 50-50 chance of 5 or 15, and Z offers a 50-50 chance of 1 or 19. All have the same expected (average) value, 10. However, in terms of risk, Z is riskier than Y, as it involves more extreme outcomes. Further, both Z and Y are riskier than X, because they both offer more extreme outcomes than X.[4]

We refer to a risk-averse decision maker as one who always prefers the least risky prospect, a risk-neutral decision maker as one who is indifferent between prospects, and a risk-lover as one who always prefers the most risky alternative

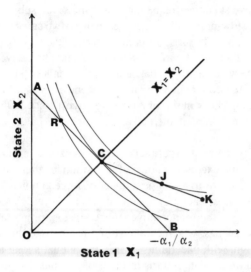

Figure 6.2 Preferences over uncertain outcomes with convex indifference curves, when prospects involve positive payoffs so that more is better. See text.

in choosing between prospects with equal expected value. In this section we show that convex indifference curves imply risk aversion for prospects with positive payoffs. That is, a diminishing marginal rate of substitution between positive payoffs implies risk aversion. However, in the case of prospects with negative, or aversive, payoffs, where less is better, a diminishing marginal rate of substitution implies a preference for the riskier prospect (risk loving) (see Section 6.5).

Figure 6.2 represents binary prospects in a world with two possible states of nature. Certain prospects are represented by points on the 45-degree line; they have the same payoff independent of the state of nature ($x_1 = x_2$). For any certain prospect, C, and any subjective probability distribution, α_1, α_2 (where $\alpha_2 = 1 - \alpha_1$), we define the locus of fair bets as those prospects with expected value equal to the certain prospect, C. The fair bet line passes through C and has a slope equal to the relative probabilities, $-\alpha_1/\alpha_2$ (line AB in Figure 6.2). Any point on AB is considered a fair bet by the decision maker.

The slope of the indifference curve where it crosses the certainty (45-degree) line gives the rate at which the decision maker, starting from a position of certainty, is just willing to trade payoffs in state 1 for those in state 2. If payoffs are assumed to be equally valuable in both states, as much of economic theory assumes, the slope of the indifference curve at point C must just equal the slope of the fair bet line (AB). Consequently, convexity of the indifference curves implies that in choosing between a certain outcome, such as C, and a fair bet, such as R, the highest indifference curve will be tangent to the fair bet line at C. An individual with these preferences is said to be risk averse.

In cases where a risk-averse individual is choosing between a certain alternative and an uncertain prospect with higher expected value, there is nothing inconsistent in choosing the risky prospect some, if not most, of the time. Point K in Figure 6.2 illustrates such a prospect. Line segment CK involves various mixes of the certain prospect with the uncertain one. As illustrated, with convex indifference curves the highest indifference curve would now be obtained by choosing a mix of prospects, point J in Figure 6.2. In the case of a discrete, single-shot choice, where mixing prospects is not permitted, choice would presumably reflect which of the two prospects, C or K, came closest to the most preferred point.

Biologists employ a survival principle to explain risk aversion for prospects offering positive payoffs. The argument goes like this: Animals forage in stochastic environments, environments that are inherently risky. In cases where the average rate of food intake from foraging is sufficient to ensure survival (budget surplus conditions), foragers should be averse to risk since their choice of more variable foraging prospects could unnecessarily jeopardize survival if a string of low-payoff outcomes was realized. Further, risk aversion should extend to a willingness to accept a lower-valued certain alternative in preference to a less certain alternative with a higher expected value. When a series of pairwise comparisons between prospects was studied, the majority of the resulting experimental data confirmed both of these predictions (for reviews of this literature, see Real and Caraco, 1986; and Caraco and Lima, 1987).

In this section, we report experiments of our own with rats that have contributed to this literature. The first series of experiments studies choice among prospects with relatively large variability in payoffs. The second series looks at prospects with smaller variability in payoffs and a skewed distribution of probabilities. In all cases, prospects employed have equal expected value so that risk aversion requires preference for the more certain alternative.

6.2a Large variability payoffs

The top half of Table 6.1 lists the prospects studied, each of which employed 45-mg Noyes food pellets as payoffs. The probability of each outcome (p_i) is shown first, followed by the payoff (x_i) for that outcome (number of food pellets delivered). In all cases, total expected food payoffs were at a level that would maintain the rat's health, but were well below satiation levels (see Section 6.3).[5]

The bottom part of Table 6.1 shows the percentage of free-choice trials allocated to the less risky alternative for the pairwise comparisons investigated.

Table 6.1. *Testing for risk aversion over gains: large variability in payoffs*

I. Prospects studied

	Subjects 210 and 211					Subjects 303 and 323			
Prospect[a]	p_1	x_1	p_2	x_2	Prospect[b]	p_1	x_1	p_2	x_2
A	1.0	10			A'	1.0	8		
B	.5	4	.5	16	B'	.5	4	.5	12
C	.5	1	.5	19	C'	.5	1	.5	15
D	.75	1	.25	37	D'	.75	1	.25	29

II. Percentage of choice of more certain alternative[c]

	210				211		
	B	C	D		B	C	D
A	87.8[d]	—	61.4 (4.14)[e]	A	95.3[d]	—	82.7 (26.6)[e]
B	—	—	77.8 (12.20)[e]	B	—	—	85.9 (11.45)[e]
C	—	—	65.0 (2.63)[f]	C	—	—	45.9 (1.17)

	303				323		
	B'	C'	D'		B'	C'	D'
A'	52.9 (3.55)[e]	—	74.7 (6.64)[e]	A'	77.1 (4.11)[e]	—	86.5 (12.66)[e]
B'	—	52.4 (.48)	78.2 (7.89)[e]	B'	—	64.7 (3.61)[e]	84.2 (7.91)[e]
C'	—	—	53.5 (0.86)	C'	—	—	57.6 (1.46)

Note: p_i = probability of payoff x_i; x_i = number of pellets.
[a]8 forced, 22 free-choice trials; 300 expected food pellets.
[b]8 forced, 17 free-choice trials; 200 expected food pellets.
[c]t-statistics in parentheses.
[d]Partial measure of preferences since prospects were not switched across levers (see Battalio, Kagel, and MacDonald 1985).
[e]Significantly different from 50.0 at the 1% level, two-tailed t-test.
[f]Significantly different from 50.0 at the 5% level, two-tailed t-test.
Source: Battalio, Kagel, MacDonald (1985).

The *t*-statistics are given in parentheses, testing the null hypothesis that mean choice frequencies were .50; that is, testing the null hypothesis of no preference for either prospect.

The data indicate that risk aversion motivated the rats; in all but one case, the average choice of the more certain alternative exceeded 50%, and commonly exceeded 60% of the free-choice trials. The only exception was subject 211, which when faced with a choice between prospects C and D, chose the less risky alternative C less than 50% of the time (and whose *t*-statistic does not allow rejection of the null hypothesis of indifference). Although preference for the less risky prospect was far from exclusive, in general there was a statistically reliable preference for the more certain prospect. Thus, the data largely support the hypothesis of risk aversion. Further, since risk aversion characterizes the data, choices satisfy weak stochastic transitivity over the several triads and the one quadrad we could compare directly; that is, preferences across sets of prospects are transitive when evaluated in terms of the criteria $L > M$ if $F(L, M) > .50$, where $F(L, M)$ is the relative frequency of choosing L over M, and $>$ indicates preference for prospect L over M.[6] This is not to say that if we established prospects explicitly designed to generate intransitivities (see, for example, Tversky, 1969), we might not find them. This is an issue we have yet to pursue.

Thus far, we have dealt with choice frequencies averaged over the session as a whole. We have not bothered to distinguish the time frame for choice, whether it corresponds to a single trial, the session as a whole, or some other portion, because the predictions from expected utility theory hold, irrespective of the time frame. However, as the animal progresses through a session, its deprivation level varies. This raises the obvious question of whether choice frequencies vary systematically over the course of a session. In addition, it is natural to inquire whether there were any systematic tendencies to vary choices on the basis of the outcome resulting from the uncertain alternative. Specifically, did the rats tend to follow a win/stay, lose/shift strategy or a win/shift, lose/stay strategy, in response to their winning or losing on the uncertain alternative? A win/shift, lose/stay strategy corresponds to the concept of "gambler's fallacy" whereby gamblers act as if previous events (winning or losing) are unlikely to repeat themselves (for some evidence that humans behave this way, see Slovic et al., 1977). We were unable to find any systematic tendencies in either of these directions under a variety of treatment conditions (Battalio, Kagel, MacDonald, 1985; Kagel, MacDonald, Battalio, White, and Green, 1986).

6.2b *Low variability in payoffs and skewed distributions*

Prospects A, B, and C in Table 6.2 were designed to test preference for a moderate, controlled amount of uncertainty, as a number of nonexpected utility formulations suggest (Coombs and Huang, 1976; Machina, 1983, 1985),

Table 6.2 *Testing for risk aversion over gains: low variability in payoffs and skewed distribution*

I. Prospects studied				
Prospect	p_1	x_1	p_2	x_2
A[a]	1.0	2.0		
B[a]	.5	3.0	.5	1.0
C[a]	.5	4.0	.5	0.0
D[b]	1.0	6.0		
E[b]	.8	5.0	.2	10.0

II. Percentage choice of more certain alternative[c]					
	303			304	
	B	C	E	B	C	E
A	51.5	73.0	—	A	87.1	87.9	—
	(0.61)	(5.95)[c]			(12.7)[c]	(13.4)[c]	
D	—	—	64.0	D	—	—	64.5
			(3.60)[c]				(2.86)[c]
	323			324	
	B	C	E	B	C	E
A	73.7	70.2	—	A	—	92.2	—
	(12.1)[c]	(9.2)[c]				(20.3)[c]	
D	—	—	51.8	D	—	—	51.3
			(0.78)				(0.43)

Note: p_i = probability of payoff x_i; x_i = number of pellets; t-statistics in parentheses.
[a]32 forced-, 68 free-choice trials; 200 expected food pellets.
[b]10 forced-, 23 free-choice trials; 198 expected food pellets.
[c]Significantly different from 50.0 at the 1% level, two-tailed t-test.

since with small variability in payoffs, and a large number of trials, there is little to lose in exercising such a taste.[7] Prospect E in Table 6.2 provides a skewed distribution of outcomes in relation to D. The skewed distribution offers a relatively small probability of a relatively large payoff, with a higher probability of being minimally worse off than with the certain alternative. Thus, it might also provide a chance of inducing risk loving between prospects with positive payoffs.

The bottom part of Table 6.2 shows the frequency with which the certain alternative was chosen in each pairwise comparison conducted. Once again risk aversion predominates in the data; in all cases, the certain alternative was preferred. Although preference for the certain alternative in the small-stakes outcomes (A, B, C) does not definitively rule out a taste for controlled, moderate amounts of risk, there is no hint of risk loving over these pairs of prospects.[8]

The skewed distribution (prospect E) does, effectively, produce indifference for two rats, 323 and 324, but a moderate degree of risk avoidance in rats 303 and 304. There is no indication of risk loving, or preference for the skewed alternative, in any of the rats. We would conjecture that it would take substantially finer gradations of outcomes, and significantly more skew, to induce in nonhuman animals anything like the gambling humans often indulge in.

The dominant and consistent preference pattern found throughout these studies is risk aversion, with both large and small variability in payoffs, and under a positively skewed distribution of payoffs. Our results are consistent with economic theory and biologists' predictions for positively valued payoffs under surplus resource conditions. In this respect our results largely replicate those of Caraco and other biologists (Caraco and Lima, 1987; Real and Caraco, 1986). Section 6.3a turns to the question of risk aversion with positively valued payoffs under deficit resource conditions, when average payoffs on the certain alternative are *not* sufficient to meet ultimate survival requirements. In Section 6.5 we return to the question of risk loving versus risk aversion, in this case for choices between prospects with negative payoffs, where less is better.

6.3 Risk preferences under varying levels of resource availability

The biologists' argument for risk aversion under surplus resource conditions is that in avoiding variability the forager minimizes the probability of a string of losses, thereby increasing the probability of survival. In contrast, foragers in an area where an overall deficit exists may well prefer a high variance alternative. When resource levels are at the point where the organism can no longer survive on the certain prospect, the chances for survival are actually increased by choosing the risky alternative, since this may produce a run of good luck (Caraco et al., 1980; Pulliam and Millikan, 1982; Stephens, 1981; Stephens and Charnov, 1982). Economists have used this argument to explain why a normally risk-averse individual might suddenly become risk loving when choosing between prospects involving quite large losses (see, for example, Machina, 1982). In effect, downside losses are truncated, since there is a threshold below which death or bankruptcy occurs.

Economists have long been concerned with the effect of wealth (or income) levels on attitudes to risk under surplus resource conditions. According to conventional wisdom, individuals become more tolerant of risk as wealth increases, or at least not less tolerant (nonincreasing absolute risk aversion according to the Arrow–Pratt measure, equation (6.3); Arrow, 1974; Pratt, 1964). Data drawn from market economies show constant or decreasing absolute risk aversion, according to most researchers (for a survey of views on this point, see Machina, 1983). In light of these views, it is interesting to see how nonhuman animals behave in this respect. Moreover, the generalized minimum-needs and generalized minimum-distance models considered in Chapters 3 and 5 yield markedly different predictions regarding changes in risk attitudes as wealth increases under surplus resource conditions. We shall consider these implications as well.

6.3a   Responses to varying resource levels

In all cases, rats chose between a certain, 8-pellet food payoff versus 29 pellets with probability .25 or 1 pellet with probability .75 (an expected payoff of 8 pellets). Resource levels were varied by altering the number of forced-choice trials across treatment conditions while holding the number of free trials fixed. The experimental treatment conditions are shown in Table 6.3 along with total expected food intake in grams.

The bottom part of Table 6.3 shows the relative frequency with which the certain alternative was chosen as total food consumption varied. With the exception of subject 323 under treatment condition 1 (the highest surplus resource condition), the certain prospect was chosen 50% of the time or more in all cases. Further, preference for the certain alternative was statistically significant in 17 out of the 20 conditions. Thus, risk aversion held over all consumption levels.

Using changes in choice frequencies to detect shifts in preferences, we see no clear, statistically significant changes in choice frequencies as incomes are varied.[9] Average choice frequencies for the certain alternative decreased somewhat as total income increased (compare conditions 4 and 1; the mean at the 24 forced-choice condition, condition 2, is somewhat misleading because of the incomplete nature of our observations there). But a paired t-test for the difference in choice frequencies between the extreme treatment conditions, 1 and 4, fails to show a significant difference at conventional levels ($t = -0.67$, d.f. = 5). In addition, an examination of the individual subject data reveals very little systematic variation in preference measures. With the exception of rat 323, no subject showed any clear systematic increase in preference for the certain alternative at lower income levels, as decreasing absolute risk aversion requires. Further, there is no switch from risk aversion at higher incomes to risk loving at lower incomes, as predicted by the biological model in going from surplus to deficit resource conditions.

Table 6.4 shows average daily weight changes associated with the different treatment conditions. The high income conditions (1 and 2) clearly resulted in resource surpluses, as evidenced by the substantial weight gains observed for all rats in these conditions. Conversely, the lowest income condition (4) clearly

Table 6.3. *Effects of varying levels of consumption on risk preferences*

	I. Experiment treatment conditions[a]		
Condition	Number of forced-choice trials	Number of free-choice trials	Expected total daily food consumption (gm)
1	32	17	17.64
2	24	17	14.76
3	8	17	9.00
4	0	17	6.12

	II. Percentage choice of certain alternative[b]				
Subject	1 [17.64]	2 [14.76]	3 [9.00]	4 [6.12]	Average across consumption levels[c]
303	68.2[d] (4)	82.4[d] (1)	64.7[d] (2)	63.0[d] (3)	69.6 (4.41)
304	—	89.4[d] (1)	90.0[d] (2)	82.9[d] (3)	87.4 (2.27)
323	45.9 (4)	68.8[d] (1)	68.3[d] (2)	78.8[d] (3)	65.4 (6.95)
324	74.1[d] (2)	—	74.1[d] (1)	80.6[d] (3)	76.3 (2.17)
333	60.0[d] (2)	—	67.1[d] (1)	54.1 (3)	60.4 (3.76)
334	73.7[d] (2)	—	54.7 (1)	76.5[d] (3)	68.3 (6.85)
Average[c]	64.4 (5.28)	80.2 (6.05)	69.8 (4.80)	72.6 (4.68)	

[a]Prospects: 8 pellets, probability $= 1.0$ vs 1 pellet, probability $= .75$ or 29 pellets, probability $= .25$.
[b]Sequence of experimental conditions in parentheses; total expected grams of food in brackets.
[c]Standard error of mean in parentheses.
[d]Significantly different from 50.0 at 1% level, two-tailed t-test.
Source: Battalio, Kagel, and MacDonald (1985).

resulted in resource deficits as all the rats lost weight. Shown in parentheses below the weight changes are mean weights, in grams, over the last five days of each treatment condition.[10]

Mean weight is important because it indicates how close subjects were to death. Although we lack precise data concerning the point at which mature rats

Table 6.4. *Effects of varying consumption levels on weight: daily weight change in grams*

	Experimental treatment conditions			
Subject	1 [17.64]	2 [14.76]	3 [9.00]	4 [6.12]
303	3.44 (310.2)	0.86 (271.4)	− 1.23 (228.4)	− 1.34 (182.8)
304	—	0.98 (273.4)	− 1.20 (231.4)	− 1.34 (186.0)
323	3.69 (286.6)	1.03 (275.2)	− 1.39 (223.6)	− 1.79 (157.4)
324	2.80 (276.8)	—	− 0.36 (173.2)	− 2.69 (174.4)
333	2.23 (278.0)	—	0.29 (193.2)	− 2.38 (189.8)
334	1.90 (261.8)	—	0.09 (189.6)	− 1.76 (184.2)
Average	2.81 (282.7)	0.96 (273.3)	− 0.63 (206.6)	− 1.88 (179.1)

Note: Mean weight in grams over last five days of each condition in parentheses.

will die from malnutrition, or disease brought on by malnutrition, in our experience we become seriously concerned about their health once weight drops below 180–200 grams. In the present experiment, all the rats weighed below 200 grams and were losing weight under the lowest income condition (condition 4 in Table 6.4), so that there was no question that our rats could not ultimately survive under this treatment condition. Yet all the rats continued to prefer the certain alternative. Indeed, we found no shift toward risk loving even during the last several days of this deficit condition when deleterious effects would have been most severe.

This absence of risk loving at the very lowest income level has also been found using water payoffs (Kagel et al., 1986), and stands in marked contrast to the work of Caraco and his associates using small birds (reviewed in Caraco and Lima, 1987), and that of Barnard and Brown (1985) using common shrews (a small rodent). Several explanations for these different results are suggested.

A number of procedural factors might be responsible for these differences. Of greatest potential significance is that the intertrial interval covaried with changing levels of resource availability both in Caraco's and in Barnard and Brown's experiments. The intertrial interval was substantially longer under deficit than under surplus conditions. In addition, in Caraco's experiments at least, the intertrial interval varied directly with a trial's outcome, so that unlucky outcomes were partly compensated (in terms of a quicker start time for the next trial) under deficit resource conditions.[11] Although we do not know the precise effect of temporal variability on choice in Caraco's experiments, we do know that, other things being equal, animals prefer greater variability in time delays (see Section 6.5). Thus, in Caraco's and Barnard and Brown's procedures, a subject's response to reward variability under changing levels of resource availability was confounded with its response to time variability. Our procedures, with their constant intertrial interval, irrespective of resource levels or the state of nature, were designed to eliminate this confound.

Aside from these procedural differences, there are important differences in daily food intake necessary for survival between relatively large mammals such as rats and the much smaller organisms used in these other studies. Barnard and Brown (1985) noted that common shrews have unusually high energy demands, are likely to die after only a few hours without food and, therefore, should be sensitive to the contingencies influencing their short-term intake. Although the relationship between daily food requirements and survival in the small birds Caraco studied is less extreme than with common shrews, it is nevertheless far more sensitive to short-term intake than it would be for rats or other relatively large mammals.

A large body weight in relation to daily consumption requirements buffers the animal against starvation between foraging periods and is a factor likely to prove critical to the predictions of the model (Barnard et al., 1985). Relatively large mammals like the rat are more likely to die from disease induced by malnutrition than from malnutrition per se. Thus, there might not be any clearly specified amount of food required for survival as there would be for a smaller organism that may simply drop from malnutrition and die from predation. In addition, given their relatively large body weights, foraging situations that require switching from risk aversion to risk loving are likely to be less frequent with large, compared to small, organisms. Consequently, large animals might be much less predisposed to change strategies in response to deteriorating resources.[12] Finally, the larger organism might have much less to gain by switching strategies, in terms of meeting its long-term resource requirements, and may be better off as a rule to play it safe, avoid risks, and take its chances on the prospects for survival improving as mean resource levels change.

In response to these results and the procedural confounds identified, Caraco and his associates have conducted an additional experiment with small birds holding the intertrial interval constant (Caraco et al., 1990). In this experiment they manipulated the temperature of the experimental chamber to induce positive and negative net energy budgets (colder temperatures require more energy). First, a baseline condition was run in which total food consumption was

measured at different temperatures to identify a resource budget that would ensure deficits at colder temperatures and surpluses at warmer ones. With this resource budget in place, temperature was associated with a clear qualitative
difference in choice. At the colder temperature, with it resource deficit, risk
aversion occurred only once and risk loving was common. In contrast, at the
warmer temperature, risk loving occurred only once and risk aversion was common. These results, correcting as they do for the procedural confound in earlier
studies, support the energy budget rule as applied to small birds. Thus, differences between these small birds and our rats are most likely explained by the
species differences discussed earlier.

6.3b Tests of competing motivational hypotheses

In expected utility theory, the value of a prospect is the probability-
weighted average of the value of the outcomes under different states of the world

$$U = \Sigma_i p_i u(x_i) \tag{6.2}$$

where p_i represents the probability of state i, x_i represents the outcome under
state i, and $u(x_i)$ is the value to the consumer of payoff x_i. The Arrow–Pratt measure of local absolute risk aversion (Arrow, 1974; Pratt, 1964) is

$$-\frac{u''(x_i)}{u'(x_i)} \tag{6.3}$$

where $u'(x_i)$ and $u''(x_i)$ are the first and second derivatives, respectively, of
the subutility function $u(x_i)$.[13] Equation (6.3) provides an invariant measure
of risk preferences with the following important property: In cases where the
Arrow–Pratt measure is decreasing (increasing), the risk premium is decreasing (increasing), as well.

The competing motivational models developed in Chapter 3 all specify particular functional forms for the valuation function $u(x_i)$. These are

$$u(x_i) = -\frac{\beta_i}{\nu}\left(\frac{\gamma_i - x_i}{\beta_i}\right)^{\nu} \quad (\gamma_i - x_i) > 0, \quad \gamma_i, \beta_i > 0, \quad \nu > 1 \tag{6.4}$$

$$u(x_i) = \frac{\beta_i}{\nu}\left(\frac{x_i - \gamma_i}{\beta_i}\right)^{\nu} \quad (x_i - \gamma_i) \geq 0, \quad \beta_i > 0, \quad \nu < 1 \tag{6.5}$$

for the generalized minimum-distance and minimum-needs hypotheses, respectively (recall equations (3.14) and (3.15)).[14] With positively valued payoffs, these valuation functions are concave throughout (the second derivatives
with respect to x_i are negative), assuming that the models' underlying restrictions are satisfied; that is, total income is less than or equal to the bliss point, in
the case of the minimum-distance hypothesis, and is greater than or equal to
survival requirements in the case of the minimum-needs model. Hence, under
surplus resource conditions, both models always predict risk aversion, which
agrees with our results as well as those of Caraco and his associates.

However, the MD and MN models yield markedly different predictions regarding changes in risk preferences with changing x_i in terms of the Arrow–Pratt measure of local risk aversion. Evaluating (6.3) in terms of (6.4) and (6.5) yields,

$$-\frac{u''(x_i)}{u'(x_i)} = (v - 1)(\gamma_i - x_i)^{-1} \tag{6.6}$$

and

$$-\frac{u''(x_i)}{u'(x)} = -(v - 1)(x_i - \gamma_i)^{-1} \tag{6.7}$$

respectively. Both (6.6) and (6.7) are positive throughout. However, for the MD model, as income grows, $(\gamma_i - x_i)$ gets smaller, so that evaluating (6.6) for different values of x_i, holding γ_i constant, yields larger positive values – and thereby increases risk aversion.[15] In contrast, evaluating (6.7) for different values of x_i, holding γ_i constant, yields smaller positive numbers – and decreases risk aversion.

Given these implications, data from our experiments and those of Caraco and his associates modestly favor the minimum-needs model, although the evidence is not as compelling as one might wish. In our food and water experiments, risk preferences did not show any statistically significant change as income varied, although mean choice levels pointed in the direction of decreasing risk aversion. Caraco and his associates sometimes report clear evidence in favor of decreasing risk aversion, consistent with the predictions of the generalized minimum-needs model. Note, however, that the potential procedural confounds identified earlier (Section 6.3a) apply to these results as well, tempering the conclusions that can be reached on the basis of these data alone. In addition, Caraco and Chasin (1984) have studied risk preferences of small birds with respect to reward skews. These tests have involved pairwise comparisons of prospects with the same mean and variance, but with different skews (different third moments about the mean). They consistently found preference for prospects with positive skew, a necessary (but not sufficient) condition for decreasing risk aversion under the Arrow–Pratt measure. Since for any given pairwise comparison intertrial times were constant, these results are free from the procedural confound noted in Section 6.3a.[16]

Our difficulty in teasing out clearly changing risk preferences as resource levels change might be rationalized under both motivational hypotheses if the set points (the minimum-needs or bliss points) varied systematically with total resource level, a sensible possibility suggested in our earlier discussions of these models (Section 3.3). Alternatively, one might argue, as many have done (for example, Kahneman and Tversky, 1979; Markowitz, 1959), that risk preferences are defined over *changes* in resource levels, not total resource levels, as expected utility theory has traditionally assumed. If this were the case, then risk preferences would depend primarily on the prospects among which the individual was choosing and would not change much with changes in income. Furthermore, this definition would predict constant risk preferences in our experiments, as the prospects and the number of free-choice trials did not themselves change; rather, the number of forced-choice trials did.

6.4 Tests of expected utility theory and the fanning-out hypothesis

One of the interesting recent developments in the study of choice under uncertainty has been the development of alternatives to expected utility (EU) theory. Evidence has accumulated documenting systematic and repeated violations of one or more of the theory's basic axioms. This section reports two experiments related to these developments. The first experiment is designed to induce Allais-type violations of the independence axiom of EU theory by mimicking conditions that reliably result in such violations with human subjects. The second experiment tests for "fanning out" of indifference curves in previously unexplored areas of the unit probability triangle. Fanning out is predicted by generalized EU theory under Machina's Hypothesis II (hereafter, referred to as H2; Machina, 1982, 1987), and by a number of other non-EU formulations as well.

6.4a Testing for Allais-type violations of expected utility theory

In verbal protocols with human subjects, cognitive psychologists and economists report systematic violations of the independence axiom of EU theory for large numbers of subjects. For example, consider choosing between the following prospects A and B (this example is from Kahneman and Tversky, 1979).

> Pair 1: Choose between A and B
> A. 3,000 Israeli pounds with prob. 1.0
> B. 4,000 Israeli pounds with prob. .80
>   0 Israeli pounds with prob. 20

Given this choice, most subjects prefer prospect A (80% of some 95 respondents in Kahneman and Tversky's sample). Now consider choosing between the following prospects C and D

> Pair 2: Choose between C and D
> C. 3,000 Israeli pounds with prob. .25
>   0 Israeli pounds with prob. .75
> D. 4,000 Israeli pounds with prob. .20
>   0 Israeli pounds with prob. .80

In choosing between these two prospects, the majority of respondents in Kahneman and Tversky's sample (65%) preferred prospect D to C. In contrast, an EU maximizer would prefer A and C or else B and D. This follows from the fact that prospect C is a reduced-form lottery consisting of a .25 chance of lottery A and a .75 chance of lottery K (where K yields zero payoff with probability 1.0), while prospect D consists of a .25 chance of lottery B and a .75 chance of lottery K. The choice of A and D violates the independence axiom of EU theory, which rules out substitutability or complementarity between prospects such as A or B when combined with any other prospect (such as K).

The independence axiom is equivalent to specifying that the preference function over prospects is linear in the probabilities (as in equation (6.3)) and that indifference curves are parallel in the unit probability triangle. It can be interpreted as follows: In terms of ultimate probabilities over the outcomes {4,000, 3,000, 0}, choosing between the mixtures $C = \lambda A + (1 - \lambda)K$, and $D = \lambda B + (1 - \lambda)K$ (where $\lambda = .25$ in this example) is the same as being offered a coin with probability λ of landing tails and probability $(1 - \lambda)$ of landing heads. If the coin comes up heads, lottery K will be won. You are asked before the coin toss whether you'd prefer A or B if the coin come up tails. Either the toss will come up heads, in which case your choice would not matter, or else it will come up tails, in which case you are back to choosing between A and B. As such, if the choice of prospects A and B are independent of K, you make the same choice as you would between A and B. Note that violations of the independence axiom in cases such as this are not random (in which case they might simply be written off as mistakes or random errors), but show consistent swings in preference from the lower-paying but more certain prospect (A) in pair 1 to the higher-paying but less certain prospect (D) in pair 2.

Although violations of the independence axiom have been reported for some time, beginning with Allais (1953), virtually all reported violations have been over hypothetical choice alternatives or small stakes outcomes (Kahneman and Tversky used hypothetical choices). In the face of these repeated violations, one of the last lines of defense of EU theory, as a descriptive theory of behavior, has been that whereas hypothetical choices were used in these studies, subjects' choices are likely to differ when they have to actually deal with the consequences of their behavior, and when they have some real experience with the outcomes (Machina, 1983). We can address this issue directly by mimicking these protocols but using real payoffs with nonhuman animals.

Of four types of systematic violations of the independence axiom reported with humans (Machina, 1982, 1987), the "common ratio" effect (Allais, 1953, p. 91) is most readily adapted to our procedures (the common ratio effect includes the "certainty effect" of Kahneman and Tversky, 1979, and the "Bergen Paradox" of Hagen, 1979, as special cases). The common ratio effect involves rankings over pairs of prospects like those in our example (the term "common ratio" derives from the equality of prob(3,000)/prob(4,000) in A versus B and C versus D).

The top part of Table 6.5 shows the prospects used in our experiments in which both food and water served as the payoffs. The prospects are directly related to those in our example: We have replaced the payoff values x_3 (4,000 Israeli pounds) $> x_2$ (3,000 Israeli pounds) $> x_1$ (0 Israeli pounds) with 13, 8, and 1 pellets of food (or cups of water). The initial probabilities of positive payoffs for prospects A and B, p (= 1.0) $> q$ (= .80), have been replaced by 1.0 and .75, respectively. The probability mix factor used to go from prospects A and B to C and D is $\lambda = 1/3$ compared with $\lambda = 1/4$ used in Kahneman and Tversky's choices. Also shown under each prospect is the expected value of the outcome. Note that the expected value of each prospect drops rather drastically as λ decreases. We decided to use a payoff of one rather than zero for the "unlucky" outcome. This decision stemmed, in part, from concern for this income effect and, in part, from the desire to avoid outcomes with no reinforcement. If a choice ended with no reinforcement, it could be argued that this zero-payoff alternative introduces a time-delay confound into choices.

The bottom part of Table 6.5 shows the mean frequencies with which the lower expected value prospects (A and C) were chosen at the two values for λ. Mean choice frequency under the initial (baseline) $\lambda = 1$ condition shows a modest preference for the 8 payoff (certain) alternative (A). Baseline conditions were chosen with this goal in mind since a necessary condition for generating Allais-type common ratio violations of EU theory is to establish preference for the certain alternative under high-probability gain conditions.[17] In contrast, a modest, but statistically significant preference for the 13-payoff alternative (D) occurs with $\lambda = 1/3$. The return to $\lambda = 1$ conditions reinstates the preference for the 8-payoff alternative (A). A paired t-test across subjects shows the changes in choice frequencies to be statistically significant, in the Allais-type direction, going from $\lambda = 1$ to $\lambda = 1/3$ ($t = 4.46$, 8 d.f., $p < .01$, two-tailed t-test) and going from $\lambda = 1/3$ back to $\lambda = 1$ ($t = -4.94$, 8 d.f., $p < .01$, two-tailed t-test). The data show Allais-type violations for most individual rats, as well.

At this point, it is important to note some important differences in procedures between the animal experiments and those with humans. During a given experimental session, human subjects will commonly choose among several different pairs of prospects like the ones in the example that started this section. In those studies in which real payoffs were used, considerably smaller monetary values are used, and after all choices have been made, one pair is randomly chosen and the preferred alternative played out. In contrast, the rats choose between a single pair of prospects (say, pair 1) repeatedly in a given experimental session, with the preferred alternative played out immediately following each choice. These choices are repeated over a number of sessions before another pair of prospects, like pair 2, is presented. This procedure differs from that used in human experiments in two important ways. First, over the course of a

Table 6.5 *Tests for Allais-type violations of expected utility theory*

I. Prospects studied			
Condition		*Prospects[a]*	*Value of* λ
1	A: 8 payoff, prob. 1.0 (8.0)	or B: 13 payoff, prob. 3/4 1 payoff, prob. 1/4 (10.0)	1.0
2	C: 8 payoff, prob. 1/3 1 payoff, prob. 2/3 (3.33)	or D: 13 payoff, prob. 1/4 1 payoff, prob. 3/4 (4.0)	1/3

II. Frequency of choosing lower expected value (8 payoff) alternative[b]

Subject	$\lambda = 1$	$\lambda = 1/3$	$\lambda = 1$
304	57.0 (1.57)	46.0 (− 0.87)	56.0 (1.71)
334	65.5 (3.46)[c]	47.5 − (0.56)	69.0 (16.9)[c]
521	57.1 (1.94)	47.5 (− 1.20)	60.4 (4.38)[c]
523	58.3 (3.50)[c]	47.9 (− 0.76)	50.4 (0.14)
524	50.0 (0.00)	42.1 (− 3.92)	47.5 (− 1.04)
631	47.5 (− 0.72)	49.2 (− 0.34)	52.1 (2.24)
632	53.8 (1.14)	49.6 (− 0.14)	57.9 (2.84)[d]
633	51.3 (0.58)	47.1 (− 1.98)	60.4 (2.98)[d]
634	57.1 (1.82)	45.8 (− 2.24)	57.5 (2.24)
Average (standard error of mean)	55.3[d] (1.79)	47.0[c] (0.74)	56.8[d] (2.13)

Note: Payoffs for rats 304 and 334 were 45 mg-Noyes food pellets; for all others they were 0.04cc cups of tap water. Sixteen forced-choice trials in all cases; 20 free-choice trials with food; 24 free-choice trials with water.

[a]Expected value in parentheses.

[b]t statistics in parentheses.

[c]Significantly different from 50.0 at 1% level, two-tailed t-test.

[d]Significantly different from 50.0 at 5% level, two-tailed t-test.

Source: MacDonald, Kagel, and Battalio (1991).

treatment condition, rats' total daily consumption levels have inevitably changed. Thus, unlike the case with humans, rats' choices are not being evaluated from a fixed level of income or wealth. This could, of course, give rise to spurious income or wealth effects that might systematically distort the rats' choices. Fortunately, however, the results of Section 6.5 give independent evidence that rats' choices among pairs of prospects are quite insensitive to wide swings in income of this sort. In addition, similar Allais-type violations have been reported with rats choosing among variable delays to reinforcement, a procedure for which there is no income variation between treatment conditions (Kagel, MacDonald, and Battalio, 1990). The second major difference is the possibility for portfolio effects, whereby the rats could mix prospects to achieve the most preferred alternative, as in choosing between prospects C and K in Figure 6.1. To guard against this, we always separated choice trials by a fixed time period (in this case, a minute and a half). Because rats have steep time discount rates (see Chapter 7), such long intertrial intervals presumably lead the rats to treat each choice trial as independent.[18]

6.4b Tests of the fanning-out hypothesis

Machina (1982, 1987) identifies three systematic violations of the independence axiom in addition to that of the common ratio effect and shows that all four violations follow from a single assumption: fanning out of the individual preference functionals.[19] Safra, Segal, and Spivak (1990) have also used fanning out to explain the preference-reversal phenomenon (Grether and Plott, 1979; Lichtenstein and Slovic, 1971; Machina, 1987). Fanning out is formalized in Machina's (1982) H2, which states that in moving from one probability distribution to another that (first-order) stochastically dominates the first, the local (linear) utility function retains the same degree of concavity, or becomes more concave at each point. In other words, preferences tend to vary systematically as a consequence of an expected income effect, so that distributions that ex ante involve more income, yield the same or more risk-averse choices.[20]

H2 can be characterized and compared with EU theory with the aid of the unit-probability triangle.[21] Consider the set of all prospects over the fixed outcome levels $x_3 > x_2 > x_1$, which can be represented by the set of all probability triples of the form $P = (p_1, p_2, p_3)$ and $\Sigma p_i = 1$. Since $p_2 = 1 - p_1 - p_3$, we can represent these prospects by points in the unit triangle in the (p_1, p_3) plane, as in Figure 6.3. Thus, with $x_1 = 1$, $x_2 = 8$, and $x_3 = 13$, the prospects employed in our tests of the independence axiom could be represented by the points $(p_1, p_3) = (0, 0)$ (prospect A); $(p_1, p_3) = (.25, .75)$ (prospect B); $(p_1, p_3) = (.67, 0)$ (prospect C); and $(p_1, p_3) = (.75, .25)$ (prospect D) (see Table 6.5 top and Figure 6.3). Upward movements in the triangle increase p_3 at the expense of p_2, shifting probability from outcome x_2 to x_3, and leftward movements reduce p_1 to the benefit of p_2, shifting probability from x_1 to x_2. These

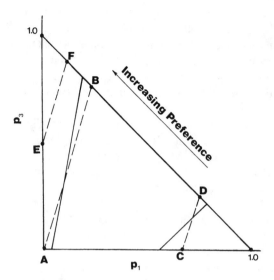

Figure 6.3 Preferences in the unit-probability triangle. Solid lines are indifference curves, dashed lines are linear combinations of the prospects employed in tests of Allais-type violations of expected utility theory (Table 6.5). Indifference curves that fan out in the unit-probability triangle are consistent with Allais-type violations.

upward and leftward movements lead to stochastically dominated prospects (recall Section 6.1), which are preferred. Finally, since indifference curves in the unit-probability triangle are given by solutions to the linear equation,

$$\bar{U} = \Sigma u(x_i)p_i = u(x_1)p_1 + u(x_2)(1 - p_1 - p_3) + u(x_3)p_3 = \text{constant} \qquad (6.8)$$

they will consist of *parallel* straight lines with slope $[u(x_2) - u(x_1)]/[u(x_3) - u(x_2)]$ within the unit-probability triangle.

We are now in a position to see how "fanning out" of indifference curves can explain Allais-type violations of the independence axiom. The prospects (A, B, C, D) used in our tests of the independence axiom form a parallelogram in the context of the unit-probability triangle. That is, the dashed lines, involving linear combinations of the prospects A and B and C and D in Figure 6.3, are parallel. Consequently, if the indifference curves are parallel, as they are in EU theory, the decision maker must choose either the pair A, C or B, D. However, if the indifference curves fan out in the unit-probability triangle, becoming steeper in moving to the northwest corner of the triangle, they are no longer parallel and thus can explain preferences for prospects A and D (Allais-type violations of EU theory), which is the case illustrated in Figure 6.3.

In other words, in EU theory equation (6.8) guides choices throughout the unit-probability triangle. And these indifference curves consist of parallel straight lines. But if we make equation (6.8) more complicated, so that the utility associated with different outcomes varies within the unit-probability triangle (as Machina's H2 assumes) and/or the probabilities associated with different outcomes are assessed differently at different points in the unit-probability triangle (as prospect theory, for example, assumes; Kahneman and Tversky, 1979), the indifference curves no longer need to be either linear or parallel. This permits more complicated choice patterns. However, any transformation of equation (6.8) to allow for more complicated choice patterns must impose some order over choices. Fanning out of indifference curves in the unit probability triangle is the choice pattern implied by a number of generalizations of EU theory (see Machina, 1983).

Most of the violations of EU theory that the fanning-out hypothesis explains have occurred in the southeast/southwest portion of the unit-probability triangle, at least for prospects with positive payoffs. The obvious question from an experimental point of view is whether choices between pairs of prospects that dominate A and B, prospects that lie to the northwest of A and B in the unit-probability triangle, such as E and F in Figure 6.3, continue to satisfy the requirements of fanning out: That is, will those who choose A and D also prefer E when offered the choice between E and F?

The top part of Table 6.6 shows the prospects employed in one of several such tests of fanning out we have conducted. Condition 1 is the same as the $\lambda = 1$ condition in our test for Allais-type violations of the independence axiom. Condition 2 (prospects X and Y in Figure 6.4, referred to as condition M-1) involves a small movement to the northwest of the $\lambda = 1$ condition. If indifference curves are linear (as a number of models suggest), and fan out, then all subjects choosing prospect A under baseline conditions will also prefer X under the M-1 condition. However, prospect Y in M-1 does not stochastically dominate prospect B. Consequently, nonlinear indifference curves of just the right shape can be used to rationalize the choice of prospect Y while still satisfying the formal requirements of Machina's H2, which underlies fanning out. Condition 3 (adjusted baseline) allows us to test for this possibility by comparing choices between prospects A and B' if subjects do show clear violations of fanning out between conditions M-1 and $\lambda = 1.0$.[22]

The bottom part of Table 6.6 shows the results of these tests, reporting for each subject and condition the frequency with which the lower expected value (8 payoff) alternative was chosen. In general, the M-1 condition produced a *decrease* in choice of the more certain alternative (prospect X in Figure 6.4) than under the $\lambda = 1.0$ condition. This is *opposite* to the pattern predicted under fanning out; rather, it is consistent with fanning in of indifference curves in terms of moving from prospects A and B to X and Y in Figure 6.4. Conducting paired

Table 6.6 *Tests of fanning out over gains*

	I. Prospects studied		
Condition	Prospects[a]		Mnemonic
1	A: 8 cups, prob. 1.0 (8.0)	or	B: 13 cups, prob. 3/4 1 cup, prob. 1/4 (10.0)	$\lambda = 1.0$ (baseline)
2	X: 13 cups, prob. 1/8 8 cups, prob. 7/8 (8.63)	or	Y: 13 cups, prob. 1/2 8 cups, prob. 3/8 1 cup, prob. 1/8 (9.63)	M-1
3	A: 8 cups, prob. 1.0 (8.0)	or	B': 13 cups, prob. 1/2 8 cups, prob. 1/3 1 cup, prob. 1/6 (9.33)	adjusted baseline

II. Frequency of choosing more certain (lower expected value) payoff[b]

Subject	Baseline $\lambda = 1$	M-1	Baseline $\lambda = 1$	M-1	Baseline $\lambda = 1$	Adjusted baseline
521	57.1 (1.94)	48.8 (− 0.24)	60.4 (4.38)[c]	55.4 (2.00)	49.2 (− 0.30)	—
523	58.3 (2.50)[d]	41.7 (− 3.84)[c]	50.4 (0.16)	42.9 (− 3.16)[d]	53.2 (12.3)[c]	—
524	50.0 (0.00)	41.3 (− 3.42)[c]	47.5 (− 1.04)	44.6 (− 3.44)[c]	47.5 (− 1.84)	—
631	47.5 (−0.72)	49.2 (−0.36)	52.1 (2.24)	45.0 (− 2.58)[d]	54.2 (2.02)	—
632	53.8 (1.14)	45.0 (− 1.48)	57.9 (2.84)[d]	47.1 (− 1.30)	50.8 (0.42)	56.7 (2.82)[d]
633	51.3 (0.58)	47.9 (− 1.62)	60.4 (2.58)[d]	48.8 (−0.36)	46.7 (− 2.06)	—
634	57.1 (−1.82)	42.1 (− 3.72)[c]	57.5 (2.28)	42.9 (− 2.78)[d]	47.1 (− 0.56)	57.5 (3.80)[c]
Average[e]	53.6 (1.56)	45.1[c] (1.32)	55.2[d] (1.94)	46.7 (1.67)	49.8 (1.13)	—

Note: Sixteen forced-choice, 24 free-choice trials; .04 cc cups.
[a]Expected value in parentheses.
[b]t-statistics in parentheses.
[c]Significantly different from 50.0 at 1% level, two-tailed t-test.
[d]Significantly different from 50.0 at 5% level, two-tailed t-test.
[e]Standard error of mean in parentheses
Source: MacDonald, Kagel, and Battalio (1991).

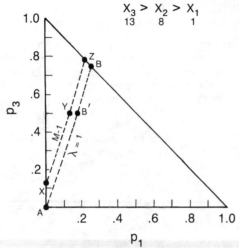

Figure 6.4 Prospects employed in tests of fanning out in previously unexplored areas of the unit-probability triangle (Table 6.6).

t-tests across subjects under the different treatment conditions, we find a statistically significant decrease in the frequency with which the more certain alternative was chosen, going from the first $\lambda = 1.0$ to the first M-1 condition ($t = 3.55$, $p < .05$, two-tailed *t*-test). Further, there is a significant increase in choice of the more certain alternative on returning to $\lambda = 1$ ($t = -6.12$, $p < .01$, two-tailed *t*-test), and, again, a statistically significant reduction in the frequency of choosing the more certain alternative on replication of the M-1 condition ($t = 5.52$, $p < .01$, two-tailed *t*-test). The average choice frequency reversed in the final replication of the baseline condition, although the difference here was not significant at conventional levels. In most cases, individual subject data show clear fanning in as well.

Also shown in Table 6.6 is the frequency with which rats 632 and 634 chose the A alternative under the adjusted baseline condition. In both cases, subjects preferred the A alternative; that is, choice frequencies were slightly greater than their average choice of A under the $\lambda = 1$ condition. Thus, for these two cases at least, the fanning-out hypothesis cannot be saved by appealing to the possibility of nonlinear indifference curves of just the right shape.

Finally, we have extended the line segment employed in the M-1 test of fanning out to the edge of the unit-probability triangle, generating prospect Z in Figure 6.4. Pairwise comparisons of prospect X and Z, and prospect Y with prospects X and Z, show that (a) X is preferred to Z, and is chosen more, on average, than A was chosen under the $\lambda = 1$ condition (56% versus 53% averaged across subjects) and (b) prospect Y is preferred to prospect X (54% choice frequency averaged across subjects) and to prospect Z (56% choice frequency averaged across subjects) (see MacDonald, Kagel, and Battalio, 1991). The first result indicates that if our M-1 test had been based on prospects X and Z, both of which lie on the *edges* of the unit-probability triangle, we would have concluded that the fanning-out hypothesis was doing relatively well. These results are symptomatic of a general pattern of behavior, namely, that fanning out does substantially better at describing behavior with prospects restricted to the edges of the unit-probability triangle than when one or more of the prospect pairs is in the interior of the triangle (Battalio, Kagel, Jiranyakul, 1990; Conlisk, 1989; Harless, 1992; MacDonald et al., 1991).

The second result, that prospect Y is preferred to prospects X and Z, indicates a failure of the betweenness axiom of EU theory: the betweenness axiom of EU theory requires that between any two pairs of prospects X and Z, if $X > Z$ (where $>$ represents preference) then $X > \lambda X + (1 - \lambda)Z > Z$, where $0 < \lambda < 1$; that is, if prospect X is preferred to Z, then any probability mix of X and Z (such as prospect Y) is preferred to Z as well. The betweenness axiom implies indifference curves that are linear in the probabilities, in contrast to the independence axiom, which implies indifference curves that are linear *and* parallel. Preference for the prospect Y in this case is indicative of convex indifference curves in the unit probability triangle, and has been observed in rats choosing among other sets of prospects as well (MacDonald et al., 1991). Note, there is no theoretical incompatibility between convexity and fanning out; one does not logically preclude the other since generalized EU theory permits nonlinear indifference curves (Machina, 1982). But since fanning out is more likely when the prospects are located on the edges of the unit-probability triangle, some relationship between violations of fanning out and violations of the betweenness axiom is suggested.

One possible explanation as to why subjects preferred alternative Y over X under M-1, but preferred A over B under $\lambda = 1$ (and A over B' under the adjusted baseline) is that the small probability of the 1-cup outcome in B and B' is exaggerated when compared with the certain 8-cup payoff in A, offsetting the attractiveness of the 13-cup payoff. However, in Y, the probability of the 1-cup outcome is reduced somewhat in relation to B and B', so that it loses its exaggerated value, particularly since prospect X drops the certainty of the 8-cup payoff in favor of a small possibility of a 13-cup payoff. This sort of explanation puts the burden on the probability-weighting function to organize deviations from EU theory, much as prospect theory does (Kahneman and Tversky, 1979), and may suggest why failures of H2 and convexity of indifference curves are related.

The results reported in Table 6.6 are but one of several tests of fanning out we have conducted in previously unexplored areas of the unit-probability triangle. These experiments have employed both human and nonhuman subjects (rats) and have been concerned with choices over losses as well as gains (Battalio et al., 1990; Kagel et al., 1990; MacDonald et al., 1991). All of these experiments show similar results: Allais-type violations of EU theory for standard manipulations like those reported in Table 6.5, and clear fanning in at previously unexplored areas of the unit-probability triangle. The breakdown of fanning out observed in these experiments is largely a negative result, because we offer no alternative model to explain the data. Although there are models, in particular prospect theory (Kahneman and Tversky, 1979), that can explain most of the results reported, these models prove deficient as well when submitted to more broadly based tests (for comprehensive tests of a number of non-EU models with human subjects, see Battalio, Kagel, Jiranyakul, 1990; Camerer, 1989; Harless, 1992; Harless and Camerer, 1991; Starmer and Sugden, 1987). Hence, we hesitate to declare a winning theory to account for our data. Nevertheless, our results do favor some sort of differential probability-weighting process or selective attention to different components of the choice problem rather than income or wealth effects in explaining deviations from EU theory. And these are essential factors underlying the formulation of prospect theory. Finally, our results also indicate some striking parallels in behavior between human and nonhuman animals and suggest a common underlying behavioral process in explaining violations of EU theory.

6.5 Risk preference in the face of aversive outcomes

Psychologists have conducted several studies of choice between constant and variable delays to reinforcement. Given equal average delays to reinforcement, they consistently find strong preference for the variable outcome alternative (for a review, see Davison, 1969; Fantino, 1967; Killeen, 1968; Mazur, 1986). We will refer to this preference for unpredictability with respect to delay to reinforcement as "risk loving."[23] The risk loving observed in such experiments can be quite striking. For example, Davison (1969) had pigeons choose between food reinforcement obtained after a certain time delay of 30 sec versus food reinforcement obtained with a 50-50 chance of a 15-sec or a 45-sec delay (for an average expected delay of 30 sec). For the five birds studied, mean choice of the certain outcome alternative was 11%. When the certain time delay was reduced to 25 sec, and the comparison repeated, the certain alternative was still chosen 37% of the time, on average.

In contrast, studies of choice between constant versus variable food reward of equal average amounts generally show risk aversion in cases where the average rate of food intake is sufficient to ensure survival (recall Tables 6.1 and 6.2). Hamm and Shettleworth (1987) tested for procedural and/or species differences to account for these different outcomes. They combined methods (conc VI–VI schedules) and subjects (pigeons) typically employed when risk loving is found, with the variable (quantity of food reinforcement) used in studies reporting risk aversion. They still observed a general pattern of risk aver-

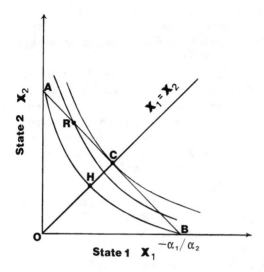

Figure 6.5 Preferences over uncertain outcomes with convex indifference curves, when prospects involve negative/aversive payoffs so that less is better. See text.

sion with amount of food and concluded that the primary factor determining whether risk loving or risk aversion is manifested is the payoff in question (delay to reinforcement versus food).

What we will argue here is that the process (diminishing marginal rate of substitution) producing risk aversion in the face of gains (where more is better) will produce risk loving when applied to aversive or negative outcomes (where less is better). Figure 6.5 illustrates this process. We have reproduced the essential elements of Figure 6.2: convex indifference curves between outcomes in different states and the fair-bet line AB. Prospect C is a certain payoff, since it yields the same amount of x in both states of nature. In contrast, prospect R involves a variable payoff, with a higher payoff in state 2 than in state 1 (since R is on the fair-bet line, it has equal expected value to C given the decision maker's assessment of the probabilities of the different states of nature).

The key difference between this case and the one discussed in Section 6.2 is that choice here is between prospects involving losses or aversive outcomes (for example, shock or delay to reinforcement), rather than prospects involving gains, so that *less* is better. Consequently, in choosing between alternatives with equal expected values, convex indifference curves result in preference for the riskier alternative, since the "highest" attainable indifference curve is now closer to the origin. For example, in choosing between the certain outcome C, and the risky alternative R, the "highest" attainable indifference curve is the one passing through R, since it is closer to the origin. The important point to note is that the manifestation of risk loving in this case results from the same process – diminishing marginal rate of substitution – as risk aversion in the case of positive payoffs.[24]

It should be noted that with negative/aversive payoffs, there is nothing inconsistent in choosing the certain prospect *if* it contains sufficiently small amounts of the bad relative to the expected value of the uncertain alternative. Such a case is illustrated in the choice between prospects H and R in Figure 6.5. Although H contains a certain loss, it is small enough in relation to R that the indifference curve closest to the origin passes through H rather than R. Note, however, that according to the theory, choice in this situation involves much more of a knife edge than in the case of positive payoffs. That is, when bad prospects are at stake, there is no mixing of certain with uncertain alternatives when the prospects have different expected values. Rather, choice is allocated exclusively to one of the alternatives, with the allocation dependent on which alternative lies on the indifference curve closest to the origin.

If our argument regarding risk loving over losses is to be strengthened, it should have some generality; that is, it should be applicable to aversive payoffs other than delay to reinforcement. To test this hypothesis, we have conducted an experiment looking at rats' choices between variable versus certain numbers of shock (Kagel et al., 1988). In each case, the rat chose between a certain number of shocks and an uncertain number with equal expected value. Water reinforcement (for thirsty rats), prior to delivery of the shock, was used to sustain responding, with the amount of water delivered independent of the lever chosen or the number of shocks to be received.

Table 6.7 shows the percentage of free-choice trials allocated to the certain alternative in this experiment. In 27 of 32 cases, the certain alternative was chosen *less* than 50% of the time (averaged across side switches), so that the majority of responses were directed toward the lever delivering variable shock. The probability that this would happen by chance alone is less than .001, assuming an equally likely chance of responding to either the variable or the certain alternative. Furthermore, averaging across subjects, for all four experimental treatment conditions, we find the certain alternative was chosen less than 50% of the time, with a null hypothesis of indifference rejected at the 5% significance level under each condition. Thus, the results in Table 6.7 confirm the robustness of risk loving in the face of losses beyond that of the time delay variable already studied.[25]

Choice frequencies reported in Table 6.7 generally lie in the interval between .40 and .60, which is less than one would anticipate under a discrete-trials choice procedure and is suggestive of rather weak preferences between the alternatives. Two explanations for these weak preferences immediately suggest

Table 6.7. *Choice between certain and uncertain shock with equal expected value: percentage choice of certain alternative*

Subject	8 shocks, $p = 1.0$ vs. 1 shock, $p = .50$ 15 shocks, $p = .50$	8 shocks, $p = 1.0$ vs. 1 shock, $p = .75$ 29 shocks, $p = .25$	4 shocks, $p = 1.0$ vs. 1 shock, $p = .50$ 7 shocks, $p = .50$	16 shocks, $p = 1.0$ vs. 1 shock, $p = .50$ 31 shocks, $p = .50$
501	37.5 $(3.48)^a$	42.4 $(3.04)^b$	46.9 (2.24)	47.4 (2.14)
502	36.9 $(3.02)^b$	42.6 $(3.26)^b$	49.6 (0.14)	47.1 (0.88)
503	43.8 $(3.24)^b$	45.0 $(2.90)^b$	46.3 (2.00)	46.9 (2.24)
504	44.4 $(3.08)^b$	43.8 $(4.72)^a$	48.1 (0.80)	49.4 (0.62)
511	46.8 (1.90)	50.0 (0.00)	51.9 (0.44)	51.9 (0.68)
512	41.3 $(3.24)^b$	43.0 $(3.06)^b$	44.2 (1.82)	43.5 (2.12)
513	50.0 (0.00)	47.5 (1.46)	46.0 (1.90)	44.4 (2.08)
514	52.5 (1.02)	46.9 (1.42)	47.5 (0.92)	48.7 (0.50)
Average[c]	44.2^b (1.96)	45.2^a (0.97)	47.6^b (0.83)	47.4^b (0.95)

Note: 1.0 ma shocks of 5-sec. duration; absolute value of t-statistic in parentheses.
[a]Significantly different from 50.0 at the 1% level, two-tailed t-test.
[b]Significantly different from 50.0 at the 5% level, two-tailed t-test.
[c]Standard error of mean in parentheses.

themselves: (1) rats may simply be relatively insensitive to variability in numbers of shock. After all, it is hard to imagine how evolutionary processes would prepare rats to be sensitive to such variability, or (2) the fact that shock was delivered 5 sec following water reinforcement undoubtedly reduces the overall aversiveness of the shock, and thus the differences between the alternatives (Deluty, 1978). This second explanation is consistent with the well-established fact that rats have rather sharp temporal discount rates (see Chapter 7). Nevertheless, the lack of extreme choice frequencies reported should not obscure the fact that the results in Table 6.7 show a clear preference for variable over constant shock levels with equal means.

6.5a Relationship to human's risk loving in the face of losses

One of the most striking differences between prospect theory (Kahneman and Tversky, 1979; Tversky and Kahneman, 1992) and EU theory, as generally applied in economics, is that prospect theory predicts risk loving in the face of losses whereas EU theory predicts risk aversion whether faced with gains or losses. The principle reason for the difference in predictions is that within prospect theory, outcomes are typically evaluated in terms of *changes* in income/asset positions, whereas in most applications of EU theory, the decision maker is viewed as basing her choice on anticipated *final* asset position. The latter assumption naturally translates losses into gains. For example, suppose you are choosing between a 50-50 chance of losing $25 or losing $0 versus a certain loss of $12.50. For these monetary losses to be meaningful, there must be some income/asset base from which they can be deducted. Suppose there is an asset base of $100 from which losses can be deducted. In terms of final asset positions, the choices involve a 50-50 chance of ending up with $75 ($100 less the $25 loss) or $100 ($100 less the $0 outcome) versus a certainty of having $87.50 ($100 less the certain $12.50 loss). Consequently, given convex indifference curves, if decisions are framed in terms of one's final asset position (one of relative gains), decision makers will act as if they are risk averse, and will choose the certain $87.50. On this, both prospect theory and EU theory agree. However, if there is no asset integration, and choices are framed in terms of *changes* in income or asset positions, then the choice variable is cast in terms of losses, where less is better, so that risk loving will result: preference for the 50-50 chance of $25 or $0. On this point, prospect theory and EU theory clearly diverge, since in most applications, economists would argue that asset integration is the most rational framework to adopt.[26]

Animal experiments provide support for the psychophysical valuation principle assumed to underlie risk loving in the face of losses, namely, diminishing marginal rates of substitution over outcomes in the loss space (see Kahneman and Tversky, 1983). With respect to the fundamental question of whether to define the utility function by *changes* in income/asset positions or the *final* (integrated) income/asset position, studies with nonhuman animals have yet to provide a resolution, since it is not clear how to establish contingencies that would permit animals to perform the translation (of losses into gains) needed to answer the question – hence, the interest in recent experimental results that show that even though humans may be more risk loving when faced with hypothetical rather than real losses, they are still generally risk loving when choosing over real losses. This risk loving with real losses indicates a general absence of asset integration (Camerer, 1989; Battalio et al., 1990). Finally, our results support Kahneman and Tversky's (1983) assertion that risk loving is likely to be found in contexts such as those involving safety, health, and quality of life. Within such contexts, outcomes are naturally framed in terms of losses and no norms are available, such as final asset position, onto which outcomes can be mapped. It is clear, then, that it is important to account for and identify naturally adopted decision frameworks if we are to understand choice under uncertainty.

6.6   Search and information acquisition in stochastic environments

In considering choices among uncertain outcomes, we have been concerned primarily with decisions in which the individual has full information concerning the set of possible terminal outcomes. For situations in which the decision maker is not fully informed, questions arise concerning search and information acquisition. A limited experimental literature, primarily originating with biologists, has begun to focus on economic issues of information acquisition and search behavior in animals. We briefly review elements of this literature in this section.

Optimization of food intake requires that the animal exploit, or allocate most of its choices to, the dominant alternative, but the animal must first discover which alternative dominates. Krebs, Kacelnik, and Taylor (1978) investigated choices between two alternatives, one of which stochastically dominated the other, when there was no prior information (via a forced-choice trial sequence) concerning which alternative was dominant. In this probability-learning experiment, birds chose between two "patches" with differing probabilities of payoff. Krebs et al. questioned whether sampling of a patch would be affected by the difference in reward probabilities between the patches. (With larger differences, less sampling is required to make an efficient exploitation decision.) A sampling was defined as the number of trials the bird took prior to devoting 90% of a sequence of 100 choice trials to the dominant alternative.

Krebs et al. found that with larger probability differences birds reliably sampled less: With a .30 versus a .20 probability of payoff on the two alternatives (a difference of .10), it took an average of just over 40 trials before the birds settled down to exploiting the dominant alternative; with a .35 versus a .15 probability of payoff (a difference of .20), the number of sampling trials dropped to a little over 20, and this pattern continued for all probability differences studied. Data from old probability-learning experiments conducted without forced-choice trials or correction procedures show similar results: with larger differences in reward probabilities, there were fewer trials prior to absorption on the dominant alternative (see, for example, North and McDonald, 1959). Data from concurrent VR–VR schedules, which are typically conducted with no forced choice trials, support this result as well: the larger the differences in VR requirements, the closer responses are to being allocated exclusively to the richer schedule (recall Section 2.5c).

The decision to sample versus exploit also depends on the number of choice trials available: If an animal is permitted fewer choice trials, then it should decide to exploit earlier since, other things being equal, there is less value to acquiring additional information. To study this question, Kacelnik (1979) (as reported in Houston, Kacelnik and McNamara, 1982) repeated the Krebs et al. experiment at each of two probability differences (.20 and .30), after birds had adapted to one of two session lengths (50 versus 250 trials per session) for a week. Measuring commitment as the proportion of the first 50 trials in the dominant patch, Kacelnik (1979) observed a substantially higher level of commitment for birds in the shorter sessions.

Psychologists reliably find that if animals are always rewarded for making a response (known as "continuous reinforcement"), they more quickly cease responding during extinction (when reinforcement is no longer provided) than when they have been rewarded less than 100% of the time ("partial reinforcement"). This is known as the partial reinforcement extinction effect (PRE) (for a review of this literature, see Mackintosh, 1974). McNamara and Houston (1980) formally model this effect in terms of optimal search under uncertainty. The essence of their argument is that animals are use to foraging in environments where patches of food can suddenly become depleted. Consequently, the higher the probability of reinforcement the animal was enjoying, the more likely it is that a run of no reinforcement means there is no food left. The exact form of the stopping rule the animal employs depends on many details, but the general conclusion of the optimal search hypothesis is that it is optimal to give up sooner, the higher the probability of reinforcement. A simple discrimination hypothesis of the PRE would argue that when reward probabilities are low, it is simply harder to know when extinction has occurred than when higher probabilities are in effect (Mowrer and Jones, 1945). In optimal search theory, the stopping rule depends on factors such as the size of the rewards involved (larger rewards imply greater persistence), the work involved in obtaining the rewards (the less work, the greater the persistence), and so on. These factors have no role to play in a pure discrimination hypothesis. In other words, in a search model, the costs and benefits of different actions are considered, in addition to the problem of simply discriminating whether an extinction schedule is in effect. No one, to our knowledge, has tried to test between these two different explanations, although alternative theories of the PRE effect have been proposed (for a discussion of the various theories, see Domjan, 1993).

It is even possible to investigate the descriptive validity of Bayes's theorem with animals. For example, Lima (1985) investigated the search behavior of birds over a set of patches that were all similar in external appearance but that, according to a random assignment rule, contained either zero or a fixed number of prey, and the prey, when present, were distributed randomly within a patch. In one particularly interesting manipulation, Lima (1985) changed the relative frequency of empty patches from 50% to 76.7% for one bird. He reports a reduced frequency of search in the empty patches. This somewhat counterintuitive result may reflect the fact that with a higher prior distribution of probabilities of finding food, failure to obtain food in the initial exploration of a patch provides a more reliable indicator of no food. This can be seen through the application of Bayes's theorem

$$P[F/S_0] = \frac{P[F]P[S_0/F]}{P[F]P[S_0/F] + P[NF]P[S_0/NF]} \tag{6.9}$$

where $P[F/S_0]$ is the probability of food being in the patch conditional on the initial exploration of the patch producing no food, $P[S_0/F]$ and $P[S_0/NF]$ is the probability that the initial exploration of the patch will produce no food conditional, respectively, on food being present or not present, and $P[F]$ and $P[NF]$ are the prior probabilities of food or no food being present in the patch. In the Lima (1985) experiment, $P[S_0/F]$ and $P[S_0/NF]$ were fixed at .625 and 1.0, while $P[F]$ was changed from .50 to .233 ($P[NF] = 1 - P[F]$). Evaluating (6.9) under the changing value of $P[F]$ shows that $P[F/S_0]$ is less than half as likely (.16 versus .385) with 76.7% of the patches empty than with 50% of the patches empty. Hence, the failure to find food in the initial exploration of a patch is a less reliable indicator of the absence of food with the more diffuse priors (50% of the patches containing food) and calls for more sampling within a given patch.

Although Bayes's rule provides a sophisticated explanation for the bird's choices, here, too, the data might be explained by the simpler discrimination hypothesis. According to this argument, as the probability of patches not containing food increases, those patches that contain food become easier to identify. In other words, discrimination of a stimulus depends on stimulus intensity in relation to background information, so that as fewer patches contain food, those that have food become easier to identify. Bayes's law assumes the ability to discriminate between alternatives but goes well beyond this, providing clear quantitative predictions as well. Thus, in this case, too, it is necessary to sort out between the decision theoretic explanation and the simpler discrimination hypothesis.

Experimental manipulations investigating Bayes's law, in addition to studies that vary the costs and benefits of search, can contribute to a better understanding of the economics of search and information acquisition. We look forward to continuing research developments in this area.

Notes

1 For example, Siegel (1961) found that probability matching (Section 3.2b), which is at odds with choice on the basis of first-degree stochastic dominance, was highly dependent on financial payoffs, and Ebbesen and Konecni (1975) could not predict the bail set by judges in a courtroom from their choices in hypothetical bail-setting problems in a laboratory situation. The literature is far from completely one-sided, however (see Bem and Allen, 1974; Camerer, in press; Grether and Plott, 1979), and indicates that propositions should be tested with real payoffs wherever possible.

2 For example, even prospect theory (Kahneman and Tversky, 1979), while permitting indirect violations of dominance in comparisons among triples of prospects, rules out direct violations under pairwise comparisons.

3 The failure to observe exclusive choice in situations such as this (as the theory predicts) gave rise to a literature on stochastic choice theories. See Luce and Suppes (1965) for a review of the literature up to this point. Also, see the interesting paper by Machina (1985), who offers a distinctly different interpretation of the basis for stochastic choices.

4 More formally, following Rothschild and Stiglitz (1970), between any pair of prospects, L and M, with the same means and with cumulative distributions, $L(x_i)$ and $M(x_i)$, if L is larger than M in the sense that

$$\sum_{i=1}^{r} L(x_i)(x_{i+1} - x_i) \leq \sum_{i=1}^{r} M(x_i)(x_{i+1} - x_i) \quad r = 1, 2, \ldots, n - 1$$
$$x_1 < \ldots < x_n$$

with strict inequality holding for at least one r, then L is said to be less risky than M. In contrast, prospects of equal expected value cannot be ranked on the basis of first-degree stochastic dominance.

5 Details of the experimental procedures can be found in Battalio, Kagel, and MacDonald (1985). One procedural detail is worth emphasizing, however. During the forced-choice trials designed to familiarize the rats with the payoffs, the random number generator controlling outcomes was programmed so that the average outcome over the entire forced-choice trial set equalled the expected outcome (although which payoff would start the forced-choice trials was varied randomly across days). In contrast, during the free-choice trials, the random number generator was allowed free rein, so that outcomes on any given trial were independent of outcomes on other trials.

6 The fact that $C > D$ or $C \approx D$ (where $\approx$ represents indifference) for 211 does not imply a violation of weak stochastic transitivity as long as risk aversion holds for the remaining pairwise comparisons for this subject. The weak stochastic transitivity prediction tested here is considerably weaker than the tests of functional equivalence reported in Navarick and Fantino (1972, 1974) (see Section 2.6).

7 Tests of strong stochastic transitivity reported in Battalio et al. (1985) also suggested the rats might prefer a moderate, controlled amount of uncertainty.

8 See MacDonald et al. (1991) for tests of the betweenness axiom of expected utility theory, reported in brief at the end of Section 6.4b. These tests indicate a preference for a linear combination of two prospects over either of the pure prospects, which is consistent with a taste for a moderate, controlled amount of risk (Coombs and Huang, 1976).

9 Caraco and his associates measured changes in risk preferences using both a certainty equivalent measure of risk preference (identifying the certain alternative that the subject is just indifferent to relative to an uncertain alternative) and the relative frequency of choice measure employed here. They reach similar conclusions using either of the two measures (compare Caraco et al., 1980, with Caraco, 1982). The frequency of choice measure is substantially less time-consuming to employ.

10 Discrepancies between weights and weight changes between periods result from intervening experimental treatment conditions.

11 For example, suppose the bird was choosing between a certain outcome of 2 millet seeds versus a 50-50 chance of 0 or 4 millet seeds under both nutritional deficit and surplus (to use one of the prospects employed in Caraco et al., 1980). With surpluses, the time between trials was 30 sec for each seed eaten during the previous trial, whereas

under deficits, it was 1 minute for each seed eaten in the previous trial. Variance in time delay to the start of the next trial for the risky choice alternative, $\Sigma_i(t_i - \bar{t})^2/n$, is 1 under the surplus conditions (where time delay is measured in minutes and $\bar{t}$ is the mean time delay), and is 4 under the deficit conditions.

12 Wunderle, Castro, and Fetcher (1987) failed to find risk loving under negative energy budgets for small birds that live in the tropics. They suggest several possible explanations for their results. One is that birds that have evolved in tropical climates, as their species had, are rarely subject to energy shortages since they can readily switch food types. In contrast, the small birds that Caraco and his associates studied, having evolved in northern climates, are frequently energy-stressed on a daily basis during harsh winters.

13 The second derivative of the valuation function $u(x_i)$ measures the degree of concavity (or convexity) of the utility function, but by itself is not invariant under linear transformations of $u(x_i)$. Under the expected utility hypothesis, utility measures are unique up to a linear transformation. Equation (6.4) in the text provides a unique measure of concavity (or convexity).

14 It is not clear what matching predicts here, although its motivational basis, melioration theory, argues that individuals choose on the basis of the average local rate of reinforcement. This would seem to imply that in choosing between equal expected value alternatives, the riskiness of the prospects will not systematically affect choice. As we have seen, this is clearly not correct.

15 This implication was recognized early on in the economics literature, leading Arrow (1974) to reject the quadratic utility function on account of evidence that favored decreasing absolute risk aversion. The primary fact underlying Arrow's observation was that people with more assets hold portfolios with a greater proportion of risky assets.

16 Hastjarjo, Silberberg, and Hursh (1990) report the effects of income on risk preferences. Unfortunately, they permitted both income level and variability in payoffs to covary in both of the experiments reported, so that pure income effects cannot be identified. They also suggest that one of the reasons Battalio et al. (1985) and Kagel et al. (1986) failed to find more sensitive risk preferences was that there were enough choices each day to ensure that aggregate reinforcement obtained from the risky alternative closely approximated its expected value. However, our experiments gave the random number generator free reign during the free-choice trials, and in Battalio et al. we employed 17 free-choice trials, compared with the 40 or more free-choice trials that Hastjarjo et al. employed.

17 However, preferences cannot be too strong here either; otherwise, there would be little opportunity to reverse them as λ is reduced, particularly since it is not possible to use very low probability outcomes, the difference between which are salient to rats.

18 Here, too, the similarity of results with time-delayed choices argues against accounting for the results in terms of portfolio effects since risk lovers do not diversify choices (see Section 6.5). Also see the results from series 2 in MacDonald et al. (1991), where for each pair of prospects, one member of the pair was a mean-preserving spread of the other, in which case the predictions of EU theory are the same, irrespective of the time frame the animal may be employing.

19 These three violations consist of (1) the common consequence effect, the most famous specific example of which is the so-called Allais Paradox, (2) oversensitivity to changes in low-probability, outlying events, and (3) the utility evaluation effect (see Machina, 1982, 1987).

20 This is not the same as arguing for increasing absolute risk aversion in terms of the Arrow–Pratt measure, in that the latter deals with changing risk preferences given non-stochastic (certain) changes in income/asset levels, whereas the present analysis deals

with stochastic differences in income/asset levels. See Nielson (1989) for clarification of this point.

21 This section relies heavily on the survey by Machina (1987), which is strongly recommended to interested readers.

22 Prospect Y does not stochastically dominate B because it has lower probability (1/2 versus 3/4) associated with the best outcome, 13 cups (recall Section 6.1). In contrast, going from prospect B′ to Y some of the probability associated with the 1-cup (worst) outcome is added to the 8-cup (a better) outcome, thereby satisfying the requirements of stochastic dominance.

23 One of our readers points out that unpredictability with respect to delay of payoffs does not carry the same consequences as unpredictability with respect to food payoffs, so that the term "risk loving" might not be appropriate here. While the distinction in terms of consequences for the animal is well taken, we will argue that the basis for preference for variability with negative payoffs is closely related to the preference for lack of variability with positive payoffs. We therefore follow the common practice of referring to preference for variability as risk loving.

24 The introduction of minimum needs or bliss points into the analysis alters these predictions. For example, Staddon and Reid (1987) show that a quadratic utility function (a leading member of the class of minimum-distance hypotheses) predicts a switch from risk loving to risk aversion with respect to time delay variability at high reinforcement rates (close to the bliss point). The truncation of the choice space resulting from the set point is responsible for the predicted change in risk preferences. This interesting prediction has yet to be verified.

25 A second phase of this experiment involved reducing the number of certain shocks while keeping the number and variability on the uncertain shock alternative unchanged. These manipulations produced reliable increases in the frequency with which the certain alternative was chosen. This result demonstrates that subjects were sensitive to the shock contingencies and suggests that one could produce preference for the certain alternative, provided the number of certain shocks was low enough.

26 Resolution of this issue is equally important for the growing number of non-EU formulations offered in the literature. For example, Machina (1982) explicitly assumes that the underlying argument of the utility function is the final asset position.

7

Intertemporal choice

Except in Section 6.5, we have not said much about how differences in the time to the arrival of commodities affect choice. This chapter considers (a) the relationship between commodities having different arrival times, and (b) the role of time discounting on choice. Experimental psychologists have done intensive research on choice between temporally differentiated commodities. In particular, they have considered choices between smaller, more immediate rewards and larger, more delayed alternatives. Much of this research has focused on the nature of the time discount function, with particular attention to those factors that promote impulsiveness versus an enhanced ability to delay gratification.

Section 7.1 presents some of the elementary economic concepts of intertemporal choice. We compare the "standard" choice model employed in the economics literature with predictions drawn from reinforcement theory in psychology. Experimental procedures employed in measuring time discount rates are discussed in Section 7.2, along with the results of a number of experiments reported in the psychology literature. These experiments show that rats and pigeons effectively employ rudimentary present discounted value calculations in deciding between alternatives. However, they also display dynamic inconsistencies, contrary to the economist's standard intertemporal choice formulation. With short delays between choice and outcomes, smaller, more immediate rewards are often preferred to larger, more delayed alternatives. However, with longer delays between choice and outcomes, the larger, more delayed alternative is preferred. We discuss the implications of time discounting for optimal foraging theory and its potential adaptive significance, along with some of the economic implications of rejecting the standard intertemporal choice formulation.

In Section 7.3, we report a new experiment concerned with the effects of differences in consumption levels (or wealth) on time discounting. We test the common conjecture in economics that as wealth increases, the preference for present over future rewards becomes less intense. Somewhat surprisingly, we find just the opposite. We consider these results in light of others reported in the literature, along with their implications for the "cycle-of-poverty" hypothesis.

Section 7.4 extends the analysis to multiperiod models of consumer choice. Of particular concern here are the conditions under which the single-period, static, choice representations developed in Chapters 2 through 5 remain unaffected when time discounting is taken into account. Section 7.5 discusses the role of time discounting for several experimental procedures discussed in Chapter 5. We review an experiment demonstrating that there are important intertemporal substitution effects in variable interval (VI) schedules (Silberberg, Warren-Boulton, and Asano, 1988). These intertemporal substitution effects help to explain the failure to maximize total food intake under concurrent VI–VR schedules. We also discuss an experiment in which time discounting influenced behavior under progressive ratio schedules (Mazur and Vaughan, 1987). Section 7.6 applies time-discounting concepts to human behavior in token economies. We show how differences in intertemporal substitution possibilities affect saving behavior in token economies. In addition, we demonstrate that in self-administered drug studies, the characteristic patterns of drug consumption reported in the literature, which have been attributed to the drugs, result instead from temporal substitution effects that are dictated by the experimental designs that have been used.

7.1 Intertemporal choice theory: Basic economic concepts and their relationship to reinforcement theory

The focus of attention in intertemporal choice problems is the consumption of commodities at different points in time. Let $x^t = (x_1^t, x_2^t, \ldots, x_n^t)$ be a vector of commodities consumed in period t, where x_i^t denotes the amount of commodity i consumed in period t (one of the commodities here may include leisure). Assume that the consumer's planning horizon extends over s periods, so that plans are made for each of s successive periods. Then in time period 1, the consumer is viewed as maximizing a utility function with the usual properties

$$U = U(x^1, x^2, \ldots, x^s) \tag{7.1}$$

where diminishing marginal rates of substitution (convex indifference curves) hold with respect to vectors of commodities consumed in different time periods.

Figure 7.1 represents choice alternatives for the two-period case. The 45° line shows the set of commodity bundles with equal consumption in each of the two time periods. Time preferences are defined in terms of the slope of the indifference curve where it crosses the 45° line. If the slope of the indifference curve is equal to one in absolute value, then the consumer has no time bias: It takes one unit of future consumption (x^{t+n}) to compensate for the loss of one unit of

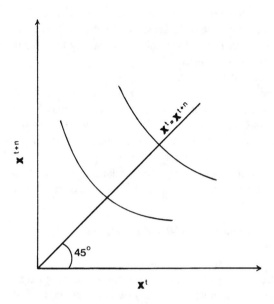

Figure 7.1 Choice between present (x^t) and future (x^{t+n}) consumption. Time bias is defined in terms of the slope of the indifference curve where it crosses the 45° line. Time bias may vary across indifference curves as the level of total consumption varies (i.e., movement along the 45° line).

current consumption (x^t). If the slope of the indifference curve is less than one in absolute value, then there is a positive time bias (impatience or impulsiveness): It takes more than one unit of future consumption to compensate for the loss of one unit of current consumption. Finally, if the slope of the indifference curve is greater than one in absolute value, then there is a negative time bias (miserliness): It takes less than one unit of future consumption to compensate for the loss of one unit of current consumption.

Note that the convexity of the indifference curves places no restriction on the nature of the time bias. That is to say, convexity does not determine whether the time bias is positive, negative, or zero. Convexity (diminishing marginal rate of substitution between consumption in different time periods) only requires that the slope of the indifference curve be negative. However, with a few notable exceptions, most economists take a positive time bias, or impulsiveness, for granted, on the basis of intuitive judgments about how individuals behave or on indirect arguments concerning the existence of positive market interest rates and uncertainty. Reinforcement theory in psychology actually predicts a positive time bias, since the principle of immediacy of reinforcement holds that, other things being equal, more immediate reinforcers are more effective than otherwise identical delayed reinforcers. Further, it is commonly conjectured, within the economics literature at least, that the time bias diminishes as one moves out along the 45° line. Consequently, at higher wealth levels there is *proportionately* more saving and more ability to defer immediate gratification, other things being equal.

The utility function, equation (7.1), permits future preferences between commodities to depend on the history of past consumption. Individuals with identical preferences but different consumption histories may behave differently. Further, the convexity of the indifference curves implies that present and future consumption are substitutable. Even with a positive time bias, one can always find a sufficiently large payoff, $x^{t+n} > x^t$, for which the decision maker is willing to "wait it out," opting for the larger, more delayed payoff. On this point, both reinforcement theory and consumer-demand theory are in complete agreement.

7.1a The standard economic model and its relationship to the matching law

Conventional assumptions within the economics literature are that the utility function is strongly separable over time (that is, the marginal rate of substitution between consumption vectors in any two time periods is independent of consumption levels in other time periods), and that the value of consumption differs between dates by a constant time bias parameter, ρ. This yields the following function:

$$U = \sum_{t=\tau}^{T} \frac{U(x^t)}{(1 + \rho)^{t-\tau}} \tag{7.2}$$

where $T - \tau$ is the decision maker's time horizon and τ is the point at which decisions are made.[1]

Equation (7.2) implies that choices are temporally consistent in the sense that choice is independent of the time, τ, at which it is made. In other words, if x_t (the smaller, immediate reward) is preferred to x^{t+n} (the larger, delayed reward) at time τ, it will also be preferred at all other times, $\tau + k$. This implied temporal consistency in choices has aroused much skepticism, beginning with Böhm-Bawerk (1923) and as emphasized by Strotz (1956).[2]

Reinforcement theory as such makes no predictions concerning temporal consistency. However, its offshoot, the matching law, predicts that preference reversals will occur as a function of the time interval between choice and receipt of reinforcement. Given alternatives x^t and x^{t+n}, the simple matching law holds that choice is based on the ratio of their consumption values times the inverse of their delay ratio:

$$\frac{x^t/(t - \tau)}{x^{t+n}/(t + n - \tau)} = \left(\frac{x^t}{x^{t+n}}\right)\left(\frac{t + n - \tau}{t - \tau}\right) \tag{7.3}$$

where $(t - \tau)$ is the time delay between the choice point, τ, and the time at which consumption takes place, t (Baum and Rachlin, 1969; Rachlin and Green, 1972). When $[x^t/(t - \tau)]/[x^{t+n}/(t + n - \tau)] > 1, x^t$ is chosen in favor of x^{t+n}.[3] However, for given values of x^t and x^{t+n}, if the time delay to both rewards is increased, there comes a point when $[x^t/(t - \tau)/[x^{t+n}/(t + n - \tau)] < 1$, and x^{t+n} would then be chosen in favor of x^t.

The matching law's prediction can be derived as a special case of discounting with a variable time bias

$$U = \sum_{t=\tau}^{T} \theta(t - \tau)U(x^t) \tag{7.4}$$

The discounted value formulation in (7.4) differs from equation (7.2) in that the exponential rate of time discounting in the standard model is replaced with a general time bias factor $\theta(t - \tau)$. When $\theta(t - \tau) = (t - \tau)^{-1}$, $\theta(t + n - \tau) = (t + n - \tau)^{-1}$, $U(x^t) = x^t$, $U(x^{t+n}) = x^{t+n}$, and consumption occurs at only one point within the relevant time horizon, equation (7.4) then yields the matching law's predictions. We refer to equation (7.4) as the variable time-bias specification because it permits the time bias to vary systematically within $t - \tau$.

7.2 Reward size, delay, and choice

In this section, we describe several laboratory studies demonstrating that time delays exert a strong influence on choice and that the temporal consistency requirements of the standard economic model are commonly violated. We begin with a detailed analysis of an experiment providing a clear demonstration of intertemporal inconsistencies (Green et al., 1981). This experiment also serves to characterize procedures employed in other experiments of this sort.

7.2a Experimental procedures

A discrete-trials choice procedure was used. Each trial consisted of a 30-sec choice period during which time the pigeon was presented with a choice between two differently illuminated response keys followed by a 10-sec outcome period. The pigeons chose between the two keys, one of which led to a small reward, x^t (2 seconds of access to a grain hopper), available at the start of the outcome period, the other of which led to a larger payoff, x^{t+n} (6 seconds of access to grain), available 4 sec later than x^t. The outcome period lasted 10 sec irrespective of the choice made, so that choosing the smaller more immediate reward did not result in any earlier start of the next choice trial. To determine consistency of intertemporal choices, the time within the 30-sec choice period when choices between the two keys were made available, τ, varied across conditions so that the time delay between choice and the outcome period $(t - \tau)$ ranged from 2 to 28 seconds.

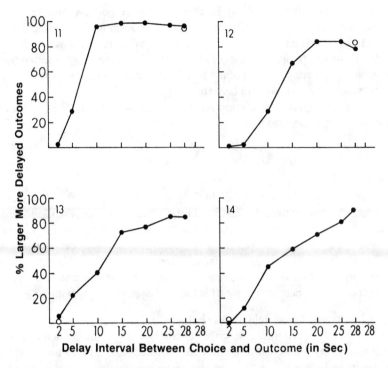

Figure 7.2 Effects of varying the time delay between choice and the outcome period on the frequency of choosing the larger, more delayed outcome. Each panel presents results from an individual pigeon. From Green et al. (1981).

There were several forced-choice trials at the beginning of each experimental session, followed by 50 free-choice trials. During the forced-choice trials, only one of the keys was illuminated and operative. These trials ensured that the pigeon experienced the consequences of responding to each key. Experimental conditions were maintained for a minimum of 15 days and were changed only when the distribution of free choices had stabilized. Pigeons were maintained at 80% of their free-feeding weights in order to ensure constancy of pretrial deprivation conditions.

7.2b Experimental results and discussion

Figure 7.2 shows the percentage of larger, more delayed outcomes chosen as a function of the delay between choice and the start of the outcome period, $t - \tau$. Values reported are means over the last five days of each experimental condition. Open circles represent a replication of each bird's initial experimental condition.

When choices became available close to the outcome period ($t - \tau < 5$), each bird strongly favored the smaller, more immediate outcome, x^t. The nearly exclusive preference for alternative x^t means that the pigeons failed to maximize total food intake. Some psychologists have (mistakenly) taken such results to be evidence against the maximization theory as currently employed in economics (Mazur, 1981).[4] Many psychologists (for example, Ainslie, 1975, 1992) have characterized this behavior as a "self-control problem," the implication being that the animals simply do not have the ability to act in their own best interest. However, although we might be surprised at the pigeons' relatively large positive time bias, or be appalled at their short time horizons, it is important to recognize that their failure to maximize food intake is perfectly consistent with economic theory.

As the delay between choice and the outcome period increased, however, choices reversed, with every bird now coming to choose the larger, more delayed outcome on more than 80% of the trials. With longer time delays, the pigeons maximized total food intake. Pigeons tend to "overvalue" more proximate satisfactions in relation to more distant ones, which Strotz (1956) and others have suggested is the "natural" state of affairs for humans. These preference reversals are, of course, incompatible with the standard economic representation, equation (7.2), although they do not contradict the more general representation in equation (7.1).[5] The reversals in preference are more in keeping with predictions of the matching law and the variable time-bias specification of equation (7.4).[6]

As in the experiments reported in Chapter 6, the pigeons fail to display exclusive preference at a number of points in Figure 7.2. Both the matching law (equation (7.3)) and variable time-bias specification (equation (7.4)) fail to account for nonexclusive preferences; to do so would require a generalization of these models in terms of probabilistic choice concepts (recall the discussion of this point in Section 6.1b). A within-session analysis of the pigeons' choices showed that x^{t+n} was chosen at nearly the same rate throughout a session. This rules out income effects, or changes in deprivation level within the experimental session, as factors responsible for the nonexclusive choice.

As already noted, the results of this experiment do not stand in isolation. Ainslie (1974), Ainslie and Herrnstein (1981), and Rachlin and Green (1972) report similar results with pigeons choosing between food rewards. The experiments reported in Section 7.3 show similar results for rats. Further, Deluty (1978) found preference reversals by rats when they chose between brief immediate shocks versus longer, delayed shocks; with short delays, rats preferred the longer but more delayed shock, only to switch their choices as the time delay between choice and the shock period increased. Reversals of this sort are to be expected since with shock, the variables x^t and x^{t+n} in equations (7.3) and 7.4) take on negative values.

In addition, research by Fantino (1966) indicates that pigeons' choices are responsive to changes in the magnitude of the payoffs, x^t and x^{t+n}, in ways that equations (7.3) and (7.4) predict (Section 7.3 reports similar results for rats).

Fantino (1966) also showed that pigeons were somewhat sensitive to postreinforcement delays when these delays were long. That is, while pigeons heavily discount future outcomes and/or have a limited time horizon, preferences can be affected by outcomes subsequent to the first reinforcement, although the effects of these later outcomes are typically not very strong (Logue, Smith, and Rachlin, 1985; Shull, Spear, and Bryson, 1981).

7.2c Implications of rejecting the standard economic model

Rejection of the standard economic model, equation (7.2), in favor of equation (7.4), has several implications for our understanding of intertemporal choice behavior. A major implication relates to the issue of consistent planning. With an intertemporal value function like that of equation (7.4), a decision maker who has complete flexibility of choice and the opportunity to revise his decisions may, upon reconsideration, come to reject a previously chosen plan. In interactive settings involving other economic agents, revision of prior commitments is typically constrained by legally binding contracts, positive transactions costs, or the possibility of a continuing series of interactions between agents. The implication that rejection of the standard model has for these situations is that one need not attribute failures of commitment only to opportunism; preference reversal after sufficient delay and time to reconsider also serves as motivation for the change in behavior.

When consistency is maintained over time, the individual is commonly characterized as exhibiting "self-control." Numerous mechanisms for achieving self-control have been proposed in the literature (Ainslie, 1975, 1992; Elster, 1979; Strotz, 1956; Logue, 1988; Thaler and Shefrin, 1981). Two such mechanisms crop up most commonly. The first is to precommit one's behavior by choosing options that make a future activity unavailable, or that increase dramatically the costs associated with alternative actions. An example would be the voluntary decision by some professors to have their nine-month salary paid in twelve installments, in order to better regulate spending in the absence of summer income. Another example, popular with large numbers of people, is to overwithhold on their income taxes as a device for saving income. The second mechanism is the learning of self-control from parental and social influences. Such learning might result either in direct modification of the discount function and/or in learning to employ both overt and covert commitment strategies when appropriate.

There is evidence that pigeons and rats can exercise "self-control" with the aid of these two mechanisms. For example, for choices between small immediate (x^t) and larger delayed (x^{t+n}) rewards, Rachlin and Green (1972) gave pigeons the opportunity to precommit in favor of x^{t+n}, or to retain flexibility by having a chance to reconsider shortly before the outcome period. When the opportunity to precommit was offered well in advance of the rewards, the pigeons preferred the larger more delayed outcome, and they chose the commitment alternative (thus ensuring receipt of the larger reward). Forced-choice trials showed that with the same delay to reinforcement, but with the commitment alternative not available, the pigeons invariably chose the small, immediate reward when required to choose again between x^t and x^{t+n} shortly before the outcome period. In other words, choice of the commitment strategy helped to enforce intertemporal consistency when the pigeons preferred the larger, more delayed alternative. This is not to say that the pigeons could have devised such a self-control strategy, but they did utilize it when it was available to help them achieve the preferred outcome.

Choosing a commitment strategy involves a cost in terms of loss of flexibility in future choices. That the pigeons chose to limit their choices is all the more striking in that they prefer choice to no choice under other circumstances. For example, if given a choice between two alternative situations, m_1 and m'_1, in which m_1 has several identical outcomes, any one of which (and only one of which) can be obtained, and m'_1 has only one of these identical outcomes, pigeons prefer the multiple-outcome alternative (Catania, 1980).

Other research shows that pigeons can be "taught" self-control. That is, with appropriate training, pigeons came to choose large, delayed outcomes in favor of small, immediate ones at short-delay intervals significantly more often than an untrained control group (Mazur and Logue, 1978). However, there was considerable variability in the effectiveness of these training methods across individual subjects.

7.2d Implications of positive discounting for optimal foraging: Constraint or adaptation?

Most optimal foraging models take long-run average rate of energy gain as the proximate currency of fitness since it correlates strongly with the organism's Darwinian fitness (Gilliam, Green, and Pearson, 1982; Turelli, Gillespie, and Schoener, 1982). As a currency of fitness, the long-run average rate of energy gain makes no distinction between the energy gained from present versus future rewards. In this context, some researchers have treated preference for smaller, more immediate rewards over larger, more delayed rewards as an impulsive constraint on foraging efficiency (e.g., Ainslie, 1975; Snyderman, 1983a). However, it is not clear to us that this is the only interpretation.

The rate of time discounting that animals exhibit in the laboratory presumably has evolved in response to selection pressures faced in nature. For species living in a competitive environment with no property rights, there is an inherent uncertainty associated with obtaining delayed outcomes. This, alone, is sufficient to generate positive time discounting. Alternatively, it is easy enough to show that uncertainty about living from one time period to the next also gives rise to a positive time bias (for a particularly elegant demonstration of this, see

Chang, 1991). Even in the absence of both of these sources of uncertainty, when an animal is close enough to starvation, the future has little fitness value unless immediate requirements are met.[7]

While the animals in a particular laboratory experiment, for all practical purposes, face zero uncertainty regarding the delivery of delayed outcomes, and zero probability of death in the intervals between reward arrivals, such was not the case in the evolutionary development of the species. Consequently, positive time bias in the laboratory represents a short-run constraint on optimal adaptation that has longer-run survival value in the natural habitat. Similar arguments apply with respect to the existence of positive time bias in humans, as we, too, are products of an evolutionary process with similar survival pressures.

7.3 Time bias under varying income levels: The cycle-of-poverty hypothesis

Many economists have conjectured that time bias varies inversely with income and wealth. This is to say, the preference for more immediate payoffs should be greater at lower income levels. Economists have been concerned with the role such preferences might play in perpetuating poverty cycles, since a higher rate of time discounting implies *proportionately* less saving as a fraction of disposable income. An early, and clear, statement of this hypothesis (which we refer to as the cycle-of-poverty hypothesis) is found in Irving Fisher (1907, quoted in Maital and Maital, 1977): "The effect will be that . . . an inequality in the distribution of capital is gradually effected, and this inequality, once achieved, tends to perpetuate itself. The poorer a man grows, the keener his appreciation of present goods is likely to become" (p. 184). Or, more succinctly, "The smaller the income, the higher is the preference for present, over future income" (p. 185).

In investigating the cycle-of-poverty hypothesis, we cannot hope to recreate the full set of cultural and socioeconomic conditions that characterize poverty in national economic systems. Rather, we focus exclusively on the wealth effects of poverty by establishing wealth differences between subjects in the laboratory and determining the effect that this treatment variable has on time discounting. If we can support Fisher's conjecture under these conditions, then we have direct evidence favoring a wealth-induced effect on time preferences, which to us, at least, is at the heart of Fisher's hypothesis. If we find no such effect on discount rates, then the data compel us to look to other conditions associated with poverty, such as discrimination and poor schooling, as explanations for the presence of poverty cycles within national economies. Distinguishing between these potential sources of poverty is essential since only a correct diagnosis of the problem will allow us to design effective policies to alleviate it.

Independent of its implications for human economic behavior, the effect of wealth on time preference is of importance to biologists and psychologists for the development of more accurate models of foraging and choice behavior. Snyderman (1983b) sees no a priori reason why higher deprivation levels should lead to either a higher or lower rate of time discounting. Logical arguments can be made for effects in either direction: Hungrier animals have a greater need for food and thus may be less impulsive; but they may also be more anxious about and in need of realizing consumption opportunities and thus have a steeper rate of time discounting. Moreover, if deprivation levels become extreme enough, there is no point in waiting for larger, more delayed rewards, since the organism's very survival may be threatened (Kagel, Green, and Caraco, 1986). (However, subjects' survival was never an issue in the experiment reported below.)

7.3a   Experimental treatment conditions

Two experiments were conducted, one using liquid and the other using food as the outcome. In both experiments, a discrete-trials choice procedure, similar to the one described in Section 7.2a, was employed. In all cases, rats chose between two alternatives. Time delays between choice opportunities were constant, irrespective of the alternative chosen, so that choosing the smaller, more immediate alternative had no effect on when the next choice trial began.

We established high and low wealth conditions by assigning rats to one of two groups distinguished by the total daily allotments of the choice commodity. In the liquid experiment, the "poor" group received a total of 7 cc of liquid per day, whereas the "wealthy" group received a total of 28 cc per day. In the food experiment, the poor group received a total of 12.4 grams of food per day, whereas the wealthy group received 20.3 grams per day.[8] Liquid rats had ad-lib access to food in their home cages between experimental sessions; likewise, food rats had ad-lib access to water in their home cages. The differences in wealth levels produced substantial weight differences. By the end of the second treatment condition, the poor-liquid (food) rats' average weight was 263.1 (294.9) grams as compared with 560.9 (414.3) grams for the wealthy group.

To maintain these weight levels, we provided measured supplemental rations of the restricted commodity in the home cages. These supplements were available to the rats approximately one-half hour after the daily experimental session ended, and they induced a clear separation between within-experiment and postexperiment consumption. In addition, in the liquid experiments, we used a 1% sodium saccharin solution in the choice sessions, with plain water as the supplemental ration. Results from studies in which rats were offered a choice show that, at equal cost, a 1% saccharin solution is much preferred to water. Satiation effects were not a problem in any of the experimental treatment conditions. Rats in both the poor and wealthy groups routinely responded without delay whenever a choice trial was presented.

The treatment conditions studied were designed to get the rats sometimes to favor the larger, more delayed (LD) alternative, and at other times to favor the smaller, more immediate (SI) outcome. In terms of the two-period choice representation shown in Figure 7.1, each treatment condition involved a different pair of alternatives, x^t and x^{t+n}. In examining choice under different treatment conditions, we can check our results for consistency with those reported in Section 7.2. In particular, we expected that increases in the delay difference between receipt of the two alternatives, as well as reductions in the difference between the reward magnitudes, would result in increased choice of the SI alternative, in accordance with elementary time discounting predictions. Also, we expected to find sensitivity to these manipulations at both income levels. Further, given the importance of temporal consistency for our acceptance or rejection of the standard economic representation, we sought to replicate the inconsistencies reported in Figure 7.2.

7.3b Experimental results and discussion

Table 7.1 shows the frequency with which the LD alternative was chosen in the liquid-payoff experiment. For example, under treatment condition A, rats chose between a 2-sec delay for 1 cup of saccharin versus a 6-sec delay for 3 cups, with the wealthy rats choosing the LD alternative 81% of the time, on average, and the poor rats choosing it 91% of the time. In terms of Fisher's cycle-of-poverty hypothesis, the wealthy group should have chosen the LD alternative more often than the poor group under each of the treatment conditions (the difference column should all have positive numbers). However, the poor group chose the LD alternative more often under treatment conditions A, B, and E, with these differences being significant at the 10% level under conditions B and E. This is the exact *opposite* of the cycle-of-poverty hypothesis. Only under the initial application of treatment condition D did the wealthy group choose the LD alternative significantly more than did the poor group, and this difference failed to replicate following treatment conditions E and F.

The food experiment yields even stronger evidence *against* the cycle-of-poverty hypothesis (see Table 7.2). Under all three treatment conditions, the poor group chose the LD alternative more often than did the wealthy group, and these differences are all statistically significant at the 5% level or better.

For the food experiment, we also looked at the effects of within-group variations in wealth levels. The original poor group was studied under wealthy conditions while the original wealthy group was plunged into poverty. The bottom part of Table 7.2 reports these results. For the original poor group, the LD alternative was chosen less often now that they were wealthy. This is consistent with the between-group differences reported in Table 7.2 and is, again, counter to the cycle-of-poverty hypothesis. However, in switching the original wealthy group to poverty conditions, the LD alternative was chosen less often than

Table 7.1 *Cycle-of-poverty experiment with liquid payoffs: choice frequency of larger, more delayed alternative*

Treatment condition	SI vs. LD[a]	Mean choice[b]		Wealthy minus poor[c]
		Wealthy	Poor	
A	2 sec - 1 cup vs	80.5	91.4	−10.9
	6 sec - 3 cups	(7.78)	(3.25)	(−1.45)
B	6 sec - 1 cup vs	69.0	88.1	−19.1
	10 sec - 3 cups	(6.71)	(4.64)	(−2.34)[e]
C	1 sec - 1 cup vs	—[d]	94.0	—
	8 sec - 3 cups		(3.39)	
D	1 sec - 2 cups vs	15.2	2.0	13.2
	20 sec - 3 cups	(4.15)	(0.55)	(3.15)[f]
E	1 sec - 2 cups vs	28.9	54.2	−25.3
	8 sec - 3 cups	(4.53)	(12.27)	(−1.93)[e]
F	13 sec - 2 cups vs	53.2	50.7	2.5
	20 sec - 3 cups	(2.85)	(0.24)	(0.87)
D′	1 sec - 2 cups vs	22.1	27.4	−5.3
replication	20 sec - 3 cups	(8.91)	(8.99)	(0.42)

[a]SI = the smaller, more immediate outcome; LD = the larger, but more delayed outcome.
[b]Standard error of mean in parentheses.
[c]*t*-test statistics in parenthesis.
[d]Not implemented for wealthy group.
[e]Significantly different from 0 at the .10 level, two-tailed *t*-test, 6 degrees of freedom.
[f]Significantly different from 0 at the .05 level, two-tailed *t*-test, 6 degrees of freedom.

when these rats were wealthy. This does *not* replicate the between-group differences reported and *is* consistent with the cycle-of-poverty hypothesis. This intriguing result serves as some justification for economists' introspections that poverty means greater impulsiveness – a notion that, after all, arises from contemplating their own response to falling from a position of relative wealth into much-reduced living conditions.[9] However, additional replications are needed before such conjectures can be confidently supported.

The crossover wealth conditions permit us to evaluate responses to the alternatives both with and without resulting weight changes. Such an evaluation helps to distinguish whether it was the difference in consumption opportunities or the weight changes that result from them, that was responsible for the between-group differences. Since it took some time for weight to stabilize following the crossover in wealth conditions, we were able to obtain two data points for each rat following the crossover, one under the altered wealth levels when there was little weight change, and a second following the weight

Table 7.2 *Cycle-of-poverty experiment with food payoffs: Choice frequency of larger, more delayed alternative*

Treatment condition	SI vs. LD[a]	Mean choice[b]		Wealthy minus poor[c]
		Wealthy	Poor	
A	1 sec – 1 pellet vs. 12 sec – 3 pellets	21.8 (5.27)	82.7 (8.18)	−60.9 (−6.26)[f]
B	12 sec – 1 pellet vs. 23 sec – 3 pellets	59.3 (7.54)	94.7 (2.78)	−35.4 (−4.41)[f]
C	2 sec – 1 pellet vs. 6 sec – 3 pellets	84.7 (2.39)	95.4 (0.28)	−10.7 (−4.44)[f]

Crossover effect	Original wealthy group when:			Original poor group when:		
	Wealthy[d]	Poor[d]	Difference[c]	Wealthy[d]	Poor[d]	Difference[c]
1 sec – 1 pellet vs. 12 sec – 3 pellets	21.8 (5.27)	5.7 (4.76)	16.1 (2.26)[e]	42.7 (12.80)	82.7 (8.18)	−40.0 (−2.64)[f]

[a]SI = the smaller, more immediate outcome; LD = the larger, but more delayed outcome.
[b]Standard error of mean in parentheses.
[c]t-test statistics in parentheses.
[d]Mean choice frequency of larger delayed alternative, with standard error of mean in parentheses.
[e]Significantly different from 0 at .10 level, two-tailed t-test, 6 degrees of freedom.
[f]Significantly different from 0 at .05 level, two-tailed t-test, 6 degrees of freedom.

change. These data show no systematic change in choice frequencies before and after the weight shifts.[10] This pattern of results indicates that income differences were directly responsible for the between-group differences, and not the weight changes.

The responses of both groups to changes in time delays and number of payoffs reported in Tables 7.1 and 7.2 are largely consistent with the results reviewed in Section 7.2. The liquid payoff for the SI alternative doubled in going from treatment condition C to E. This change resulted in a sharp reduction in the poor rats' choice of the LD alternative (from 94% to 54%). A reduction in the time delay to the LD alternative between treatment conditions D and E in the liquid experiment resulted in increased choice of the LD alternative for both groups (an increase from 2% to 54% for the poor group and from 15% to 29% for the wealthy group).

Our data are also consistent with the preference reversals others have reported. Increasing the time delay to both alternatives for the food rats resulted in a statistically significant increase in choice of the LD alternative for the wealthy group ($t = 4.41$, d.f. $= 3$, $p < .05$, paired t-test) from 22% under treatment condition A to 59% under condition B. For the liquid rats, increasing the time delay to both alternative in going from treatment conditions E to F resulted in a significant increase in choice of the LD alternative for the wealthy group ($t = 4.75$, d.f. $= 3$, $p < .05$, paired t-test) from 29% to 53%. Although there was less frequent choice of the LD alternative with the addition of a constant time delay in going from treatment condition A to B for the wealthy liquid rats, the change in choice frequency fails to achieve statistical significance ($t = 1.65$, d.f. $= 2$, paired t-test).[11] Finally, as shown in Table 7.2, the original poor group chose the LD alternative substantially more often under wealthy conditions than did the original wealthy group (43% versus 22%, $t = 1.51$, d.f. $= 6$, $p = .09$, one-tailed t-test). This is consistent with Logue et al.'s (1984) studies, which suggest that a history of choosing a larger, more delayed outcome carries over into a relatively lower rate of time discounting under new choice conditions (also see Grosch and Neuringer, 1981).

It should be clear that our data do not support the cycle-of-poverty hypothesis, as a general proposition. If anything, our results suggest just the opposite, namely, that time discount rates decrease with reductions in income levels. While these results may not be generalizable beyond rats and the particular procedures employed, we are still justified in rejecting the cycle-of-poverty hypothesis as a general economic phenomenon. We are also skeptical of claims based on field data suggesting that low-income levels by themselves are responsible for any observed increase in time discount rates.[12] Consequently, to the extent that data from national economic systems suggest that poverty is associated with proportionately lower saving rates, or with a general inability to delay gratification, our results suggest that factors other than income and wealth may well be responsible for the behavior. For example, heightened uncertainty regarding the delivery of deferred rewards is another factor generally associated with poverty and might be more effectively targeted by policy instruments in attempts to overcome long-term poverty.

There are a few other animal experiments dealing with the effects of deprivation levels on time discount rates. Logue and her associates found no effect of deprivation level on the frequency with which pigeons chose the larger, more delayed alternative (Logue and Peña-Correal, 1985; Logue et al., 1988). Other studies, with other species in other situations, yield mixed results, with at least one study showing a positive relationship between increased deprivation level and increased frequency of choosing the larger, more delayed alternative (Christensen-Szalanski et al., 1980), and at least one study showing the opposite pattern (Snyderman, 1983b; see also Eisenberger, Masterson, and Lowman, 1982). Additional experiments will be required to determine what, if any, procedural and/or species differences are responsible for these different outcomes, or whether they are simply the result of different responses to different parameter values, as in our liquid experiment during the initial application of treatment condition D.

7.4 Toward a more molecular theory: Multiperiod models of consumer choice

The data reported in Figure 7.2 and in Tables 7.1 and 7.2 show rather sharp rates of time discounting by the animals. One clear implication of these time-discount patterns is that in the labor-supply and commodity-choice experiments reported in Chapters 2 through 5, the animal does not plan for the choice session as a whole; or, at least, at the beginning of an experimental session, the animal heavily discounts rewards to be received in the latter part of the session. We ignored time discounting in our modeling of consumer-choice and labor-supply decisions in earlier chapters, but a number of psychologists would prefer to see it included (see the published commentary on Rachlin et al., 1981). Although this approach provides a fine description of behavior, we now consider a multiperiod consumer-choice model that incorporates a moving time horizon and permits replanning on the part of the decision maker. In particular, we want to show the conditions under which the single-period, static choice representations developed in Chapters 2 through 5 remain unaffected given the animals' high rate of time discounting (readers uninterested in this particular question may wish to skip this section).

7.4a Structure of the model

Section 7.1 considered a consumer whose planning horizon extended over s periods and who could be viewed as maximizing, in time period 1, a well-behaved utility function

$$U = U^1(x^1, x^2, \ldots, x^s) \tag{7.5}$$

where x^t denotes a vector of commodities consumed in period t. At the beginning of time period 2, the consumer's time horizon extends to period $s + 1$, and the consumer now maximizes the utility function

$$U = U^2(\hat{x}^1, x^2, \ldots, x^{s+1}) \tag{7.6}$$

where $\hat{x}^1$ represents the consumption vector actually realized in period 1. This process repeats itself at the beginning of time periods 3, 4, and so on. In other words, our consumer has a moving time horizon, of some finite duration, and the concepts governing our plotting of indifference curves extend to representing preferences among commodity bundles in different time periods, as well as within a given time period.

An interesting, multiperiod consumption model must explicitly describe how future opportunities affect present choices and how past choices affect current and future behavior. In typical economic modeling efforts, the consumer's ability to borrow and lend through organized markets serves this purpose by providing an obvious vehicle for shifting consumption and income from one period to the next. Clearly, in our animal experiments there are no organized markets for borrowing and lending at established market interest rates. However, in terms of modeling strategies, two obvious alternatives suggest themselves. One is to model explicitly the fact that some commodities – for example, food and, to a lesser extent, water – can be stored internally for future consumption ("assets under the belt"). In doing this, one introduces a new set of constraints that involve storage costs, carrying-capacity limitations, and depreciation rates over time, as well as any differential costs of meeting current consumption requirements from internal stores or outside purchases. Such modeling efforts would require an intimate understanding of animal physiology.

Alternatively, all commodities can be modeled as involving consumption flows, with different patterns of substitutability between elements of the consumption vectors at different points in time depending on consumption histories up to that point. This alternative would, of necessity, have to be adopted for commodities such as leisure, which cannot be stored. The advantage of adopting this alternative for all commodities is that it makes writing the budget constraint particularly easy since the explicit modeling of commodity carryover relationships between time periods is not required. To be sure, the preference structure linking some commodities, such as food and water, in different time periods, would depend on the animal's physiology and consumption pattern prior to that point in time. But this is no different from the within-period relationships for these commodities, which depend on physiological factors as well. It is this alternative that we adopt here and that suffices for the level of modeling detail intended.

Since there are no organized markets for borrowing or lending across time periods, a separate budget constraint applies to each time period; that is, the consumer must satisfy s time constraints in maximizing the utility function, equation (7.5), in period 1

$$\sum_i p_i^t x_i^t = M^t \qquad t = 1, 2, \ldots, s \qquad (7.7)$$

(Note that by definition, $\sum_t M^t = M$, where M is session-total income.)

Assume that all consumption in period t is obtained through own labor-supply effort or through unearned income opportunities that are specific to that time period. These were, in fact, the conditions that prevailed in our open-economy, labor-supply experiments with pigeons (Section 4.3b) and in our commodity-choice experiments (Section 2.2). This means that each of the s budget constraints is identical in structure to the session-total budget constraint originally specified, except that the budget constraints now apply to consumption within a restricted time period, rather than for the session as a whole.[13] Thus, both the labor-supply and commodity-choice experiments may be reformulated to have the animal maximizing a multiperiod utility function. The commodity bundles among which the animal is choosing have the same arguments (e.g., consumption and leisure, food and water) as in the original single-period framework, only now each commodity bundle has a time superscript as well. In the following subsections, (a) we compare the static structure of the optimal solution to this problem with the single-period (molar) model originally specified, and (b) we analyze dynamic aspects of the solution as well.

7.4b Static behavioral relationships

First, consider the within-period allocation rule between commodities. In all cases, the marginal rate of substitution between commodity flows within a given time period must equal the ratio of commodity prices in that period.

$$\frac{U_i^t}{U_j^t} = \frac{p_i^t}{p_j^t} \qquad i, j = 1, 2, \ldots, n; \qquad t = 1, 2, \ldots, s \qquad (7.8)$$

where $U_i^t = \partial U / \partial x_i^t$.[14] This is the *same* allocation rule dictated by the single-period (molar) choice model, except that choices there referred to session-total values, whereas here they refer to within-period values.

A molecular formulation requires the specification of a between-period allocation rule. The marginal rule of substitution between flows of the same commodity in two different time periods will not, in general, equal their relative prices in the two periods. Rather, time discounting factors come into play

$$\frac{U_i^t}{U_i^k} = \frac{p_i^t \lambda^t}{p_i^k \lambda^k} \qquad i = 1, 2, \ldots, n; \qquad t, k = 1, 2, \ldots, s \qquad (7.9)$$

where λ^t represents the marginal value of income in time period t, and the ratio λ^t / λ^k represents the relative value of income in the two periods t and k.

Note that with identical commodity prices in all periods, the marginal rate of substitution across time periods for the same commodity reduces to

$$\frac{U_i^t}{U_i^k} = \frac{\lambda^t}{\lambda^k} \qquad (7.10)$$

so that intertemporal consumption patterns depend only on the discount factor, λ. What this means, in terms of the commodity-choice experiments analyzed in Chapters 2 and 3, is that since commodity prices were constant *within* an experimental session, the only intertemporal choice decision the animal faced was how fast to use up its allotted number of lever presses. This, in turn, would be dictated strictly by time preferences. In this context, the steep time-discount rates identified in this chapter can be used to explain why the animals typically used their daily allotment of lever presses within a fraction of the total time period allotted.[15]

In terms of the labor-supply experiments, the timing of the delivery of the unearned reinforcements can be quite important from the animal's point of view. Unearned income delivered at the end of an experimental session would be heavily time-discounted at the beginning of the session. One would need to know the rate of time discounting with some precision in order to devise accurate, compensated wage-change schedules. The open-economy experiments with pigeons were designed to skirt this issue. The unearned income was delivered unpredictably throughout an experimental session during which within-session wage rates remained constant. In this way, we minimized the effects of intertemporal substitution on consumption-leisure substitution, since the latter was of principal interest.

7.4c Dynamic aspects of behavior

As the consumer moves through time, the consumption plan is revised and extended (compare equation (7.5) with equation (7.6)). Even assuming that all prices remain constant over time and that the form of the utility function does not vary with time, the consumer's expenditure patterns will generally vary between time periods because past consumption affects current and future choices. Further, for any two consumers with identical preferences and the same budget constraint, their consumption patterns will generally differ in any given time period if they have had different consumption histories.

The open-economy experimental procedure, in which animals are maintained at a constant body weight or deprivation level at the start of each experimental session, was employed with a view to minimizing the effects that past consumption may have on current choice. With this control in place, and if there are no explicit intertemporal substitution effects resulting from variations in commodity prices, the single-period (molar) model yields accurate predictions, since relative price changes affect within-period choices (equation (7.8)), and not between-period choices (equation (7.10)). To be sure, the molar model cannot, and is not intended to, describe the time pattern of consumption (or work–leisure substitution) *within* a given experimental session. However, the absence of intertemporal price and income variations ensures that there are no implicit intertemporal substitution effects that cannot be accounted for by the single-period model. Moreover, the within-period equilibrium between relative price and relative marginal utility of different commodities (equation (7.8)) is the same as in the molar model, although the point at which these relationships are evaluated varies over the course of the experimental session.

By contrast, in closed-economy experiments, the animal's body weight and relative deprivation level will vary between experimental conditions as well as day to day within a given condition (at least until some sort of steady-state choice pattern is established and body weights have stabilized within a given treatment condition). These variations in the subject's state between treatment conditions may confound the single-period (molar) model's predictions. That is, such changes may introduce a source of variability that is not accounted for by the single-period choice model but that may be of some importance. However, for pairwise comparisons over temporally contiguous time periods involving compensated price or wage changes, this uncontrolled source of variability is unlikely to be very important since real income levels and consumption patterns are not likely to deviate that much between conditions.

In sum, economic models are capable of providing a more detailed, molecular analysis of choice behavior than we indicated in previous chapters. However, accurate and informative characterizations of consumption patterns over time require considerably more information about the structure of preferences than anything we have been willing to assume so far. More important, in the absence of temporal variations in prices and/or income availability, such detailed modeling efforts would do little to enhance the predictive accuracy of the single-period (molar) choice models developed in Chapters 2 through 5. Of course, there is a gap in terms of the single-period model's ability to explain the pattern of consumption over the course of an experimental session, but the models were not developed or applied with this goal in mind.

7.5 Time discounting in schedules of reinforcement: Responding on VI versus VR schedules and on progressive ratio schedules

Although we have argued that time discounting does not materially affect the results of our consumer-demand and labor-supply experiments, the same cannot be said for behavior under some of the other schedules of reinforcement discussed to this point. In what follows, we explicitly account for the role of time discounting on differential response rates on VI (variable interval) versus VR (variable ratio) schedules of reinforcement and in PR (progressive ratio) schedules of reinforcement.

Silberberg, Warren-Boulton, and Asano (1988) investigated the role of time discounting in producing "excessive" response rates on VI schedules (recall that on a VI schedule, a single response after a variable time interval produces reinforcement, whereas on a VR schedule, reinforcement is delivered following a variable number of responses). Responding is typically lower on VI than on VR schedules with approximately equal rates of reinforcement. In our earlier analysis (Section 5.2b), these differences in response rates were accounted for strictly in terms of consumption–leisure trade-offs that result from the higher marginal reinforcement rate that VR schedules provide (Figure 5.1). However, critics (Prelec, 1982) have challenged this analysis, arguing that response rates on VI schedules still seem too high to be consistent with optimization principles, since virtually the same VI reinforcement rate could be obtained with substantially fewer responses.

Silberberg, Warren-Boulton, and Asano (1988) reasoned that an important factor underlying the "excessive" number of responses on VI schedules results from temporal discounting on the animal's part. Responding on a VI schedule affects not only the amount of reinforcement obtained, but also the immediacy of reinforcement. More rapid responding results in a slightly higher reinforcement rate and in more immediate delivery of reinforcers once they have been set up on the VI schedule. Thus, differential response rates on VI and VR schedules involve not only substituting consumption for leisure, but also involve an implicit substitution of labor expended for greater immediacy of reward.

To test their hypothesis, Silberberg et al. (1988) devised a VI schedule that would eliminate the temporal motivation for responding. Each food payoff that would have been received immediately after completion of the VI requirement was replaced with a conditioned reinforcer (a light flash) that signaled that a food payoff had been earned but could not be consumed until the end of the session. On the assumption that the value of immediate access to the conditioned reinforcer (the light flash) would be less than the value of food, the time discounting factors promoting excessive responding on VI schedules would be suppressed in relation to a traditional VI schedule.

It was desirable to use a species with a relatively low rate of time discounting (or one that could easily be trained to accept delayed rewards); otherwise, delaying food reward for any significant period of time might completely suppress responding. For this, the researchers studied adult Japanese macaques (*Macaca fuscata*). In addition, the macaques were studied in a control condition, a VR schedule with the same characteristics as those of the VI schedule – food reinforcement replaced with the light flash and all food rewards delivered at the end of the session.

Silberberg et al. used an ABA design: The A phase compared response rate on a standard VI with a standard VR schedule, and the B phase compared response rates under the conditions in which food was delayed until the session's end.[16] Their basic dependent variable was the differential response rate between VR and VI schedules (VR responses minus VI responses; VR–VI measure). For the two subjects studied, there was more than a 50% increase in the VR–VI measure when food delivery was delayed until session's end in comparison with when food was delivered within the session. Reductions in the VI response rate were largely responsible for the increase in the VR–VI measure.

The results of Silberberg et al.'s experiment gives some insight into responding on concurrent VI–VR schedules as well. Recall that on such schedules, the VI timer continues to operate and sets up reinforcers on the VI schedule while the animal is working on the VR schedule. Assume for the moment that the VI schedule holds all rewards once they are set up. Then, to maximize reward rates, the animal should spend all of its time on the VR schedule, switching over to the VI schedule only to collect rewards at the end of the session. However, because more immediate rewards have greater value than delayed payoffs, the animal will not wait until the end of the session to collect VI reinforcers. Further, once subjects have switched to the VI schedule, they will respond "excessively" as they reduce leisure for the sake of greater immediacy of reinforcement as Silberberg et al. (1987) have shown. (For additional analysis of this argument, see Rachlin, Green, and Tormey, 1988). In following these strategies, the animal will neither be maximizing its rate of food intake nor minimizing its labor per unit of food consumed. Rather, it is substituting reduced consumption and leisure for more immediate access to food.

There are implicit temporal trade-offs in progressive ratio (PR) schedules (with reset) as well. Recall (Section 5.2d) that under this procedure subjects have a choice of responding on the PR schedule (a fixed ratio [FR] schedule with increasing work requirements following each reinforcer) or switching to a stationary FR schedule, completion of which resets the value of the PR to the beginning of the sequence. With the first several ratio requirements on the PR schedule below the value of the stationary FR schedule, minimizing work requires that the subject switch from the PR to the stationary FR well before the work requirement on the PR equals that on the stationary FR. However, assuming a constant time cost for each response (a reasonable approximation), optimal switching from the PR to the stationary FR means giving up a more immediate reward in favor of a more delayed payoff. For example, assume that the stationary FR requirement is 120 and that the initial value of the PR is 10 and the requirement increases by 20. In order to minimize work, the subject should switch from the PR after completion of the ratio 50 requirement. Assuming it takes 1 sec to complete each response, switching early means forgoing a 70-sec delay to the next reward on the PR in place of a 120-sec delay on the stationary FR. However, in switching to the stationary FR, the next several rewards come much sooner, since the PR resets to FR 10. Thus, there is an immediate cost to switching at the optimal point in return for deferred benefits.

To demonstrate the role of time delays in choice in PR schedules (with reset), Mazur and Vaughan (1987) added an intertrial interval (ITI) following each payoff. That is, after each reward from either the PR or the stationary FR, there was a fixed time delay before their pigeons could begin working again for more food (delays of 25 and 50 sec were used). Behavior with and without the ITI was compared. The introduction of an ITI does nothing to alter the switch point that minimizes total work requirements. However, if the rewards for switching (the immediate reset of the PR) are further delayed, there is less incentive to switch early since deferred rewards are valued less than more immediate ones. Switching occurred later with the ITI than without it.

Mazur and Vaughan conclude that their results are inconsistent with an optimization model that assumes that subjects are simply trying to minimize *total* labor supply. They note, however, that their results are not incompatible with all theories that assume some sort of underlying optimization process: "Indeed, the theory of delayed reinforcement we have described (and use as an explanation for the data) can be called an optimality analysis because it assumes that the subject will choose whichever alternative has the greater value at the moment of choice" (pp. 260–1). That is, rats and pigeons employ some sort of present discounted-value calculation in choosing between schedules that involve either explicit or implicit temporal substitution effects. When these effects are present, they can have a large influence on choice.

7.6 Time discounting in applied behavioral research

Economists place considerable emphasis on the forward-looking nature of economic behavior. Indeed, Gary Becker (1993) notes that one of the hallmarks of the economic approach to the study of human choice is that behavior is forward looking. Individuals try as best they can to anticipate the uncertain consequences of their actions. Although operant psychologists place considerable emphasis on the role of future payoffs and time discounting on choice, applied psychologists have often overlooked the effects of these variables, which can radically affect the conclusions reached. In this concluding section we illustrate the role of time effects in applied behavior settings. In one case, self-administered drug consumption, a relatively simple accounting of time effects points to a very different conclusion from that of the authors.

All of the studies considered in this section were conducted in "token economies." Token economies are organized systems in which individuals receive tokens, or points, for work performed. The tokens are, in turn, exchangeable for current or future consumption goods. Token economies were originally developed by psychologists for the purpose of establishing therapeutic environments for institutionalized populations such as psychiatric patients, prejuvenile delinquents, stutterers, and school children (for a review of these therapeutic applications, see Kazdin and Bootzin, 1972). In addition, token economies have been successfully established specifically as research environments designed to investigate socioeconomic behavior using volunteer subjects (Bigelow, Emurian, and Brady, 1975; Kagel, Battalio, and Miles, 1980; Miles et al., 1974).

As economic systems, token economies are subject to systemic effects, which, when not taken into account, can thwart therapeutic objectives and distort understanding of behavioral relationships manifested in them. For example, in a therapeutic token economy, increasing the wage rate for a target activity, such as personal hygiene care, may lead to reductions in other, equally important, income-earning activities and thereby offset the therapeutic gains originally intended. While psychologists have long been aware of the interrelationships between activities, the implications of these interdependencies have often been overlooked (Winkler, 1980; Winkler and Burkhard, 1990). This is particularly true with respect to subjects' valuations of immediate versus delayed rewards.

At the most basic level of an economy, the manner in which tokens can be exchanged for primary goods, and the tokens' value on leaving the economy, will have a critical impact on token-saving behavior. Consider the following two token economies. In one, volunteer marijuana smokers lived for 98 days in an experimental token economy where they could earn points for simple construction tasks. The points earned could be exchanged for marijuana and other goods within the token economy, or could be exchanged for cash (without penalty) when subjects left the experiment (Kagel et al., 1980; Miles et al., 1974). The second economy was the Central Islip token economy operating on a chronic ward of a state psychiatric institution (Battalio et al., 1973; Kagel et al., 1977). In the Central Islip economy, tokens could not be exchanged for cash and were valueless outside the economy.

These structural differences severely restricted saving within the therapeutic economy as compared with the experimental economy. Predictably, in the experimental economy a large portion of the tokens earned went into savings (averaging some 60% of earned income; Kagel et al., 1975), with the stock of savings in the economy increasing continuously over time. In the ward economy, however, almost all token income went into consumption, so much so that total net savings for 38 people over a seven-week period was +3 tokens. During this period, participants added to and subtracted from their stock of savings, but these transactions largely canceled each other out (Winkler, 1980). Such differences in savings patterns are not surprising since in the ward economy anything saved was ultimately lost upon leaving the ward. Once savings had reached a level required to smooth transactions across earnings periods, there was no further incentive to save. In contrast, in the experimental economy, savings were convertible into dollars upon leaving the economy, so that there was a genuine saving motive for future, expanded consumption opportunities once the experiment was completed.

7.6a *The effects of time on self-administered drug consumption*

Studies of self-administered drug use often take place in token economies with differing degrees of complexity and different underlying economic structures. Often there are important differences between these economies in terms of the subject's ability to transfer token earnings to currency upon leaving the economy, and/or in the restrictions placed on income earning and consumption opportunities within the economy. These differences have significant effects on labor supply and drug consumption. More important, these differences in experimental design result in important differences in intertemporal substitution possibilities whose impact on labor supply and drug use often goes unrecognized.

For example, consider the research on work-contingent alcohol consumption by Nathan et al. (1970, 1971, 1972) and Mello and Mendelson (1972). The experimental design used in these studies involves a baseline condition in which no alcohol is available. However, during the baseline, points can be earned for future alcohol consumption or for the purchase of, at most, one other commodity that is available during baseline as well as later in the study (time out from isolation in the case of Nathan et al., 1970, 1971, 1972, and cigarettes in Mello and Mendelson, 1972). Following the baseline period, unlimited amounts of alcohol are available for purchase, concurrent with the same token-earning opportunities that were in effect during the baseline condition. Further, tokens have no value outside the economy. The pattern found during the experimental phase of all the studies cited shows that once alcohol became available, there was an immediate drinking spree, during which time subjects slowed down or completely stopped working. Subjects only resumed working when they were completely out of points or in imminent danger of running out. The authors view this spree drinking, with the associated reduction in labor supply, as characteristic of self-administered alcohol consumption.

The conclusions regarding a characteristic alcohol drinking spree may be unwarranted. Rather, economic conditions alone may well account for the behavior. The economic contingencies were such that the subject was first allowed to work with one consumption activity, but not alcohol, which was immediately available. Subjects knew that in a short period of time a highly preferred commodity, whose consumption was likely to interfere with optimal job performance, would become available. Moreover, there was no incentive to save tokens except for within-session consumption since they were valueless beyond the confines of the economy. Under this experimental design, working and saving during baseline, followed by spending and consumption of the highly preferred commodity, is largely a response to the specific economic contingencies rather than a response to the pharmacological properties of the commodity under investigation. This analysis gains support from the contrasting results obtained in another study of alcoholics' work-contingent behavior (Mello et al., 1968). In this experiment, there was no baseline period during which alcohol was withheld (although here, too, tokens were valueless outside the economy). Rather, from the start subjects had a choice of working and saving to finance periods of any duration of extended drinking without work, or of closely matching working and drinking. Under these circumstances, virtually all subjects closely matched income earning with drinking, but the "characteristic" spree behavior found in other studies was by and large absent.

As a second example, consider the conclusions that Mendelson and Meyer (1972) draw concerning the work-consumption pattern of individuals in a marijuana study they conducted:

The most significant feature of this (work) behavior was that, almost without exception, every subject earned the maximum number of reinforcement points each day. . . . This finding is in marked contrast to the results obtained in alcohol-related research in which alcoholics have periodic complete cessation of work output when they are consuming alcohol. (Mendelson and Meyer, 1972, p. 94)

Marijuana users, they assert, work steadily while smoking whereas alcoholics go on periodic sprees, with the implication that these differences in working and consumption are due to the different drugs. What the authors fail to take into account is that in their marijuana study, points were exchangeable for currency on completion of the study, and daily point earnings were limited by a binding income ceiling. Hence, in this study, there was an incentive to keep working because earnings could be transferred outside the experiment and because there was a constraint on work-consumption sprees since there was a sharp limit on maximum daily earnings. By contrast, in the alcohol study by Mello and Mendelson (1972), unexpended points were valueless at the end of the experiment and no limits were placed on daily earnings. Hence, there was no incentive to keep working for the sake of postexperiment income, plus there was no constraint on work-consumption sprees. Given these design differences, any attempt to assign differences in work-consumption behavior to drug differences is completely confounded by variations in the value of labor and drugs imposed by temporal factors built into the experiments.

Notes

1 The assumptions embodied in equation (7.2) are sufficient to ensure consistent intertemporal choice. See Hadar (1971, pp. 233–2) for a good discussion of necessary and sufficient conditions.
2 Changes in absolute differences in delay values, besides changes in the ratio of the values, also affect choice (Green and Snyderman, 1980; Navarick and Fantino, 1976).
3 Failures to maximize food intake have also been observed in our labor-supply experiments (Chapters 4 and 5) and our uncertainty experiments (Chapter 6).
4 To do so would require intransitivities in choice, which were not tested for here. The violations of temporal consistency described here are analogous to the common ratio

effect in decision making under uncertainty (recall Section 6.4). Loewenstein and Prelec (1992) refer to preference reversals of this sort as the common difference effect.

5 Kagel, Green, and Caraco (1986) provide a functional form for the variable time-bias specification. Kagel and Green (1987) discuss alternative decision-making formulations that are capable of organizing the data (see also Loewenstein and Prelec, 1992).

6 Rachlin et al. (1986) have argued that probabilistic reinforcers are functionally equivalent to delayed reinforcers. See their paper for details, along with the work of Mazur (1989) who tests their model and modifies it.

7 In this context, we might expect the time-discount function to vary systematically across species, depending on their evolutionary histories. Perhaps organisms without predators tend to discount future rewards less than those organisms subject to predation while foraging, and perhaps an animal foraging with a group of competitors discounts the future to a greater degree than does a solitary forager.

8 When the wealthy group reached mature body weight (at the end of the second treatment condition), total food intake was reduced to 18.0 grams per day.

9 Mark Isaac first drew our attention to this interpretation of the data.

10 Mean choice frequencies for the LD alternative were 41.7% (8.7) versus 42.7% (12.8) for the original poor group and 6.4% (3.7) versus 5.7% (4.8) for the original wealthy group, with the initial response to the change in consumption opportunities listed first, and standard errors of the mean reported in parentheses.

11 Only three of the four rats in this group were exposed to treatment condition A. The between treatment t-statistic is 1.12 with 5 d.f., which is also not statistically significant.

12 Savings behavior in developing countries has been subject to relatively intensive study and is related to the cycle-of-poverty hypothesis. Although there are numerous problems with data accuracy, and it is difficult to know what to count as savings, the data tend to show that average savings rates remain a constant proportion of per capita income under conditions of steady growth (Mikesell and Zinser, 1973, p. 19). That is, the Keynesian model's prediction of increased marginal and average propensities to save as a function of national income (which is consistent with the cycle-of-poverty hypothesis) is not supported.

13 The corresponding session budget constraint is $\sum p_i x_i = M$.

14 See Hadar (1971) for a straightforward mathematical derivation of this relationship.

15 Fluctuating commodity prices between different time periods within a given experimental session are present in multiple schedules of reinforcement. A multiple schedule is one in which two or more schedules of reinforcement are presented successively throughout a session, with each component schedule associated with a distinct exteroceptive stimulus. The present formulation can be extended to deal with multiple schedules. We make no effort to do so here, however, because such an extension would add little to the analysis of such schedules. Staddon's (1982) theory of behavioral competition comes closest in spirit to the structure of such a model. Williams (1983) reviews multiple-schedule performance, critically evaluating Staddon's behavioral competition model (however, see Staddon, 1982, for a rebuttal to Williams's objections).

16 To control for possible differences in average rates of reinforcement on the two schedules, food setups for subjects when working on the VI schedule were yoked to the time it took the subjects to complete the response requirement for each reinforcer on the VR schedule (recall Figure 5.1, and the related discussion in Section 5.2b).

8

Summing up

This chapter summarizes our applications of individual choice theory from economics to the study of animal behavior. Our research program has been guided by three primary goals. First and foremost, our goal has been to investigate experimentally important implications of economic choice theory using real, highly valued payoffs. By studying the behavior of individual subjects under rigorous experimental methods, we have been able to investigate economic choice theory without having to rely on the string of auxiliary assumptions usually required when using field data (assumptions about functional forms, measurement of variables, etc., which are often of questionable validity; see, for example, Pencavel, 1986). Our second goal has been to test between the different explanations of the data. This has led to an extensive dialogue, published primarily in psychology journals, in which economic choice theory has been contested with the matching law, a prominent model of choice in the animal psychology literature. Our third goal has been to shed some light on important and complex social issues, such as the cycle of poverty and characteristics of earnings distributions. Here we have used the unique advantages of experiments and the animal model to manipulate treatment variables (such as income level) which cannot easily be done (or are prohibitively expensive to do) with volunteer human subjects. In addition, we have focused on a few select variables – such as pure wealth effects in the cycle of poverty. This "tunnel vision" is both a strength and a weakness of the experimental methodology: a strength in that we are able to isolate the causal effect of a particular variable; a weakness in that there is considerably more to complicated social issues than can be incorporated within any single variable such as income.

8.1 Tests of individual choice theory

In static models of consumer-demand and labor-supply behavior, *the* important prediction relates to the direction of the subject's response to income-compensated price changes. Our studies offer rather overwhelming support for this aspect of the theory in a simple, two-commodity world with such goods (reinforcers) as food and water (essential commodities) and different-flavored fluids (nonessential commodities), in both labor-supply (Section 4.4) and commodity-choice (Section 2.3) experiments. In addition, the predictions have been verified in both closed and open economies and under a number of different experimental procedures. Arguably, these studies constitute the first real tests of consumer-demand theory: The unit of analysis is the behavior of individual subjects and the experiments are free of the string of auxiliary assumptions that are required when attempts are made to apply the theory to field data (these auxiliary assumptions are often said to have broken down when the data are inconsistent with the theory).

We and others have demonstrated the existence of a Giffen good, a good whose consumption increases when its price increases (at least in some portion of the choice space). The difficulty in identifying a Giffen good was in finding a commodity that satisfied the initial conditions of the theory; it had to be a strongly inferior good that takes up a large portion of the budget constraint. The importance of the Giffen good lies not in suggesting that this class of commodities is likely to be observed in national economies. Indeed, our experience suggests quite the opposite. Rather, the important point is that we have reliably demonstrated this far-from-obvious implication of consumer-choice theory.

Tests of the representative consumer hypothesis show that the weak form of the hypothesis is satisfied. That is, the behavior of individual pigeon and rat consumers is similar enough that the same system of demand equations best characterizes their choices. However, the strong form of the hypothesis, which requires that tastes be sufficiently homogeneous so that the stringent criteria required to achieve consistent aggregation across individuals are satisfied, fails in both labor-supply and commodity-choice experiments. Experimental evaluation of the strong form of the representative consumer hypothesis is important because a large body of theory and empirical research relies on it to draw powerful implications from consumer-demand theory for aggregate labor-supply behavior and for macroeconomic models as well. Since animals bred for genetic similarity and raised in virtually identical environments fail to satisfy the strong representative consumer hypothesis, it strikes us as highly unlikely that people will do so either, even after allowing for age, education, and other objective differences.

A generalized minimum-needs hypothesis (as embodied in a generalized CES utility function) provides a useful functional form for organizing subjects' choices of normal goods in both commodity-choice and labor-supply experiments (Sections 3.3 and 5.3). The model implies that commodities become more substitutable as income increases, in contrast to a bliss-point formulation (as embodied in a generalized quadratic utility function) in which commodities become less substitutable at higher income levels. The estimates of minimum needs are both plausible and consistent with independent experimental evidence. However, the generalized MN model clearly cannot fit all of our data. It fails to account for the existence of inferior goods and Giffen goods. Moreover, there is some evidence from labor-supply experiments that expansion paths become nonlinear at very high unearned-income levels, and that they collapse to a bliss point instead. However, the model has proved useful for interpreting data from our experiments and from others as well (e.g., Shurtleff, Warren-Boulton, and Silberberg, 1987).

When our studies were extended to choice under uncertainty we found strong parallels between the choice behavior of humans and rats. Both species exhibit Allais-type violations of expected utility theory, and these violations are more common for choices on the edges, rather than in the interior, of the unit-probability triangle (Section 6.4). Generalizations of EU theory that explain these Allais-type violations in terms of the fanning out of indifference curves in the unit-probability triangle (which in turn reflects an anticipated income effect on choice) are found to fail for both humans and rats in previously unexplored areas of the probability triangle (Section 6.4b, and Kagel et al., 1990). Our conclusion is that violations of EU theory in both humans and rats are better explained by some sort of differential probability weighting process, or selective attention to different components of the choice problem, factors that are essential ingredients of prospect theory (Kahneman and Tversky, 1979).

Under surplus resource conditions and positive payoffs, choice under uncertainty is commonly characterized by risk aversion (Section 6.2). This finding is consistent with survival arguments offered by biologists. Risk-averse choice is also consistent with the economic assumption of diminishing marginal rates of substitution underlying the characterization of preferences in both consumer-demand and labor-supply models that do not incorporate uncertainty. Biologists' predictions regarding the change from risk aversion to risk loving under deficit resource conditions are found to be satisfied for small birds and rodents. Such animals experience harsh winters that lead to considerable variability in resource levels. However, this prediction is not supported by our results with rats, which have substantially larger food stores and omnivorous eating capabilities. Nor is the change in risk preferences seen among small birds that have evolved in tropical climates and that are rarely subjected to energy shortages since there is a wider variety of food types from which to select (Section 6.3a). Species differences in risk taking under deficit resource conditions appear to be explained by the greater range of options available to rats and tropical birds in response to nutritional deficits. Such animals can switch food sources or, in the case of the rat with its relatively large body mass, can play it safe and wait for foraging conditions to improve.

Diminishing marginal rates of substitution imply risk loving over losses, where less is better. The established preference of rats and pigeons for variable over fixed delays to reinforcement is consistent with this implication. A new experiment is reported supporting the generality of this prediction by extending it to choice over variable levels of shock (Section 6.5). These results are related to prospect theory, which postulates risk loving when high probability losses are used. Our results support the motivational process underlying this prediction.

In choosing over time-dated goods, where one can substitute current for future consumption, the choices of rats and pigeons are well organized using a present discounted value formulation. Temporal inconsistencies in choice, analogous to the common ratio effect, are reported. With relatively short delays to reinforcement, smaller more immediate rewards are preferred to larger but more delayed rewards. The addition of a constant time delay to both alternatives (with no change in their payoffs), results in a reversal in preference—the larger but more delayed alternative is now preferred (Section 7.2). There are strong similarities between human and animal choices here as well (e.g., Green, Fry, and Myerson, 1994; Loewenstein and Prelec, 1992; Navarick, 1982; Rachlin, Raineri, and Cross, 1991). Preference for smaller, more immediate rewards over larger, more delayed outcomes is often characterized as a "self-control" problem. We argue that such preferences can also reflect a useful adaptation to circumstances in the natural environment, although they can prove dysfunctional under other circumstances.

8.2 Alternative explanations

One possible explanation for why our commodity-choice and labor-supply data are consistent with predictions from economic theory is that the subjects engage in essentially random behavior. Becker (1962; also Chant, 1963) has shown that random behavior by a collection of individuals, in conjunction with changes in the budget constraint, can result in negatively sloped aggregate demand curves. However, our work with individual subject data and the rigorous control afforded by our laboratory methods have led us to conclude that these random behavior models do not provide explanations for our data (Sections 3.1 and 5.1).

The matching law is an effort by psychologists to quantify the "law of effect" (Herrnstein, 1961, 1970): greater reinforcement produces greater response strength.[1] The matching law achieved considerable success in describing choice under concurrent VI–VI schedules and concurrent VR–VR schedules when the same commodity serves as reinforcement on both schedules (Section 3.2b). Our early research showed that both of these results can also be explained by consumer-choice theory. In contrast, when choosing between qualitatively different reinforcers (gross complements such as food and water) consumer-choice theory predicts antimatching (a reversal in sign of the exponent in the matching equation; see Section 3.2c), as is consistent with observed data.

Proponents of the matching law could argue that their model was never intended to explain choices between qualitatively different reinforcers (just the sort of thing economic choice theory is designed to explain). Analysis then shifted to labor-supply behavior. Labor-supply theory predicts higher response rates on VR than on VI schedules (provided reinforcement rates are high enough to meet minimum survival requirements) and that labor-supply curves are likely to eventually bend back on themselves at higher wage rates (higher levels of reinforcement). In contrast, the matching law by itself is silent with regard to differences in response rates on VI compared with VR schedules and predicts that labor-supply curves will be positively sloped throughout. A number of laboratories have found support for both of the predictions from labor-supply theory (Section 5.2a and 5.2b).

Proponents of the matching law showed that subjects fail to maximize total food intake on concurrent VI–VR schedules, thereby presumably refuting the maximization model underlying the explanation for matching under concurrent VI–VI schedules. However, it is easy to show that there are implicit consumption-leisure substitution effects involved in concurrent VI–VR procedures that predict the failure to maximize total food intake. Subsequent experimental research has demonstrated that these substitution effects provide only a partial explanation of behavior under this procedure (Section 5.2c). Additional research (Silberberg et al., 1988; Section 7.5) suggests that implicit intertemporal substitution effects also account for the failure to maximize total food intake on concurrent VI–VR schedules.

The debate between maximizing and matching accounts of behavior continues in the animal psychology literature. Even though the authors of this text clearly are biased in their opinion of who is winning the argument, it is fairly safe to say that economic choice theory, with its emphasis on income and substitution effects between different commodities, between consumption and leisure, and between present and future consumption, has more than held its own. One of the primary problems with the matching law, in terms of quantifying the intuition underlying the law of effect, is that it does not adequately take into account the effect of income changes on choice (Sections 3.2c and 5.2a). (Recall, for example, that it is the income effect that produces the backward-bending portion of the labor-supply curve, contrary to the matching law's prediction of a positively sloped curve throughout.) The concept of income-compensated price changes has been the economists' solution to the problem that the sign of an income effect cannot, in general, be predicted, and that the income effect can, at times, offset predictions based solely on the substitution effect. In fact, predictions based on income-compensated price changes have much in common with the intuition underlying the law of effect—which is that greater reinforcement (lower prices) must always lead one to select a commodity-choice bundle containing more of the good whose reinforcement rate increased. Some sort of formal adjustment of the matching law to account for income effects would seem to be required as well.

What our experiments do demonstrate is that hyperrational economic agents are not required for behavior to be consistent with economic choice theory. Presumably pigeons and rats are not consciously trying to maximize utility or fitness by their actions. Rather, they are likely to be following some fundamental behavioral principle, like the law of effect (as we have just characterized it), in determining what choices to make. This, in conjunction with the notion that changes in income levels can have strong, systematic effects on choices, is really all that is needed to explain most of our data.

8.3 Social policy implications

In reporting our results, we have touched on several complicated social policy issues. Our experiments validate predictions based on static models of labor supply that welfare programs have a disincentive effect on work at the margin (Section 4.5a). This, however, does not imply that such programs should be eliminated. Rather, we must accept and account for these disincentive effects in our efforts to improve individual and societal welfare. With respect to more dynamic considerations, our results are consistent with a small welfare trap effect. However, shifts in labor supply resulting from exposure to unearned income are far too small to suggest major shifts in preferences. To the extent that our results are generalizable to humans, they suggest that any constancy of individuals on welfare roles does not result from any nefarious shift in preferences.

Earnings distributions for rat and pigeon workers are quite compact but nevertheless are far from exhibiting perfect equality, even though a number of factors that promote income inequality in national economies have been removed. Further, the unevenness in earnings is not simply a result of random variability unrelated to individuals. The ranks of individuals within the earnings distribution remain relatively stable across changes in wage rates. This stability in rankings suggests that the earnings differences result from inherent differences in the desire for consumption versus leisure. One conclusion that we think can safely be drawn from these results is that there is a lower bound to the equality of earnings that can be achieved after eliminating most of the sources of inequality that economists commonly cite. Whether our Gini coefficients – most of which fall in the range of 0.05 to 0.20 (Table 5.2) – are relatively large or small given that most common sources of inequality have been eliminated, we leave to the individual reader to decide.[2]

We find no evidence for a welfare trap effect: Poorer rats do not seem to have higher rates of time discounting or a greater inability to defer gratification than wealthy rats. Rather, if anything, we see just the opposite pattern in choices across income levels. As such, we reject the cycle-of-poverty hypothesis as a general economic phenomenon. Of course, it is perfectly possible, as one of our colleagues has suggested, that people might behave differently with respect to food on the table compared with money in the bank. But this kind of criticism does not invalidate generalizing our results to the human condition. Rather, it indicates the need to conduct additional experiments that operationalize the essential motivational differences between food on the table and money in the bank.

Notes

1 The matching law is quite different from probability matching theory. Probability matching fails to explain choices on concurrent VR–VR schedules (Section 3.2b) and in tests of first-degree stochastic dominance that do not use correction procedures (Section 6.1b).
2 The Gini coefficients for animal workers are substantially less than for the U.S. economy as a whole and somewhat less than reported for homogeneous groups of full-time workers in the United States and the United Kingdom (Section 5.4).

BIBLIOGRAPHY

Ainslie, G. W. 1974. Impulse control in pigeons. *Journal of the Experimental Analysis of Behavior* 21:485–9.

1975. Specious reward: A behavioral theory of impulsiveness and impulse control. *Psychological Bulletin* 82:463–96.

1992. *Picoeconomics: The strategic interaction of successive motivational states within the person.* Cambridge University Press.

Ainslie, G. W., and R. J. Herrnstein. 1981. Preference reversal and delayed reinforcement. *Animal Learning and Behavior* 9:476–82.

Allais, M. 1953. Le comportement de l'homme rationnel devant le risque, critique des postulats et axiomes de l'école Americaine. *Econometrica* 21:503–46.

Allison, J. 1979. Demand economics and experimental psychology. *Behavioral Science* 24:403–15.

1981. Economics and operant conditioning. In *Advances in analysis of behaviour.* Vol. 2, *Predictability, correlation, and contiguity,* ed. P. Harzem and M. D. Zeiler. Wiley.

Allison, J., M. Miller, and M. Wozny. 1979. Conservation in behavior. *Journal of Experimental Psychology: General* 108:4 – 34.

Arrow, K. J. 1974. *Essays in the theory of risk-bearing.* North-Holland.

1987. Rationality of self and others in an economic system. In *Rational Choice,* ed. R. M. Hogarth and M. W. Reder. University of Chicago Press.

Atkinson, A. B. 1975. *The economics of inequality.* Oxford University Press.

Barnard, C. J., and C. A. J. Brown. 1985. Risk-sensitive foraging in common shrews (*Sorex araneus* L.). *Behavioral Ecology and Sociobiology* 16:161–4.

Barnard, C. J., C. A. J. Brown, A. I. Houston, and J. M. McNamara. 1985. Risk-sensitive foraging in common shrews: an interruptive model and the effects of mean and variance on reward rate. *Behavioral Ecology and Sociobiology* 18:139–46.

Barofsky, I., and D. Hurwitz. 1968. Within ratio responding during fixed ratio performance. *Psychonomic Science* 11:263–4.

Battalio, R. C., G. P. Dwyer, Jr., and J. H. Kagel. 1987. Tests of competing theories of consumer choice and the representative consumer hypothesis. *The Economic Journal* 97: 842–56.

Battalio, R. C., L. Green, and J. H. Kagel. 1981. Income-leisure tradeoffs of animal workers. *American Economic Review* 71:621–32.

Battalio, R. C., J. H. Kagel, R. C. Winkler, E. B. Fisher, Jr., R. L. Basmann, and L. Krasner. 1973. A test of consumer demand theory using observations of individual consumer purchases. *Western Economic Journal* 11:411–28.

Battalio, R. C., J. H. Kagel, H. Rachlin, and L. Green. 1981. Commodity-choice behavior with pigeons as subjects. *Journal of Political Economy* 89:67–91.

Battalio, R. C., and J. H. Kagel. 1985. Consumption-leisure tradeoffs of animal workers: effects of increasing and decreasing marginal wage rates in a closed economy experiment. *Research in Experimental Economics*. Vol. 3, ed. V. L. Smith. JAI Press.

Battalio, R. C., J. H. Kagel, and D. N. MacDonald. 1985. Animals' choices over uncertain outcomes: Some initial experimental results. *American Economic Review* 75:597–613.

Battalio, R. C., J. H. Kagel, and K. Jiranyakul. 1990. Testing between alternative models of choice under uncertainty: Some initial results. *Journal of Risk and Uncertainty* 3:25–50.

Battalio, R. C., J. H. Kagel, and C. A. Kogut. 1991. Experimental confirmation of the existence of a Giffen good. *American Economic Review* 81:961–70.

Baum, W. M. 1974. On two types of deviations from the matching law: bias and undermatching. *Journal of the Experimental Analysis of Behavior* 22:231–42.

Baum, W. M., and H. Rachlin. 1969. Choice as time allocation. *Journal of the Experimental Analysis of Behavior* 12:861–74.

Bauman, R. 1991. An experimental analysis of the cost of food in a closed economy. *Journal of the Experimental Analysis of Behavior* 56:33–50.

Becker, G. S. 1962. Irrational behavior and economic theory. *Journal of Political Economy* 70:1–13.
1968. crime and punishment: an economic approach. *Journal of Political Economy* 76:169–217.
1971. *Economic theory*. Knopf.
1981. *A treatise on the family*. Harvard University Press.
1993. Nobel lecture: the economic way of looking at behavior. *Journal of Political Economy* 101:385–409.

Bem, D. J., and A. Allen. 1974. On predicting some of the people some of the time. *Psychological Review* 81:506–20.

Bickel, W. K., R. J. DeGrandpre, J. R. Hughes, and S. T. Higgins. 1991. Behavioral economics of drug self-administration. II. A unit-price analysis of cigarette smoking. *Journal of the Experimental Analysis of Behavior* 55:145–54.

Biddle, J. E., and D. S. Hamermesh. 1990. Sleep and the allocation of time. *Journal of Political Economy* 98:922–43.

Bigelow, G., H. Emurian, and J. V. Brady. 1975. A programmed environment for the experimental analysis of individual and small group behavior. In *Experimentation in controlled environments and its implications for economic behavior and social policy making*, ed. C. G. Miles. Addiction Research Foundation of Ontario.

Bigelow, G., and I. Liebson. 1972. Cost factors controlling alcoholic drinking. *The Psychological Record* 22:305–14.

Böhm-Bawerk, E. V. 1923. *The positive theory of capital*. (Trans. by W. Smart). G. E. Stechert and Co.

Boland, L. A. 1981. On the futility of criticizing the neoclassical maximization hypothesis. *American Economic Review* 71:1031–6.

Brown, J. S. 1988. Patch use as an indicator of habitat preference, predation risk, and competition. *Behavioral Ecology and Sociobiology* 22:37–47.

Browning, E. K., and J. M. Browning. 1983. *Microeconomic theory and applications*. 1st ed. Little, Brown.

Brunswik, E. 1939. Probability as a determiner of rat behavior. *Journal of Experimental Psychology* 25:175–97.

Bruner, J. S., J. J. Goodnow, and G. A. Austin. 1956. *A study of thinking*. Wiley.

Camerer, C. 1989. An experimental test of several generalized utility theories. *Journal of Risk and Uncertainty* 2:61–104.

In press. Individual decision making. In *Handbook of Experimental Economics,* eds. J. Kagel and A. Roth. Princeton University Press.

Caraco, T. 1981. Energy budgets, risk and foraging preferences in dark-eyed juncos (*junco hyemalis*). *Behavioral Ecology and Sociobiology* 8:213–17.

1982. Aspects of risk-aversion in foraging white-crowned sparrows. *Animal Behaviour* 30:719–27.

Caraco, T., W. U. Blanckenhorn, G. M. Gregory, J. A. Newman, G. M. Recer, and S. M. Zwicker. 1990. Risk-sensitivity: ambient temperature affects foraging choice. *Animal Behaviour* 39:338–45.

Caraco, T., and M. Chasin. 1984. Foraging preferences: response to reward skew. *Animal Behaviour* 32:76–85.

Caraco, T., and S. L. Lima. 1987. Survival, energy budgets and foraging risk. In *Quantitative analyses of behavior.* Vol. 6, *Foraging,* ed. M. L. Commons, A. C. Kacelnik, and S. J. Shettleworth. Erlbaum.

Caraco, T., S. Martindale, and T. S. Whittam. 1980. An empirical demonstration of risk-sensitive foraging preferences. *Animal Behaviour* 28:820–30.

Catania, A. C. 1980. Freedom of choice: a behavioral analysis. In *The psychology of learning and motivation,* ed. G. W. Bower. Academic Press.

Catania, A. C., T. J. Matthews, T. J. Silverman, and R. Yohalem. 1977. Yoked variable-ratio and variable-interval responding in pigeons. *Journal of the Experimental Analysis of Behavior* 28:155–61.

Catania, A. C., and G. S. Reynolds. 1968. A quantitative analysis of the responding maintained by variable interval schedules of reinforcement. *Journal of the Experimental Analysis of Behavior* 11:327–84.

Chang, F. 1991. Uncertain lifetimes, retirement and economic welfare. *Economica* 58:215–32.

Chant, J. F. 1963. Irrational behavior and economic theory: a comment. *Journal of Political Economy* 71:505–10.

Charnov, E. L. 1976. Optimal foraging, the marginal value theorem. *Theoretical Population Biology* 9:129–36.

Chiang, A. C. 1974. *Fundamental methods of mathematical economics.* McGraw-Hill.

Christensen-Szalanski, J. J., A. D. Goldberg, M. E. Anderson, and T. R. Mitchell. 1980. Deprivation, delay of reinforcement, and the selection of behavioral strategies. *Animal Behaviour* 28:341–6.

Collier, G. 1982. Determinants of choice. In *Response structure and organization: 1981 Nebraska symposium on motivation,* ed. D. J. Bernstein. University of Nebraska Press.

1986. The dialogue between the house economist and the resident physiologist. *Nutrition and Behavior* 3:9–26.

Collier, G., E. Hirsch, and P. H. Hamlin. 1972. The ecological determinants of reinforcement in the rat. *Physiology and Behavior* 9:705–16.

Collier, G., and W. Jennings. 1969. Work as a determinant of instrumental performance. *Journal of Comparative and Physiological Psychology* 68:659–62.

Collier, G., and D. F. Johnson. 1990. The time window of feeding. *Psychology and Behavior* 48:771–7.

Conlisk, J. 1968. Simple dynamic effects in work – leisure choice: a skeptical comment on the static theory. *Journal of Human Resources* 3:324–6.

1989. Three variants on the Allais example. *American Economic Review* 79:392–407.

Conover, W. J. 1971. *Practical nonparametric statistics.* Wiley & Sons.

Coombs, C. H., and L. C. Huang. 1976. Tests of the betweenness property of expected utility. *Journal of Mathematical Psychology* 13:323–37.

Cowie, R. J. 1977. Optimal foraging in great tits. *Nature* 268:137–9.

Cowie, R. J., and J. R. Krebs. 1979. Optimal foraging in patchy environments. In *Population dynamics,* ed. R. M. Anderson, B. D. Turner, and L. R. Taylor. Blackwell Scientific.

Davison, M. 1969. Preference for mixed-interval versus fixed-interval schedules. *Journal of the Experimental Analysis of Behavior* 12:247–52.

Davison, M., and D. McCarthy. 1981. Undermatching and structural relations. *Behaviour Analysis Letters* 1:67–72.

1988. *The matching law: a research review.* Erlbaum.

Deaton, A., and J. Muellbauer. 1980. *Economics and consumer behavior.* Cambridge University Press.

Deluty, M. Z. 1978. Self-control and impulsiveness involving aversive events. *Journal of Experimental Psychology: Animal Behavior Processes* 4:250–66.

Domjan, M. 1993. *The principles of learning and behavior.* 3d ed. Brooks/Cole.

de Villiers, P. 1977. Choice in concurrent schedules and a quantitative formulation of law of effect. In *Handbook of operant behavior,* ed. W. K. Honig and J. E. R. Staddon. Prentice-Hall.

Dougan, J. D. 1992. Inelastic supply: an economic approach to simple interval schedules. *Journal of the Experimental Analysis of Behavior* 58:415–29.

Dougan, W. R. 1982. Giffen goods and the law of demand. *Journal of Political Economy* 90:809–15.

Dwyer, G. P., Jr., and C. M. Lindsay. 1984. Robert Giffen and the Irish potato. *American Economic Review* 74:188–92.

Ebbesen, E. B., and V. J. Konecni. 1975. Decision making and information integration in the courts: the setting of bail. *Journal of Personality and Social Psychology* 32:805–21.

Ehrlich, I. 1973. Participation in illegitimate activities: a theoretical and empirical investigation. *Journal of Political Economy* 81:521–67.

Eisenberger, R., F. A. Masterson, and K. Lowman. 1982. Effects of previous delay of reward, generalized effort, and deprivation on impulsiveness. *Learning and Motivation* 13:378–89.

Elsmore, T. F., G. V. Fletcher, D. G. Conrad, and F. J. Sodetz. 1980. Reduction of heroin intake in baboons by an economic constraint. *Pharmacology Biochemistry and Behavior* 13:729–31.

Elster, J. 1979. *Ulysses and the sirens: studies in rationality and irrationality.* Cambridge University Press.

Engerman, S. L., and R. W. Fogel. 1974. *Time on the cross: the economics of American negro slavery.* Little, Brown.

Estes, W. K. 1959. The statistical approach to learning theory. In *Psychology: A study of a science.* Vol. 2., ed. S. Koch. McGraw-Hill.

1962. Learning theory. *Annual Review of Psychology* 13:107–44.

1964. Probability learning. In *Categories of human learning,* ed. A. W. Melton. Academic Press.

Fantino, E. 1966. Immediate reward followed by extinction vs. later reward without extinction. *Psychonomic Science* 6:233–234.

1967. Preference for mixed versus fixed-ratio schedules. *Journal of the Experimental Analysis of Behavior* 10:35–43.

Ferster, C. B., and B. F. Skinner. 1957. *Schedules of reinforcement.* Appleton-Century-Crofts.

Fleshler, M., and H. S. Hoffman. 1962. A progression for generating variable-interval schedules. *Journal of the Experimental Analysis of Behavior* 5:529–30.

Friedman, D. 1985. Experimental economics: comment. *American Economic Review* 25:264.

Gilliam, J. F., R. F. Green, and N. E. Pearson. 1982. The fallacy of the traffic policeman: a response to Templeton and Lawlor. *American Naturalist* 119:875–8.

Green, J. K., and L. Green. 1982. Substitution of leisure for income in pigeon workers as a function of body weight. *Behaviour Analysis Letters* 2:103–12.

Green, L., E. B. Fisher, Jr., S. Perlow, and L. Sherman. 1981. Preference reversal and self-control: choice as a function of reward amount and delay. *Behaviour Analysis Letters* 1:43–51.

Green, L., and D. E. Freed. 1993. The substitutability of reinforcers. *Journal of the Experimental Analysis of Behavior* 60:141–58.

Green, L., A. Fry, and J. Myerson. 1994. Discounting of delayed rewards: A life-span comparison. *Psychological Science* 5:33–6.

Green, L., and J. H. Kagel. In press. *Advances in behavioral economics.* Vol. 3. Ablex.

Green, L., J. H. Kagel, and R. C. Battalio. 1982. Ratio schedules of reinforcement and their relationship to economic theories of labor supply. In *Quantitative analyses of behavior.* Vol. 2, *Matching and maximizing accounts,* ed. M. Commons, R. J. Herrnstein, and H. Rachlin. Ballinger.

1987. Consumption-leisure tradeoffs in pigeons: effects of changing marginal wage rates by varying amount of reinforcement. *Journal of the Experimental Analysis of Behavior* 47:17–28.

Green, L., and H. Rachlin. 1991. Economic substitutability of electrical brain stimulation, food, and water. *Journal of the Experimental Analysis of Behavior* 55:133–43.

Green, L., H. Rachlin, and J. Hanson. 1983. Matching and maximizing with concurrent ratio-interval schedules. *Journal of the Experimental Analysis of Behavior* 40:217–24.

Green, L., and M. Snyderman. 1980. Choice between rewards differing in amount and delay: toward a choice model of self control. *Journal of the Experimental Analysis of Behavior* 34:135–47.

Greenwood, M., D. Quartermia, P. Johnson, J. Cruce, and J. Hirsch. 1974. Food motivated behavior in genetically obese and hypothalamic-hyperphagic rats. *Psychology and Behavior* 13:687–92.

Grether, D. M., and C. R. Plott. 1979. Economic theory of choice and the preference reversal phenomenon. *American Economic Review* 62:623–38.

Grosch, J., and A. Neuringer. 1981. Self-control in pigeons under the Mischel paradigm. *Journal of the Experimental Analysis of Behavior* 35:3–21.

Gustavson, C. R. 1977. Comparative and field aspects of learned food aversions. In *Learning mechanisms in food selection,* ed. L. M. Barker, M. R. Best, and M. Domjan. Baylor University Press.

Hadar, J. 1971. *Mathematical theory of economic behavior.* Addison-Wesley.

Hagen, O. 1979. Towards a positive theory of preferences under risk. In *Expected utility hypotheses and the Allais paradox: contemporary discussions of decisions under uncertainty with Allais' rejoinder,* ed. M. Allais and O. Hagen. D. Reidel.

Hamblin, R. L., and H. L. Miller, Jr. 1977. Matching as a multivariate power law: frequency of behavior versus frequency and magnitude of reinforcement. *Learning and Motivation* 8:113–26.

Hamm, S. L., and S. J. Shettleworth. 1987. Risk aversion in pigeons. *Journal of Experimental Psychology: Animal Behavior Processes* 13:376–83.

Harless, D. W. 1992. Predictions about indifference curves in the unit probability triangle: a test of competing decision theories. *Journal of Economic Behavior and Organization* 18:391–414.

Harless, D. W., and C. F. Camerer. 1991. *The predictive utility of generalized expected utility theories.* Drexel University Department of Economics working paper.

Hastjarjo, T., A. Silberberg, and S. R. Hursh. 1990. Quinine pellets as an inferior good and a Giffen good in rats. *Journal of the Experimental Analysis of Behavior* 53:263–71.

Heiner, R. A. 1985. Experimental economics: comment. *American Economic Review* 75:260–3.

Henle, P. 1972. Exploring the distribution of earned income. *Monthly Labor Review* 95:16–27.

Herrnstein, R. J. 1961. Relative and absolute strength of response as a function of frequency of reinforcement. *Journal of the Experimental Analysis of Behavior* 4:267–72.

1970. On the law of effect. *Journal of the Experimental Analysis of Behavior* 13:243–66.

Herrnstein, R. J., and G. M. Heyman. 1979. Is matching compatible with reinforcement maximization on concurrent variable-interval variable-ratio? *Journal of the Experimental Analysis of Behavior* 31:209–23.

Herrnstein, R. J., and D. H. Loveland. 1975. Maximizing and matching on concurrent ratio schedules. *Journal of the Experimental Analysis of Behavior* 24:107–16.

Herrnstein, R. J., and D. Prelec. 1989. Giffen goods in rats: a reply to Battalio et al. Paper presented at Southern Economic Association meetings.

——— 1991. Melioration: A theory of distributed choice. *Journal of Economic Perspectives* 5:137–56.

Herrnstein, R. J., and W. Vaughan, Jr. 1980. Melioration and behavioral allocation. In *Limits to action: the allocation of individual behavior,* ed. J. E. R. Staddon. Academic Press.

Hicks, J. R. 1946. *Value and capital.* 2d ed. Clarendon.

Hill, T. P. 1959. An analysis of the distribution of wages and salaries in Great Britain. *Econometrica* 27:355–81.

Hineline, P. N., and F. J. Sodetz. 1987. Appetitive and aversive schedule preferences: Schedule transitions as intervening events. In *Quantitative analyses of behavior.* Vol. 5, *Reinforcement value—the effects of delay and intervening events,* ed. M. L. Commons, H. Rachlin, and J. Mazur. Erlbaum.

Hogan, J. A., and T. J. Roper. 1978. A comparison of the properties of different reinforcers. In *Advances in the study of behavior,* vol. 8, ed. J. S. Rosenblatt, R. A. Hinde, C. Beer, and M-C. Busnel. Academic Press.

Hollard, V., and M. C. Davison. 1971. Preference for qualitatively different reinforcers. *Journal of the Experimental Analysis of Behavior* 16:375 – 80.

Houston, A. I., A. Kacelnik, and J. McNamara. 1982. Some learning rules for acquiring information. In *Functional ontogeny,* ed. D. McFarland. Pittman.

Houston, A., and D. J. McFarland. 1980. Behavioral resilience and its relation to demand functions. In *Limits to action: the allocation of individual behavior,* ed. J. E. R. Staddon. Academic Press.

Houston, A., and B. H. Sumida. 1987. Learning rules, matching and frequency dependence. *Journal of Theoretical Population Biology* 126:289–308.

Hubbard, S. F., and R. M. Cook. 1978. Optimal foraging by parasitoid wasps. *Journal of Animal Ecology* 47:593–604.

Hull, C. L. 1942. *A behavior system.* Yale University Press.

Hursh, S. R. 1978. The economics of daily consumption controlling food- and water-reinforced responding. *Journal of the Experimental Analysis of Behavior* 29:475–91.

——— 1980. Economic concepts for the analysis of behavior. *Journal of the Experimental Analysis of Behavior* 34:219–38.

——— 1984. Behavioral economics. *Journal of the Experimental Analysis of Behavior* 42:435–52.

——— 1991. Behavioral economics of drug self-administration and drug abuse policy. *Journal of the Experimental Analysis of Behavior* 56:377–93.

Hursh, S. R., and B. H. Natelson. 1981. Electrical brain stimulation and food reinforcement dissociated by demand elasticity. *Physiology and Behavior* 26:509–15.

Kacelnik, A. 1979. Studies of foraging behaviour in great tits. Unpublished D. Phil. diss., University of Oxford.

Kacelnik, A., A. I. Houston, and J. R. Krebs. 1981. Optimal foraging and territorial defence in the great tit (*parus major*). *Behavioral Ecology and Sociobiology* 8:35–40.

Kagel, J. H. 1987. Economics according to the rats (and pigeons too): what have we learned and what can we hope to learn? In *Laboratory Experimentation in Economics,* ed. A. E. Roth. Cambridge University Press.

Kagel, J. H., R. C. Battalio, and L. Green. 1983. Matching versus maximizing: comments on Prelec's paper. *Psychological Review* 90:380–4.

Kagel, J. H., R. C. Battalio, L. Green, and H. Rachlin. 1980. Consumer demand theory applied to choice behavior of rats. In *Limits to action: the allocation of individual behavior,* ed. John E. R. Staddon, Academic Press.

Kagel, J. H., R. C. Battalio, and C. G. Miles. 1980. Marihuana and work performance: results from an experiment. *Journal of Human Resources* 15:373–95.

Kagel, J. H., R. C. Battalio, H. Rachlin, L. Green, R. L. Basmann, and W. R. Klemm. 1975. Experimental studies of consumer demand behavior using laboratory animals. *Economic Inquiry* 13:22–38.

Kagel, J. H., R. C. Battalio, R. C. Winkler, and E. B. Fisher, Jr. 1977. Job choice and total labor supply: an experimental analysis. *Southern Economic Journal* 44: 13–24.

Kagel, J. H., R. C. Battalio, R. C. Winkler, E. B. Fisher, Jr., C. G. Miles, R. L. Basmann, and L. Krasner. 1975. Income, consumption, and saving in controlled environments: further economic analysis. In *Experimentation in controlled environment,* ed. C. G. Miles. Addiction Research Foundation of Ontario.

Kagel, J. H., G. P. Dwyer, Jr., and R. C. Battalio. 1985. Bliss points vs. minimum needs: tests of competing motivational processes. *Behavioural Processes* 11:61–77.

Kagel, J. H., and L. Green. 1987. Intertemporal choice behavior: evaluation of economic and psychological models. In *Advances in behavioral economics.* Vol. 1, ed. L. Green and J. H. Kagel. Ablex.

Kagel, J. H., L. Green, and T. Caraco. 1986. When foragers discount the future: constraint or adaptation? *Animal Behaviour* 34:271–83.

Kagel, J. H., D. N. MacDonald, and R. C. Battalio. 1990. Tests of "fanning out" of indifference curves: results from animal and human experiments. *American Economic Review* 80:912–21.

Kagel, J. H., D. N. MacDonald, R. C. Battalio, S. White, and L. Green. 1986. Risk aversion in rats under varying levels of resource availability. *Journal of Comparative Psychology* 100:95–100.

Kagel, J. H., D. N. MacDonald, L. Green, and R. C. Battalio. 1988. Risk preferences over losses in rats: responses to variable shock levels and delays to reinforcement. Mimeographed, Univ. of Pittsburgh.

Kahneman, D., and A. Tversky. 1979. Prospect theory: an analysis of decision under risk. *Econometrica* 47:263–91.

1983. Choices, values, and frames. *American Psychologist* 39:341–350.

Kazdin, A. E., and R. R. Bootzin. 1972. The token economy: an evaluative review. *Journal of Applied Behavior Analysis* 5:343–72.

Kendall, M. G., and A. Stuart. 1969. *The advanced theory of statistics.* Hafner.

Killeen, P. 1968. On the measurement of reinforcement frequency in the study of preference. *Journal of the Experimental Analysis of Behavior* 11:263–9.

Krebs, J. R., A. I. Houston, and E. I. Charnov. 1981. Some recent developments in optimal foraging. In *Foraging behavior: ecological, ethological and psychological approaches,* ed. A. C. Kamil and T. D. Stuart. Garland Press.

Krebs, J. R., A. Kacelnik, and P. Taylor. 1978. Tests of optimal sampling by foraging great tits. *Nature* 275:27–31.

Kuznets, S. 1955. Economic growth and income inequality. *American Economic Review* 45:1–28.

Lancaster, K. 1966. A new approach to consumer theory. *Journal of Political Economy* 74:132–57.

Lea, S. E. G. 1978. The psychology and economics of demand. *Psychological Bulletin* 85:441–66.

1981. Animal experiments in economic psychology. *Journal of Economic Psychology* 1:245–71.

Lichtenstein, S., and P. Slovic. 1971. Reversals of preference between bids and choice in gambling decisions. *Journal of Experimental Psychology* 89:46–55.

Lima, S. L. 1985. Sampling behavior of starlings foraging in simple patchy environments. *Journal of Behavioral Ecology and Sociobiology* 16:135–42.

Lobb, B., and M. C. Davison. 1975. Performance in concurrent interval schedules: a systematic replication. *Journal of the Experimental Analysis of Behavior* 24:191–8.

Loewenstein, G., and D. Prelec. 1992. Anomalies in intertemporal choice: evidence and an interpretation. *Quarterly Journal of Economics* 429:573–98.

Logan, F. A. 1964. The free behavior situation. In *Nebraska symposium on motivation,* ed. D. Levine. University of Nebraska Press.

    1965. Decision making by rats: delay versus amount of reward. *Journal of Comparative and Physiological Psychology* 59:1–12.

Logue, A. W. 1988. Research on self-control: an integrating framework. *Behavioral and Brain Sciences* 11:665–79.

Logue, A. W., A. Chavarro, H. Rachlin, and R. W. Reader. 1988. Impulsiveness in pigeons living in the experimental chamber. *Animal Learning and Behavior* 16:31–9.

Logue, A. W., and T. E. Peña-Correal. 1985. The effect of food deprivation on self-control. *Behavioural Processes* 10:355–68.

Logue, A. W., M. L. Rodriguez, T. E. Peña-Correal, and B. C. Mauro. 1984. Choice in a self-control paradigm.: quantification of experience-based differences. *Journal of the Experimental Analysis of Behavior* 41:53–67.

Logue, A. W., M. E. Smith, and H. Rachlin. 1985. Sensitivity of pigeons to prereinforcer and postreinforcer delay. *Animal Learning and Behavior* 13:181–6.

Luce, R. D., and P. Suppes. 1965. Preference, utility and subjective probability. In *Handbook of mathematical psychology,* vol. 3, ed. R. D. Luce, R. R. Bush, and E. Galanter. J. Wiley and Sons.

McCloskey, D. 1989. The open fields of England: rent, risk and the rate of interest. 1300–1815. In *Markets in history: economic studies of the past,* ed. D. Galenson, Cambridge University Press.

MacDonald, D., J. H. Kagel, and R. C. Battalio. 1991. Animals' choices over uncertain outcomes: further experimental results. *Economic Journal* 101:1067–84.

Mackintosh, N. J. 1974. *The psychology of animal learning.* Academic Press.

McNamara, J. M., and A. I. Houston, 1980. The application of statistical decision theory to animal behavior. *Journal of Theoretical Biology* 85:673–90.

Machina, M. J. 1982. "Expected Utility" analysis without the independence axiom. *Econometrica* 50:277–324.

    1983. The economic theory of individual behavior toward risk: theory, evidence and new directions. Tech. Report 433, Center for Research on Organizational Efficiency. Stanford University.

    1985. Stochastic choice functions generated from deterministic preferences over lotteries. *Economic Journal* 95:575–94.

    1987. Choice under uncertainty: problems solved and unsolved. *Journal of Economic Perspectives* 1:121–54.

Maital, S., and S. Maital. 1977. Time preference, delay of gratification and the intergenerational transmission of economic inequality: a behavioral theory of income distribution. In *Essays in labor market analysis,* ed. O. C. Ashenfelter and W. E. Oates. Halsted Press.

Manser, M., and M. Brown. 1980. Marriage and household decision-making: a bargaining analysis. *International Economic Review* 21:31–44.

Markowitz, H. 1959. *Portfolio selection: efficient diversification of investments.* Yale University Press. Maynard-Smith, J. 1978. Optimization theory in evolution. *Annual Review of Ecological Systems* 9:31–56.

Mazur, J. E. 1981. Optimization theory fails to predict performance of pigeons in a two-response situation. *Science* 214:823–5.

    1986. Fixed and variable ratios and delays: further tests of an equivalence rule. *Journal of Experimental Psychology: Animal Behavior Processes* 12:116–24.

    1989. Theories of probabilistic reinforcement. *Journal of the Experimental Analysis of Behavior* 51:87–99.

Mazur, J. E., and A. W. Logue. 1978. Choice in a self-control paradigm: effects of a fading procedure. *Journal of the Experimental Analysis of Behavior* 30:11–17.

Mazur, J. E., and W. Vaughan, Jr. 1987. Molar optimization versus delayed reinforcement as explanations of choice between fixed-ratio and progressive-ratio schedules. *Journal of the Experimental Analysis of Behavior* 48:251–61.

Meisch, R., and T. Thompson. 1972. Determinants of ethanol intake in rats: food intake and ethanol concentration. Reports from the Research Laboratories, PR-72-3. Department of Psychiatry, University of Minnesota.

———. 1973. Ethanol as a reinforcer: effects of fixed-ratio size and food deprivation. *Psychopharmacologia* (Berlin) 28:171–83.

Mello, N. K., H. B. McNamee, and J. H. Mendelson, 1968. Drinking patterns of chronic alcoholics: gambling and motivation for alcohol. In *Clinical research in alcoholism*, ed. J. O. Cole. Psychiatric Research Report 24. American Psychiatric Association.

Mello, N. K., and J. H. Mendelson. 1972. Drinking patterns during work-contingent and noncontingent alcohol acquisition. *Psychosomatic Medicine* 1972:139–64.

Mendelson, J. H., and R. E. Meyer. 1972. Behavioural and biological concomitants of chronic marihuana smoking by heavy and casual users. *A Signal of Misunderstanding*. Technical papers of the first Report of the National Commission on Marihuana and Drug Abuse. Vol. 1. Superintendent of Documents, U.S. Government Printing Office, Washington, D.C.

Mikesell, R. F., and J. E. Zinser. 1973. The nature of the savings function in developing countries: a survey of the theoretical and empirical literature. *Journal of Economic Literature* 11:1–26.

Miles, C. G., G. R. S. Congreve, R. J. Gibbins, J. Marshman, R. Devenyi, and R. C. Hicks. 1974. An experimental study of the effects of daily cannabis smoking on behavior patterns. *Acta Pharmacologica et Toxocologica* Supp. I:1–44.

Miller, H. L., Jr. 1976. Matching-based hedonic scaling in the pigeon. *Journal of the Experimental Analysis of Behavior* 26:335–47.

Mogenson, G., and J. Cioé. 1977. Central reinforcement. In *Handbook of operant behavior*, ed. W. K. Honig and J. E. R. Staddon. Prentice-Hall.

Morgan, P. B., and D. Tustin. 1992. The perception and efficiency of labour supply choices by pigeons. *Economic Journal* 102:1134–48.

Motheral, M. S. 1982. *Optimal allocation of behavior: ratio schedules*. Ph.D. diss., Department of Psychology, Duke University.

Mowrer, O. H., and H. M. Jones. 1945. Habit strength as a function of the pattern of reinforcement. *Journal of Experimental Psychology* 35:293.

Murdoch, W. W. 1969. Switching in general predators: experiments on predator specificity and stability of prey populations. *Ecological Monographs* 39:335–54.

Myers, D. L., and L. E. Myers. 1977. Undermatching: a reappraisal of performance on concurrent variable interval schedules of reinforcement. *Journal of the Experimental Analysis of Behavior* 27:203–14.

Myerson, J., and S. Hale. 1988. Choice in transition: a comparison of melioration and the kinetic model. *Journal of the Experimental Analysis of Behavior* 49:291–302.

Nathan, P. E., M. S. Goldman, S. A. Lisman, and A. A. Taylor. 1972. Alcohol and alcoholics: a behavioral approach. *Transactions of New York Academy of Science* 34:602–27.

Nathan, P. E., J. S. O'Brien, and L. M. Lowenstein. 1971. Operant studies of chronic alcoholism: interaction of alcohol and alcoholics. In *Biological aspects of alcohol*, ed. M. K. Roach, W. M. McIsaac, and P. J. Creaver. University of Texas Press.

Nathan, P. E., N. A. Titler, L. M. Lowenstein, P. Soloman, and A. M. Rossi. 1970. Behavioral analysis of chronic alcoholism. *Archives of General Psychiatry* 22:419–30.

Navarick, D. J. 1982. Negative reinforcement and choice in humans. *Learning and Motivation* 13:361–77.

Navarick, D. J., and E. Fantino. 1972. Transitivity as a property of choice. *Journal of the Experimental Analysis of Behavior* 18:389–401.

1974. Stochastic transitivity and undimentional behavior theories. *Psychological Review* 81:426–41.

1976. Self-control and general models of choice. *Journal of Experimental Psychology: Animal Behavior Processes* 2:75–87.

Nielson, W. S. 1989. Behavior in the probability triangle. Texas A&M University. Photocopy.

North, A. J., and R. D. McDonald. 1959. Discrimination learning as a function of the probability of reinforcement. *Journal of Comparative and Physiological Psychology* 52:342–44.

Osborne, S. R. 1977. The free food (contra-freeloading) phenomenon: a review and analysis. *Animal Learning and Behavior* 5:221–35.

Parker, G. A., and R. A. Stuart. 1976. Animal behavior as a strategy optimizer: evolution of resource assessment strategies and optimal emigration thresholds. *American Naturalist* 110:1055–76.

Pear, J. J. 1975. Implications of the matching law for ratio responding. *Journal of the Experimental Analysis of Behavior* 23:139–40.

Pencavel, J. 1986. Labor supply of men: a survey. In *Handbook of labor economics,* vol. 1, ed. O. C. Ashenfelter and R. Layard. North-Holland.

Plant, M. W. 1984. An empirical analysis of welfare dependence. *American Economic Review* 74:673–84.

Pollak, R. A. 1971. Additive utility functions and linear Engel curves. *Review of Economic Studies* 38:401–13.

Pollak, R. A., and T. J. Wales. 1980. Comparison of the quadratic expenditure system and translog demand systems with alternative specifications of demographic effects. *Econometrica* 48:595–612.

Pratt, J. W. 1964. Risk aversion in the small and in the large. *Econometrica* 32:122–36.

Prelec, D. 1982. Matching, maximizing, and the hyperbolic reinforcement feedback function. *Psychological Review* 89:189–230.

1983. The empirical claims of maximization theory: a reply to Rachlin and to Kagel, Battalio, and Green. *Psychological Review* 90:385–9.

Pulliam, H. R., and G. C. Millikan. 1982. Social organization in the non-reproductive season. In *Avian biology,* vol. 6, ed. D. S. Farner and J. R. King. Academic Press.

Rachlin, H. 1978. A molar theory of reinforcement schedules. *Journal of the Experimental Analysis of Behavior* 30:345–60.

1983. How to decide between matching and maximizing: a reply to Prelec. *Psychological Review* 90:376–9.

Rachlin, H., R. Battalio, J. Kagel, and L. Green. 1981. Maximization theory in behavioral psychology. *The Behavioral and Brain Sciences* 4:371–417 (with commentaries).

Rachlin, H., and L. Green. 1972. Commitment, choice and self-control. *Journal of the Experimental Analysis of Behavior* 17:15–22.

Rachlin, H., L. Green, J. H. Kagel, and R. C. Battalio. 1976. Economic demand theory and psychological studies of choice. In *The psychology of learning and motivation,* ed. G. Bower. Academic Press.

Rachlin, H., L. Green, and B. Tormey. 1988. Is there a decisive test between matching and maximizing? *Journal of the Experimental Analysis of Behavior* 50:113–23.

Rachlin, H., J. H. Kagel, and R. C. Battalio. 1980. Substitutability in time allocation. *Psychological Review* 87:355–74.

Rachlin, H., A. W. Logue, J. Gibbon, and M. Frankel. 1986. Cognition and behavior in studies of choice. *Psychological Review* 93:33–45.

Rachlin, H., A. Raineri, and D. Cross. 1991. Subjective probability and delay. *Journal of the Experimental Analysis of Behavior* 55:233–44.

Rapport, D. J. 1971. An optimization model of food selection. *American Naturalist* 105:575 – 87.

Real, L. A. 1981. Uncertainty and pollinator-plant interactions: the foraging behavior of bees and wasps on artificial flowers. *Ecology* 62:20–6.

Real, L. A., and T. Caraco. 1986. Risk and foraging in stochastic environments. *Annual Review of Ecological Systems* 17:371–90.

Rees, A. 1974. An overview of the labor-supply results. *Journal of Human Resources* 9:158–80.

Robbins, L. 1930. On the elasticity of demand for income in terms of effort. *Economica* 29:123–9.

Roth, A. E. In press. Introduction to experimental economics. In *Handbook of experimental economics*, ed. J. H. Kagel and A. E. Roth. Princeton University Press.

Rothschild, M., and J. E. Stiglitz. 1970. Increasing risk I: a definition. *Journal of Economic Theory* 2:225–43.

Safra, A., U. Segal, and A. Spivak. 1990. Preference reversals and nonexpected utility behavior. *American Economic Review* 80:922–30.

Samuelson, P. A. 1947. *Foundations of economic analysis.* Harvard University Press.

Sawhill, I. V. 1988. Poverty in the U.S.: why is it so persistent? *Journal of Economic Literature* 26:1073–119.

Schrader, S. M., and L. Green. 1990. The economics of leisure in psychological studies of choice. In *Advances in Behavioral Economics*, vol. 2, ed. L. Green and J. H. Kagel. Ablex.

Shafer, W., and H. Sonnenschein. 1982. Market demand and excess demand functions. In *Handbook of mathematical economics*, ed. K. J. Arrow and M. Intriligator. North-Holland.

Shimp, C. P. 1969. Optimal behavior in free-operant experiments. *Psychological Review* 76:97–112.

Shull, R. L., D. J. Spear, and A. E. Bryson. 1981. Delay or rate of food delivery as a determiner of response rate. *Journal of the Experimental Analysis of Behavior* 35:129–43.

Shurtleff, D., and A. Silberberg. 1990. Income maximizing on concurrent ratio-interval schedules of reinforcement. *Journal of the Experimental Analysis of Behavior* 53:273–84.

Shurtleff, D., F. R. Warren-Boulton, and A. Silberberg. 1987. Income and choice between different goods. *Journal of the Experimental Analysis of Behavior* 48:263–75.

Sidman, M. 1960. *Tactics of scientific research.* Basic Books.

Siegel, S. 1961. Decision making and learning under varying conditions of reinforcement. *Annuals of New York Academy of Sciences* 89:766–83.

Silberberg, A., J. R. Thomas, and N. Berendzen. 1991. Human choice on concurrent variable-interval variable-ratio schedules. *Journal of the Experimental Analysis of Behavior* 56:575–84.

Silberberg, A., F. R. Warren-Boulton, and T. Asano. 1987. Inferior-good and Giffen-good effects in monkey choice behavior. *Journal of Experimental Psychology: Animal Behavior Processes* 13:292–301.

   1988. Maximizing present value: a model to explain why moderate response rates obtain on variable-interval schedules. *Journal of the Experimental Analysis of Behavior* 49:331–8.

Silberberg, A., and J. M. Ziriax. 1985. Molecular maximizing characterizes choice on Vaughan's (1981) procedure. *Journal of the Experimental Analysis of Behavior* 43:83–96.

Silberberg, E. 1978. *The structure of economics: a mathematical analysis.* McGraw-Hill.

Simon, H. 1979. Rational decision making in business organization. *American Economic Review* 69:493–513.

Skinner, B. F. 1938. *The behavior of organisms,* Appleton-Century.

   1948. Superstition in the pigeon. *Journal of Experimental Psychology* 38:168–72.

   1953. *Science and human behavior.* Macmillan.

Slovic, P., B. Fishoff, S. Lichtenstein, B. Corrigan, and B. Combs. 1977. Preference for insuring against probable small losses: insurance implications. *Journal of Risk and Insurance* 44:237–58.

Smith, V. L. 1982. Microeconomic systems as an experimental science. *American Economic Review* 72:923–55.

Snyderman, M. 1983a. Optimal prey selection: partial selection, delay of reinforcement and self control. *Behaviour Analysis Letters* 3:131–47.

1983b. Optimal prey selection: the effects of food deprivation. *Behaviour Analysis Letters* 3:359–70.

Sonnenschein, H. 1973. Do Walras' identity and continuity characterize the class of community excess demand functions? *Journal of Economic Theory* 6:345–54.

Staddon, J. E. R. 1979a. Operant behavior as adaptation to constraint. *Journal of Experimental Psychology: General* 108:48–67.

1979b. Regulation and time allocation: comment on "conservation in behavior". *Journal of Experimental Psychology: General* 108:35–40.

1980. Optimality analyses of operant behavior and their relation to optimal foraging. In *Limits to action*, ed. J. E. R. Staddon. Academic Press.

1982. Behavioral competition, contrast and matching. In *Quantitative analyses of behavior.* Vol. 2, *Matching and maximizing accounts*, ed. M. Commons, R. J. Herrnstein, and H. Rachlin. Ballinger.

1988. Quasi-dynamic choice models: melioration and ratio invariance. *Journal of the Experimental Analysis of Behavior* 49:303–20.

Staddon, J. E. R., and S. Motheral. 1978. On matching and maximizing in operant choice experiments. *Psychological Review* 85:436–45.

Staddon, J. E. R., and A. Reid. 1987. Adaptation to reward. In *Foraging behavior,* ed. A. C. Kamil, J. R. Krebs, and H. R. Pulliam. Plenum Press.

Starmer, C., and R. Sugden. 1987. Violations of the independence axiom: an experimental test of some competing hypotheses. Economics Research Center Discussion Paper 24, University of East Anglia.

Stephens, D. W. 1981. The logic of risk-sensitive foraging preferences. *Animal Behaviour* 29:628–9.

Stephens, D. W., and E. L. Charnov. 1982. Optimal foraging: some simple stochastic models. *Behavioral Ecology and Sociobiology* 10:251–63.

Stephens, D. W., and J. R. Krebs. 1986. *Foraging theory.* Princeton University Press.

Stigler, G. J. 1947. Notes on the history of the Giffen paradox. *Journal of Political Economy* 55:152–6.

1948. A reply. *Journal of Political Economy* 56:61–2.

1987. *The theory of price.* 4th ed. Macmillan.

Stigler, G. J., and G. S. Becker. 1977. De gustibus non est disputandum. *American Economic Review* 67:76–90.

Stone, J. R. N. 1954. Linear expenditure systems and demand analysis: an application to the pattern of British demand. *Economic Journal* 64:511–27.

Strotz, R. H. 1956. Myopia and inconsistency in dynamic utility maximization. *Review of Economic Studies* 23:165–80.

Stubbs, D. A., and S. S. Pliskoff. 1969. Concurrent responding with fixed relative rate of reinforcement. *Journal of the Experimental Analysis of Behavior* 12:887–95.

Sutherland, N. S., and N. J. Mackintosh. 1971. *Mechanisms of animal discrimination learning.* Academic Press.

Taylor, R., and M. Davison. 1983. Sensitivity to reinforcement in concurrent arithmetic and exponential schedules. *Journal of the Experimental Analysis of Behavior* 39:191–8.

Thaler, R., and H. M. Shefrin. 1981. An economic theory of self-control. *Journal of Political Economy* 89:392–406.

Thiel, H. 1975. *Theory and measurement of consumer demand.* Vol. 1. American Elsevier.

Thistle, P. 1983. *Essays in labor supply.* Ph.D. diss. Texas A&M University.

Thorndike, E. L. 1911. *Animal intelligence.* Macmillan.

Thurstone, L. L. 1931. The indifference function. *Journal of Social Psychology* 2:139–67.

Timberlake, W. 1977. The application of the matching law to simple ratio schedules. *Journal of the Experimental Analysis of Behavior* 25:215–17.

——— 1980. A molar equilibrium theory of learned performance. In *The psychology of learning and motivation,* Vol. 14, ed. G. H. Bower. Academic Press.

Timberlake, W., and B. F. Peden. 1987. On the distinction between open and closed economies. *Journal of the Experimental Analysis of Behavior* 48:35–60.

Turelli, M., J. H. Gillespie, and T. W. Schoener. 1982. The fallacy of the averages in ecological optimization theory. *American Naturalist* 119:879–84.

Tversky, A. 1969. Intransitivity of preferences. *Psychological Review* 76:31–48.

Tversky, A., and D. Kahneman. 1992. Advances in prospect theory: cumulative representation of uncertainty. *Journal of Risk and Uncertainty* 5:297–323.

Varian, H. R. 1992. *Microeconomic analysis.* W. W. Norton.

Vaughan, W., Jr. 1985. Choice: a local analysis. *Journal of the Experimental Analysis of Behavior* 43:383–405.

Vaughan, W., Jr., and R. J. Herrnstein. 1987. Stability, melioration, and natural selection. In *Advances in behavioral economics,* Vol. 1, ed. L. Green and J. H. Kagel. Ablex.

Vaughan, W., Jr., and H. L. Miller, Jr. 1984. Optimization versus response-strength accounts of behavior. *Journal of the Experimental Analysis of Behavior* 42:337–48.

Wanchisen, B. A., T. A. Tatham, and P. N. Hineline. 1988. Pigeons' choices in situations of diminishing returns: fixed- versus progressive-ratio schedules. *Journal of the Experimental Analysis of Behavior* 50:375–94.

——— 1992. Human choice in "counterintuitive" situations: Fixed- versus progressive-ratio schedules. *Journal of the Experimental Analysis of Behavior* 58:67–85.

Williams, B. A. 1983. Another look at contrast in multiple schedules. *Journal of the Experimental Analysis of Behavior* 39:345–84.

Winkler, R. C. 1980. Behavioral economics, token economies, and applied behavior analysis. In *Limits to action: the allocation of individual behavior,* ed. J. E. R. Staddon. Academic Press.

Winkler, R. C., and B. Burkhard. 1990. A systems approach to behavior modification through behavioral economics. In *Advances in behavioral economics,* Vol. 2, ed. L. Green and J. H. Kagel. Ablex.

Wunderle, J. M., M. Santa Castro, and N. Fetcher. 1987. Risk-averse foraging by bananaquits on negative energy budgets. *Behavioral Ecology and Sociobiology* 21:249–55.

INDEX

activity distribution, preferred, 61–2
See also bliss points
adventitious reinforcement, 93
Ainslie, G. W., 179, 180, 181
Allais, M., 153
Allais Paradox, 171n.19
Allais violations
  conditions for generating, 154
  described in fanning out of indifference
    curves, 156–62
  of expected utility theory, 7, 152–3
  identification, 3
Allison, J., 25, 87, 90
Arrow, K. J., 71, 146, 150
Arrow–Pratt measure of risk aversion, 146,
  150, 151
Asano, T., 28, 60, 120, 174, 192, 193
Atkinson, A. B., 130
Austin, G. A., 55

Barnard, C. J., 148, 149
Barofsky, I., 87
Battalio, R. C., 26, 56, 59, 67f, 69t, 70, 84, 87,
  95, 97t, 98f, 116, 123t, 128, 142t, 143,
  144t, 147t, 148t, 155t, 156, 159t, 161,
  162, 166, 196
Baum, W. M., 54, 59, 177
Becker, G. S., 2, 30, 36, 47, 48, 50, 68, 90,
  195, 203
behavior. *See* adventitious reinforcement;
  labor supply; random behavior
  models; search behavior; superstitious
  behavior
Berendzen, N., 119
Bergen paradox, 153
betweenness axiom. *See* expected utility
  theory

Bickel, W. K., 90
Biddle, J. E., 36
Bigelow, G., 87, 88f, 196
bliss points
  conditions for, 62–3
  testing, 6
Böhm-Bawerk, E. V., 176
Boland, L. A., 95
Bootzin, R. R., 195
Brady,, J. V., 196
brain stimulation. *See* electrical stimulation of
  the brain (EBS)
Brown, C. A. J., 148, 149
Brown, M., 2, 36
Browning, E. K., 106
Browning, J. M., 106
Bruner, J. S., 55
Brunswik, E., 35, 55
Bryson, A. E., 180
budget constraint/budget line
  changing, 24
  in commodity-choice theory, 11
  function of, 10–11
  with income-compensated price change,
    11–13
  with income-constant price change,
    14–17
  in irrational choice model, 47
Burkhard, B., 196
Camerer, C., 162, 166
Caraco, T., 134, 137, 141, 145, 148, 149,
  151, 183
Catania, A. C., 113, 181
certainty effect, 153
Chang, F., 182
changeover delay (COD), 114, 116